HEDGEBROOK

Plays

volume one

WhitPress

Seattle, Washington • Jackson Hole, Wyoming • www.WhitPress.org

To you all, our most heartfelt thanks and gratitude.

This Whit Press book is made possible in major part by the generous support of Margot Snowdon, Arianna Snowdon, Ted and Addie Donnan, Nancy Nordhoff, Connie Kemmerer, Elizabeth Rudolf, Shauna Woods, Paul and Paula Butzi, Emily Knobloch, Nell Fuqua, Cecile Lamb, Annette Cummings, Janet Heron, Kathy Karahadian, Teresa Meadows, our individual donors and the following organizations and businesses:

- The Hill-Snowdon Foundation
- Community Foundation of Jackson Hole
- Seattle Office of Arts & Cultural Affairs
- 4 Culture King County Percent for Art

Cover and interior design by: Tracy Lamb, Laughing Lamb Design, Jackson, Wyoming

ISBN: 978-0-9836983-2-6

Library of Congress Control Number: 2012944699

First Edition: November 2012

Published by:

Whit Press
4701 SW Admiral Way, #125, Seattle, WA 98116
252 East Pearl, PO Box 13275, Jackson WY 83002
www.whitpress.org 206-295-1670

FOREWORD

What an amazing time to be alive, to be a woman, and to be a playwright.

Now at the beginning of the 21st century, massive environmental shifts are waking us up to our fragile relationship with mother earth. We are experiencing a cultural sea change as old systems break down and paradigms shift. Technology is speeding up our ability to connect around the globe in seconds, and the information overload is both overwhelming and exhilarating. There is a sense of urgency surrounding the real or imagined timelines of the "end" or the "new beginnings" that will follow in the aftermath of change.

Hedgebrook
WOMEN AUTHORING CHANGE

It is essential in this time that we hear from women.

Hedgebrook's mission is to "support visionary women writers whose stories and ideas shape our culture now and for generations to come." If we believe that our stories shape who we are, as individuals and as a people, then who gets to be the storyteller becomes a critical question. And what better place for stories to be shared than in the *theatron*, the "seeing place" where we enact our stories, provoke a dialogue and envision our way forward together?

And yet, as of 2012 less than 20% of the plays being produced around the country each year are by women, a statistic that hasn't gone up significantly in the 15 years we've been producing the Hedgebrook Women Playwrights Festival.

A national movement is calling for "50/50 in 2020," with a vision that by the year 2020, at least 50% of the plays being produced in America will be by women. To this end, Hedgebrook is convening our alumnae and other women playwrights, artistic directors, literary managers, dramaturgs, directors, agents, and producing partners to brainstorm ways we can work together to reach that ambitious goal. We're hosting conversations in partnership with The Lark Play Development Center in New York, creating opportunities for playwrights to build relationships with the people and organizations who develop new work. We're partnering with theatres around the country—Seattle's

ACT Theatre, Seattle Repertory Theatre, Denver Theatre Center, and Oregon Shakespeare Festival, to name a few—to develop plays by women playwrights under commission, so that our festival becomes a pipeline for women's plays to go from genesis to production.

By publishing this first volume of groundbreaking plays, Hedgebrook and Whit Press are deepening our commitment to women playwrights by putting their work in your hands.

The next step is yours. Devour these plays, share them with everyone you know, produce them, teach them, and work with Hedgebrook to build an audience and create the demand for more work by women to be seen on all stages. We have eight years to get to 50/50. Let's make it happen.

— **Amy Wheeler,**
playwright, alumna and
Executive Director of Hedgebrook, April 2012

PREFACE

It all starts with a seed. A seed gets planted, sprouts, takes root, grows, bears fruit, and multiplies. The same happens with playwriting: seeds of ideas take form, root around for awhile, are nurtured and cultivated, develop, and grow into plays. As gardeners in this process, we have been looking for a way to bring these plays from their home soil to other patches of fertile ground. Since the Hedgebrook Women Playwrights Festival was founded in 1998, 50 new plays have emerged from the Hedgebrook soil. With this anthology, we offer you a chance to sample the fruits of our labor and to share in a wide range of voices, stories, humor, and heart.

The plays featured in this book grew out of playwrights' residencies at Hedgebrook, where the Whidbey Island retreat's unique blend of communion and solitude, invigorating conversation and thoughtful reflection, good food and radical hospitality create an environment where plawrights can do their best work. The results are some of the most compelling new plays in the country: award-winners as well as works that may be less well-known but are no less provocative or inspiring. From the heartfelt whimsy of Sarah Ruhl's *The Clean House* to the acerbic wit of Ellen McLaughlin's *Helen*, from the warmth and intimacy of Kathleen Tolan's *Memory House* to the epic imagination of Naomi Iizuka's *Ghostwritten* and the keen re-imagining of history in Lynn Nottage's *Las Meniñas*, *Hedgebrook Plays, Volume One* offers a rich and varied bounty.

We are immensely grateful to the playwrights who have so generously shared their work, to the theatres that have supported our efforts (notably ACT and Seattle Repertory Theatres), and to the visionaries at Hedgebrook who helped us see that we can create the world we want to live in, one play at a time.

The idea to publish a collection of Hedgebrook plays has been percolating for a long time. For several years, we actively searched for but never found the right publisher. Until Whit Press. Claudia Mauro's passionate dedication to disseminating the works of women writers makes her the perfect partner in this long-awaited endeavor. Seeds need water and sunshine to grow. Because of Claudia and Whit Press, this volume is finally photosynthesizing.

**— Liz Engelman and Christine Sumption,
Editors**

Liz Engelman *is a freelance dramaturg who splits her time between Whidbey Island, Washington and Ely, Minnesota. She has worked in new play development at the Playwrights' Center in Minneapolis, Bay Area Playwrights Festival, New York Theatre Workshop, the O'Neill Playwrights Conference, Denver Theater Center, and numerous other venues. She is the founder and director of Tofte Lake Center at Norm's Fish Camp, a creative retreat up in the Boundary Waters of Minnesota. She is also the Alumnae Relations Coordinator at Hedgebrook. She has served as a dramaturg with the Hedgebrook Women Playwrights Festival for nine of the past fifteen years.*

Christine Sumption *is a freelance dramaturg who lives in Seattle. She has served as a dramaturg for Sundance Theatre Lab, ACT Theatre, Seattle Children's Theatre, and Seattle Repertory Theatre, where she was on the artistic staff for nine years, edited* Prologue *magazine, and produced the annual Hedgebrook Women Playwrights Festival. She is Co-Curator of the Construction Zone at ACT Theatre and teaches at Cornish College of the Arts. She has served as a dramaturg with the Hedgebrook Women Playwrights Festival for twelve of the past fifteen years.*

This book is dedicated to Nancy Nordhoff,

whose vision and generosity have made Hedgebrook

the beating heart of a global community of women writers.

Hedgebrook
WOMEN AUTHORING CHANGE

INTRODUCTION

by Mame Hunt

Each time I drive down Useless Bay Road toward the farm on South Whidbey Island, I wonder if the things I most love about Hedgebrook will have changed. And each time I discover that Hedgebrook looks and feels the same as it did at our first Hedgebrook Women Playwrights Festival in 1998. Same wonderful food, big-hearted staff, banana slugs, and little wood stoves in each cottage that we must learn to stoke and maintain. In each of the six cottages in the woods resides a collection of journals written in by those who have stayed there before—playwrights like Tanya Barfield, Eisa Davis, Cherrie Moraga, Theresa Rebeck, Regina Taylor, and Alice Tuan tucked in among the novelists, poets, and filmmakers. Still here are the traditional journal entries—the tributes to the owls and expressions of gratitude for Hedgebrook's unique blend of solitude and community.

But let me return to the beginning . . .

The Hedgebrook Women Playwrights Festival began in 1998, the brainchild of Leslie Swackhamer, then interim artistic director of ACT Theatre, and Janice Kennedy, playwright and Hedgebrook board member. Each year, about 50 women playwrights are nominated by a select panel of dramaturgs, artistic directors, and other theatre artists nationwide, and that list is winnowed down to four chosen writers. These playwrights journey to Hedgebrook to workshop whichever new play of theirs they need to hear/develop/pay attention to. Here playwrights revisit and rework their plays with the support of dramaturgs and the gracious Hedgebrook staff. The process is a combination of walks in the woods, coffee in the cottages, readings after dinner, random encounters in the bathhouse. If there is a real life equivalent, I suspect it's at Microsoft...

There are astonishing peonies and artichokes in the organic garden at Hedgebrook. We're invited to snip and assemble our own bouquets, and the artichokes are served for supper. After a sumptuous meal in the farmhouse, playwrights and dramaturgs gather around the fire to hear a revised play and discuss the pros and cons of the new choices that have been made: more ambiguity or less, more reality or less, more music, perhaps? Some nights we simply share our stories of life in the theatre.

Our futures and the futures of these plays live in a hundred different places, but we are here. For two weeks or more. The rocks we collect on the beach are proof.

At the end of our time, the playwrights return to their lives and the dramaturgs to ours. We'll email back and forth many times in the coming year or so, as the plays are revised further, heard again, are perhaps scheduled for production in Seattle or elsewhere. The bonds created at the Hedgebrook Women Playwrights Festival are tenacious ones, built on a combination of work, admiration, and laughter that is completely unique. And the work itself reflects the friendships that are forged here. Whatever challenges the Festival and Hedgebrook have faced and will face in the future, our signature is proudly written on the pages of the American theatre. And we will sign it again and again and again and again…

Mame Hunt is the Lead Dramaturg for Sundance Theatre Lab and teaches at Georgetown University. She has served as a dramaturg with the Women Playwrights Festival for six of the past fifteen years.

ACKNOWLEDGMENTS

Braden Abraham, Christy Bain, Sara Bathum, Kurt Beattie, Linda Bowers, Paul and Paula Butzi, Sue Ellen Case, Matthew Clapp, Jr., Elizabeth Crane, Allan and Norah Davis, Michael Bigelow Dixon, Gordon Edelstein, David Esbjornson, Oskar Eustis, Cynthia Fuhrman, Mary Kay Haggard, Adrien-Alice Hansel, Philip Himberg, Rosa Joshi, Janice Kennedy, Doug Langworthy, Margaret Layne, Ashley Leasure, Jim Loder, Kevin Maifeld, Emily Mann, Jerry Manning, Louise McKay, Claudia Mauro, Anita Montgomery, Benjamin Moore, Nancy Nordhoff, Christine O'Connor, Sharon Ott, Janice Paran, Annie Ready, Elizabeth Rudolf, Carlo Scandiuzzi, Bruce Sevy, Elizabeth Sumption, Jacquelin K. Sumption, Leslie Swackhamer, Ten Eyck Swackhamer, Tammy Talman, Kevin Tighe, Susan Trapnell, Gary Tucker, Paula Vogel, Amy Wheeler, Richard E.T. White, Sharon Williams, Shauna Woods, Chay Yew, Dorit Zingarelli, Vito Zingarelli, and the incomparable Hedgebrook staff.

HWPF PLAYWRIGHTS

Valetta Anderson, Tanya Barfield, Neena Beber, Rhada Blank, Leanna Brodie, Laurie Carlos, Eugenie Chan, Julia Cho, Darrah Cloud, Kia Corthron, Frances Ya-Chu Cowhig, Migdalia Cruz, Eisa Davis, Joann Farías, Lillian Garrett-Groag, Gina Gionfriddo, Jessica Goldberg, Danai Gurira, Quiara Alegría Hudes, Naomi Iizuka, Julie Jensen, Honour Kane, Sherry Kramer, Lisa Loomer, Michele Lowe, Ellen McLaughlin, Molly Smith Metzler, Cherrie Moraga, Lenelle Moïse, Julie Marie Myatt, Lynn Nottage, Lizzie Olesker, Jamie Pachino, Regina Porter, Theresa Rebeck, Alva Rogers, Sarah Ruhl, Laura Schellhardt, Gwendolyn Schwinke, Rosanna Staffa, Susan Soon-he Stanton, Deborah Isobel Stein, Victoria Stewart, Lydia Stryk, Caridad Svich, Regina Taylor, Kathleen Tolan, Sarah Treem, Alice Tuan, Erin Cressida Wilson, and Karen Zacarías.

HWPF DRAMATURGS

Lue Morgan Douthit, Liz Engelman, Mame Hunt, Anita Montgomery, Carrie Ryan, and Christine Sumption.

HWPF DIRECTORS

Nikki Appino, Kurt Beattie, Kathleen Collins, Lue Morgan Douthit, David Esbjornson, Rita Giomi, Ellen Graham, Adam Greenfield, Pam MacKinnon, Jerry Manning, Allison Narver, Valerie Curtis-Newton, Kristin Newbom, Sharon Ott, Victor Pappas, Bartlett Sher, Robin Lynn Smith, Christine Sumption, Leslie Swackhamer, Liesl Tommy, Daniela Varon, M. Burke Walker, Richard E.T. White, and Paul Willis.

CONTENTS

HEDGEBROOK

Plays

volume one

Naomi Iizuka

Ellen McLaughlin

Lynn Nottage

Sarah Ruhl

Kathleen Tolan

EDITED BY:
LIZ ENGELMAN & CHRISTINE SUMPTION

NOTES ON THE CLEAN HOUSE
by Sarah Ruhl

When I was invited to Hedgebrook, I had just finished the first two acts of *The Clean House.* I had heard Act One out loud at the McCarter Theatre, but I hadn't heard Act Two before, and certainly not in public. I was terribly nervous to hear it in public, and in fact was hoping to just hear Act One again, while I privately scribbled on Act Two. Then I met my cohorts—Julia Cho, Karen Zacarías, and Kathleen Tolan. We were all to become close friends— our short two weeks together have now stretched into years of friendship.

Somehow in a week we had established among ourselves a fellowship in which anything could be discussed—including love, art, and money. These three formidable women, and the formidable Chris Sumption, encouraged me to be brave and hear the full draft of *The Clean House* at Seattle Repertory Theatre, directed by Kristin Newbom, and I did. Their encouragement was a touchstone of that play's life— of the play's forging ahead, out of my brain and into the world.

Later, the three playwrights would encourage me in three different cities. Julia and I saw each other often in Santa Monica where we both lived at the time, taking long walks, talking about writing, eating together. Ah, the meals Julia cooked me when I was pregnant. Hamburgers, dumpling soup, fish…And Karen and I saw each other when I had plays done in Washington, DC. She was at the opening night of *Passion Play* and *Dead Man's Cell Phone*. When I was newly pregnant in DC, she was too, but didn't know it; we both madly ate gazpacho and lemon squares without realizing why they tasted so good. And Kathleen and I saw each other in New York, and still do. Kath came to the first preview of *The Clean House* in New York, as she would later come to previews of *Eurydice* and *Dead Man's Cell Phone*. Her notes and support were always vital to my mental health during previews. Her daughters still sing songs to my daughter, and Kath tried to teach me how to potty-train a toddler by singing songs to her.

I mention artistic embarrassments like births and toddlers because

I think there was something unique about four women coming together and supporting each other's literal and figurative births. Balancing a domestic life and a writing life is something that Virginia Woolf didn't have to do to the same extent—she had a cook, and, to her sorrow, no children. But many of us are constantly negotiating between the ravings and beckonings of our imaginations and the ravings and beckonings of the other beings in our households. To have four women to speak freely with about these things has been a small miracle. There they all are on my desk: a picture of Julia, Kath, and Karen—with her arms up in triumph—in front of the Seattle Repertory Theatre, June 4th-7th, 2003.

Much has been made lately of the new studies about why women playwrights don't get produced as often as men. The studies are interesting in their specificity, as opposed to our ancient collective groan. For example, the fact that theatre departments receive fewer plays by women than men. Does this have to do with a confidence gap—women wanting to squirrel their plays away rather than have them see the light of day (as I did when I didn't want the second act of *The Clean House* to be read in public)? Is there a child-rearing gap—women are spending some of their imaginatively fertile years on their reproductive lives? Is there an economic gap, in that women still make less per dollar than men, so have to work harder to finance their writing lives, either by teaching, or some other work? All I know is that simple talk among women helps to close all of these gaps, whereas isolation seals them off. At Hedgebrook, we encouraged each other to send our plays into the world, we problem-solved about child care, and we talked about crass things like money that we otherwise wouldn't dare talk about in mixed company.

We all need to remember that, though statistics may be demoralizing, women own this art form as much as men do. We have our Aphra Behns, we have our Lorraine Hansberrys, we have our Suzan-Lori Parkses, our Paula Vogels, our Caryl Churchills, our Maria Irene Forneses, and we have each other. We need make no apologies for our sex in this art form. And the more we talk to each other, the less, I think, we spend time apologizing to everyone else.

—**Sarah Ruhl**

BIOGRAPHY

Sarah Ruhl's plays include *The Clean House* (Susan Smith Blackburn Award, 2004, Pulitzer Prize finalist, Pen Award), *Melancholy Play, Eurydice, Late: a cowboy song, Orlando, Demeter in the City* (NAACP Image Award nomination), *Passion Play* (Fourth Forum Freedom Award, Kennedy Center), *Dead Man's Cell Phone* (Helen Hayes Award), and *In the Next Room (or the vibrator play)*. Her plays have been performed at Lincoln Center Theater, Second Stage, Playwrights Horizons, the Goodman Theatre, Yale Repertory Theatre, Woolly Mammoth Theatre Company, Berkeley Repertory Theatre, the Wilma Theatre, Cornerstone Theater Company, Madison Repertory Theatre, Clubbed Thumb, and the Piven Theatre Workshop, among other theaters across the country. Her plays have been translated into German, Polish, Korean, Russian, and Spanish, and have been produced internationally in Canada, Germany, Latvia, and Poland. Sarah received her M.F.A. from Brown University, and is originally from Chicago. She is the recipient of a Helen Merrill award, Whiting Writers' Award, PEN/Laura Pels award, and a MacArthur Fellowship. She is a proud member of New Dramatists and 13P.

ACKNOWLEDGMENTS

The world premiere of *The Clean House* was produced by Yale Repertory Theatre, New Haven, Connecticut; James Bundy, Artistic Director; Victoria Nolan, Managing Director. It was subsequently produced by New York's Lincoln Center Theater in 2006.

The first act of *The Clean House* was commissioned by McCarter Theatre.

THE CLEAN HOUSE
by Sarah Ruhl

CHARACTERS

LANE, a doctor, a woman in her early fifties. She wears white.

MATILDE, Lane's cleaning lady, a woman in her late twenties. She wears black. She is Brazilian. She has a refined sense of deadpan.

VIRGINIA, Lane's sister, a woman in her late fifties.

CHARLES, Lane's husband, a man in his fifties. A compassionate surgeon. He is childlike underneath his white coat. In the first Act, Charles plays Matilde's father.

ANA, a woman who is older than Lane. She is Argentinean. She is impossibly charismatic. In the first Act she plays Matilde's mother.

NOTE: Everyone in this play should be able to tell a really good joke.

SET A white living room.
White couch, white vase, white lamp, white rug.
A balcony.

PLACE A metaphysical Connecticut. Or, a house that is not far from the city and not far from the sea.

A NOTE ON DOUBLE CASTING

It is important that Ana and Charles play Matilde's mother and father in the first act.

How much can they create, without speaking, a sense of memory and longing, through silence, gesture and dance? Ana's transformation at the end of the play should create a full circle for Matilde, from the dead to the living and back again.

A NOTE ON LULLABIES

There are many beautiful Brazilian lullabies. We chose this one for the first production:

Se essa rua, se essa rua fosse minha
Eu mandava, eu mandava ladrilhar
Com pedrinhas, com pedrinhas de brilhante
P'ra Matilde, só p'ra Matilde passar

If that street, if that street were mine
I would have it, I would have it paved
With little stones, with little diamond stones
For Matilde, only for Matilde to go by.

I have bracketed the lullaby sections because some productions have chosen not to include the singing. I am happy with either choice. If you don't choose to use a lullaby in the production, whether because of a lack of singers or because the ending seems to fly better without the moment of singing, they are worth listening to while you are discovering the tone of the play.

A NOTE ON SUBTITLES

The director might consider projecting subtitles in the play for some scene titles and some stage directions. I would suggest these:

A woman tells a joke in Portuguese.
Lane.
Virginia.
Matilde.

Virginia takes stock of her sister's dust.
Matilde tries to think up the perfect joke.
Virginia and Lane experience a primal moment in
which they are 7 and 9 years old.
Virginia has a deep impulse to order the universe.
Charles performs surgery on the woman he loves.
Ana.
Charles.
They fall in love.
They fall in love some more.
They fall in love completely.
Ana's balcony.
Matilde tries to think up the perfect joke.
Lane makes a house-call to her husband's soul mate.
Lane forgives Ana.
Lane calls Virginia.
Lane guards Ana the way a dog would guard a rival
dog, if her rival were sick.
The funniest joke in the world.

A NOTE ON JOKES

*I want the choice of jokes to be open, allowing for the possibility that
different productions may come up with different and more perfect
Brazilian jokes. So please use these jokes as you will.*

JOKE #1, TO BE TOLD ON PAGE 25:

Um homem tava a ponto de casar e ele tava muito nervosa ao
preparar—se pra noite de nupias porque ele nunca tuvo sexo en la
vida de ele. Enton ele

vai pra médico e pergunta: "O que que eu devo fazor?" O médico
fala: "Não se preocupa. Voce coloca uma nota de dez dolares na bolso
direito y voce practica 10, 10, 10."

Enton el homen vai pra casa y practica todo semana 10,10,10. Aí
ele volta pra médico y lhe fala: "Muito bem! Agora você coloca uma nota
de 10 no bolso direito e uma nota do 20 (vinte) no bolso esquerdo e
practica: "10, 20; 10, 20."

Ele foi pra casa praticou toda semana 10,20; 10,20; 10,20. Ele volta pra medico y ele falou: "É isso aí! Agora você coloca uma nota de 10 no bolso direito, uma de 20 no bolso esquerdo e uma de 100 (cem) na frente. Aí você practica: 10, 20, 100.

Aí ele casou. A noite de núpcias chegou. Ele tava con sua mulher todo bonita e gustosa e ele comencou a fazer amor "10, 20, 100; 10, 20, 100; 10, 20— Ai, que se foda o trocado: 100, 100, 100!!!"

Translation:
A man is getting married. He's never had sex and he's very nervous about his wedding night. So, he goes to a doctor and he says, "I'm really nervous, what should I do?" The doctor says, "Don't worry about it. Go home and put a ten dollar bill in your right pocket and you practice 10! 10! 10!, moving your hips to the left."

So, he goes home and after a week of practice, he returns to the doctor who says "Very good. Now, go back home and put a ten dollar bill in your right hand pocket, a twenty dollar bill in your left hand pocket and go 10! 20! 10! 20!" (*The joke teller moves hips from side to side.*)

So, he practices, does very well, returns to the doctor who says "Perfect! Now you're going to put a 10 dollar bill in your left hand pocket, a 20 dollar bill in your right hand pocket and a 100 dollar bill in front, where you will go like this 10! 20! 100!!"

The man practices as he is told, goes back to the doctor who says "Perfect! You're ready to go!" The big day arrives and the man is very excited about his night with his wife. The time comes and he is in bed and he starts with his wife "10! 20! 100! 10! 20! 100! 10! 20—Oh, fuck the change 100! 100! 100!"

JOKE #2, TO BE TOLD ON PAGE 52:
Por que os homens na cama são como comida de microondas? Estão prontos em trinta segundos.

Translation:
Why are men in bed like microwave food? They're done in thirty seconds.

JOKE #3, TO BE TOLD ON PAGE 63:

O melhor investimento que existe é comprar um argentino pelo valor que ele vale e depois vendê-lo pelo valor que ele acha que vale.

Translation:

The best investment ever is to buy an Argentinean for what he is really worth and later sell him for what he thinks he is worth.

A NOTE ON PRONUNCIATION

Matilde is pronounced by the Americans in the play as Ma-til-da. It is pronounced by Ana as Ma-til-da until she realizes that Matilde is Brazilian. And it is pronounced by Matilde and the more observant characters in the play as Ma-chil-gee, the correct Brazilian pronunciation.

*This play is dedicated to
the doctors in my life, Tony and Kate.*

ACT ONE

1. Matilde.

Matilde tells a long joke in Portuguese to the audience.
We can tell she is telling a joke even though we might not
understand the language.
She finishes the joke.
She exits.

2. Lane.

Lane, to the audience.

LANE: It has been such a hard month.

My cleaning lady—from Brazil—decided that she was depressed one day and stopped cleaning my house.

I was like: clean my house!

And she wouldn't!

We took her to the hospital and I had her medicated and she Still Wouldn't Clean.

And—in the meantime—*I've* been cleaning my house!

I'm sorry, but I did not go to medical school to clean my own house.

3. Virginia.

Virginia, to the audience.

VIRGINIA: People who give up the *privilege* of cleaning their own houses—they're insane people.

If you do not clean: how do you know if you've made any progress in life? I love dust. The dust always makes progress. Then I remove the dust. That is progress.

If it were not for dust I think I would die. If there were no dust to clean then there would be so much leisure time and so much thinking time and I would have to do something besides thinking and that thing might be to slit my wrists.

Ha ha ha ha ha ha just kidding.

I'm not a morbid person. That just popped out!

My sister is a wonderful person. She's a doctor. At an important hospital. I've always wondered how one hospital can be more important than another hospital. They are places for human waste. Places to put dead bodies.

I'm *sorry*. I'm being morbid again.

My sister has given up the privilege of cleaning her own house. Something deeply personal—she has given up. She does not know how long it takes the dust to accumulate under her bed. She does not know if her husband is sleeping with a prostitute because she does not smell his dirty underwear. All of these things, she fails to know.

I know when there is dust on the mirror. Don't misunderstand me— I'm an educated woman. But if I were to die at any moment during the day, no one would have to clean my kitchen.

4. Matilde

Matilde, to the audience.

MATILDE: The story of my parents is this. It was said that my father was the funniest man in his village. He did not marry until he was sixty-three because he did not want to marry a woman who was not funny. He said he would wait until he met his match in wit.

And then one day he met my mother. He used to say: your mother— and he would take a long pause— (*Matilde takes a long pause.*)—is funnier than I am. We have never been apart since the day we met, because I always wanted to know the next joke.

My mother and father did not look into each other's eyes. They laughed like hyenas. Even when they made love they laughed like hyenas. My mother was old for a mother. She refused many proposals. It would kill her, she said, to have to spend her days laughing at jokes that were not funny.

(*Pause.*)

I wear black because I am in mourning. My mother died last year. Have you ever heard the expression 'I almost died laughing?' Well that's what she did. The doctors couldn't explain it. They argued, they said she choked on her own spit, but they don't really know. She was laughing at one of my father's jokes. A joke he took one year to make up, for the anniversary of their marriage. When my mother died laughing, my father shot himself. And so I came here, to clean this house.

5. Lane and Matilde

Lane enters.
Matilde is looking out the window.

LANE: Are you all right?

MATILDE: Yes.

LANE: Would you please clean the bathroom when you get a chance?

MATILDE: Yes.

LANE: Soon?

MATILDE: Yes.

> *Matilde looks at Lane.*

LANE: The house is very dirty.

> *Matilde is silent.*

LANE: This is difficult for me. I don't like to order people around. I've never had a live-in maid.

> *Matilde is silent.*

LANE: Matilde—what did you do in your country before you came to the United States?

MATILDE: I was a student. I studied humor. You know—jokes.

LANE: I'm being serious.

MATILDE: I'm being serious too. My parents were the funniest people in Brazil. And then they died.

LANE: I'm sorry.
That must be very difficult.

MATILDE: I was the third funniest person in my family. Then my parents died, making me the first funniest. It is terrible to be the first funniest, so I left.

LANE: That's very interesting. I don't always—understand the arts. Listen. Matilde. I understand that you have a life, an emotional life— and that you are also my cleaning lady. If I met you at—say—a party— and you said, I am from a small village in Brazil, and my parents were comedians, I would say: that's very interesting. You sound like a very interesting woman.

But life is about context.

And I have met you in the context of my house, where I have hired you to clean. And I don't want an interesting person to clean my house. I just want my house—cleaned.

> *Lane is on the verge of tears.*

MATILDE: Is something wrong?

LANE: No, it's just that—I don't like giving orders in my own home. It makes me—uncomfortable. I want you to do all the things I want you to do without my having to tell you.

MATILDE: Do you tell the nurses at the hospital what to do?

LANE: Yes.

MATILDE: Then pretend I am your nurse.

LANE: Okay.
Nurse—would you polish the silver, please.

MATILDE: A doctor does not say: Nurse—would you polish the silver, please.
A doctor says: Nurse—polish the silver.

LANE: You're right. Nurse: polish the silver.

MATILDE: Yes, doctor.

> *Matilde gets out silver polish and begins polishing.*
> *Lane watches her for a moment, then exits.*

6. Matilde.

> *Matilde stops cleaning.*

MATILDE: This is how I imagine my parents.

> *Music.*

A dashing couple appears.

MATILDE: They are dancing.
They are not the best dancers in the world.
They laugh until laughing makes them kiss.
They kiss until kissing makes them laugh.

> *They dance.*
> *They laugh until laughing makes them kiss.*
> *They kiss until kissing makes them laugh.*
> *Matilde watches.*

7. Virginia and Matilde.

> *The doorbell rings.*
> *The music stops.*
> *Matilde's parents exit.*
> *They blow kisses to Matilde.*
> *Matilde waves back.*
> *The doorbell rings again.*
> *Matilde answers the door.*

MATILDE: Hello.

VIRGINIA: Hello. You are the maid?

MATILDE: Yes.

You are the sister?

VIRGINIA: Yes.
How did you know?

MATILDE: I dusted your photograph.
My boss said: this is my sister. We don't look alike. I thought:
you don't look like my boss. You must be her sister.

My name is Matilde. *(Brazilian pronunciation of Matilde.)*

VIRGINIA: I thought your name was Matilde. (*American pronunciation of Matilde.*)

MATILDE: Kind of.

VIRGINIA: Nice to meet you.

MATILDE: Nice to meet you. I don't know your name.

VIRGINIA: Oh! My name is Virginia.

MATILDE: Like the state?

VIRGINIA: Yes.

> *Matilde continues to stand in front of the door.*

MATILDE: I've never been to Virginia.

VIRGINIA: Maybe I should go.

MATILDE: To Virginia?

VIRGINIA: No. I mean—am I interrupting you?

MATILDE: No. I was just—cleaning. Your sister is at work.

VIRGINIA: She's always at work.

MATILDE: Would you like to come in?

VIRGINIA: Yes. Actually—I came to see you.

MATILDE: Me?

VIRGINIA: Lane tells me that you've been feeling a little blue.

MATILDE: Blue?

VIRGINIA: Sad.

MATILDE: Oh. She told you that?

VIRGINIA: Come, sit on the couch with me.

MATILDE: Okay.

> *Virginia goes to sit on the couch.*
> *She pats the couch.*

Matilde sits down next to her.

VIRGINIA: Do you miss home?

MATILDE: Of course I do. Doesn't everyone?

VIRGINIA: Is that why you've been sad?

MATILDE: No. I don't think so. It's just that—I don't like to clean houses. I think it makes me sad.

VIRGINIA: You don't like to clean houses.

MATILDE: No.

VIRGINIA: But that's so simple!

MATILDE: Yes.

VIRGINIA: Why don't you like to clean?

MATILDE: I've never liked to clean. When I was a child I thought: if the floor is dirty, look at the ceiling. It is always clean.

VIRGINIA: I like cleaning.

MATILDE: You do? Why?

VIRGINIA: It clears my head.

MATILDE: So it is, for you, a religious practice?

VIRGINIA: No. It's just that: cleaning my house—makes me feel clean.

MATILDE: But you don't clean other people's houses. For money.

VIRGINIA: No—I clean my own house.

MATILDE: I think that is different.

VIRGINIA: Do you feel sad *while* you are cleaning?
Or before? Or after?

MATILDE: I am sad when I think about cleaning. But I try not to think about cleaning while I am cleaning. I try to think of jokes. But sometimes the cleaning makes me mad. And then I'm not in a funny mood. And *that* makes me sad. Would you like a coffee?

VIRGINIA: I would *love* some coffee.

> *Matilde goes to get a cup of coffee from the kitchen.*
> *Virginia puts her finger on the table-tops to test the dust.*
> *Then she wipes her dirty finger on her skirt.*
> *Then she tries to clean her skirt but she has nothing to*
> *clean it with. Matilde comes back and gives her the coffee.*

VIRGINIA: Thank you.

MATILDE: You're welcome.

> *Virginia drinks the coffee.*

VIRGINIA: This is good coffee.

MATILDE: We make good coffee in Brazil.

VIRGINIA: Oh—that's right. You do!

MATILDE: Does that help you to place me in my cultural context?

VIRGINIA: Lane didn't describe you accurately. How old are you?

MATILDE: Young enough that my skin is still good.
Old enough that I am starting to think: is my skin still good?
Does that answer your question?

VIRGINIA: Yes. You're twenty-seven.

> *Matilde nods.*

MATILDE: You're good.

VIRGINIA: Thank you.
Listen. Matilde. (*American pronunciation.*)

MATILDE: Matilde. (*Brazilian pronunciation.*)

VIRGINIA: Yes.
I have a proposition for you.

MATILDE: A proposition?

VIRGINIA: A deal.
I like to clean. You do not like to clean. Why don't I clean for you.

MATILDE: You're joking.

VIRGINIA: No.

MATILDE: I don't get it. What do you want from me?

VIRGINIA: Nothing.

MATILDE: Then—why?

VIRGINIA: I have my house cleaned by approximately 3:12 every afternoon. I have folded the corner of every sheet. The house is quiet. The gold draperies are singing a little lullaby to the ottoman. The silverware is gently sleeping in its box. I tuck in the forks, the spoons, the knives. I do not have children.

MATILDE: I'm sorry.

VIRGINIA: *(Faster and faster.)* Don't be sorry. My husband is barren. I never thought that the world was quite good enough for children anyway. I didn't trust myself to cope with how sick and ugly the world is and how beautiful children are and the idea of watching them grow into the dirt and mess of the world—someone might kidnap them or rape them or otherwise trample on their innocence, leaving them in the middle of the road, naked, in some perverse sexual position, to die while strangers rode past on bicycles and tried not to look. I've thought about doing some volunteer work, but I don't know who to volunteer for.

> *A pause. She looks at Matilde.*

VIRGINIA: Since I was twenty-two, my life has gone downhill, and not only have I not done what I wanted to do, but I have lost the qualities and temperament that would help me reverse the downward spiral—and now I am a completely different person.

I don't know why I am telling you all of this, Mathalina.

> *Matilde and Virginia look at each other.*
> *Matilde thinks about correcting Virginia. She doesn't.*

MATILDE: Go on.

VIRGINIA: I used to study Greek literature. One summer my husband

and I went to Europe. It was supposed to be relaxing but I have trouble relaxing on vacations. We were going to see ruins and I was going to write about ruins but I found that I had nothing to say about them. I thought: why doesn't someone just sweep them up! Get a very large broom!

I'm sorry. I was trying to say...

MATILDE: You were telling me how your life has gone down-hill since you were twenty-two.

VIRGINIA: Yes. The point is: every day my house is cleaned by 3 o'clock. I have a lot of—time.

I'd be very happy to come here and·clean Lane's house before Lane gets home from work. That is what I'm telling you. Only don't tell her. She wouldn't like it.

MATILDE: I will let you clean the house if it will make you feel better.

VIRGINIA: Let's start in the bathroom. I love cleaning the toilet. It's so dirty, and then it's so clean!

8. Lane and Matilde.

> *Matilde is reading the funny papers.*
> *Lane enters.*

LANE: It's so clean!

MATILDE: Yes.

LANE: The medication is helping?

MATILDE: I'm feeling much better.

LANE: Well—that's terrific.

> *Lane exits.*

Matilde takes out her medication.
She undoes the bottle,
takes one pill out,
looks at it,
and throws it in the garbage can.

9. Matilde.

Matilde, to the audience.

MATILDE: The perfect joke makes you forget about your life. The perfect joke makes you remember about your life. The perfect joke is stupid when you write it down. The perfect joke was not made up by one person. It passed through the air and you caught it. A perfect joke is somewhere between an angel and a fart.

This is how I imagine my parents:

Music.
Matilde's mother and father appear.
They sit at a cafe.

My mother and father are at a cafe.
My mother is telling my father a joke.
It is a dirty joke.
My father is laughing so hard that he is banging his knee on the underside of the table.
My mother is laughing so hard that she spits out her coffee.
I am with them at the cafe. I am eight years old.
I say: what's so funny?
(I *hate* not understanding a joke.)
My mother says:
Ask me again when you're thirty.
Now I'm almost thirty. And I'll never know the joke.

Matilde's mother and father look at her. They exit.

10. Virginia and Matilde.

The next day.
Virginia folds laundry.
Matilde watches.
Virginia is happy to be cleaning.

MATILDE: You're good at that.

VIRGINIA: Thank you.

MATILDE: You want to hear a joke?

VIRGINIA: Not really.

MATILDE: Why?

VIRGINIA: I don't like to laugh out loud.

MATILDE: Why?

VIRGINIA: I don't like my laugh. It's like a wheeze. Someone once told me that. Who was it—my husband? Do you have a husband?

MATILDE: No.

VIRGINIA: That's good.

MATILDE: Do you like your husband?

VIRGINIA: My husband is like a well-placed couch. He takes up the right amount of space. A man should not be too beautiful. Or too good in bed. A man should be—functional. And well-chosen. Otherwise you're in trouble.

MATILDE: Does he make you laugh?

VIRGINIA: Oh, no. Something uncontrollable would come out of my mouth when he wanted it to. I wouldn't like that.

MATILDE: A good joke cleans your insides out. If I don't laugh for a week, I feel dirty. I feel dirty now, like my insides are rotting.

VIRGINIA: Someone should make you laugh. I'm not the person to do it.

MATILDE: Virginia. My mother once said to me: Matilde, in order to tell a good joke, you have to believe that your problems are very small, and that the world is very big. She said: if more women knew more jokes, there would be more justice in this world.

> *Virginia starts folding underwear.*
> *Matilde watches.*

VIRGINIA: I've never seen my sister's underwear before.

MATILDE: Her underwear is practical. And white.

> *Virginia continues to fold underwear.*

VIRGINIA: I wonder if Lane has gone through menopause yet. Her underwear is very white. Some women throw out underwear when they get a blood-stain. Other women keep washing the stain.

MATILDE: I can't afford to throw away underwear. If I could, believe me, I would. I would buy new underwear every day: purple, red, gold, orange, silver…

> *Virginia folds a pair of men's underwear.*

VIRGINIA: It's a little weird to be touching my brother-in-law's underwear.
He's a very handsome man.
When he and Lane first met, I thought: Lane gets the best of everything. A surgeon. With a specialty. He's—charismatic.

> *Virginia touches her brother-in-law's underwear as she folds.*

Then I thought: it's better to have a husband who is not too handsome. Then you don't worry about him.

> *Virginia comes across a pair of women's black underwear.*

VIRGINIA: These don't look like Lane.

MATILDE: No.

VIRGINIA: Too shiny.

MATILDE: Too sexy.

> *Matilde and Virginia look at each other.*

11. Lane and Virginia have coffee.

Lane and Virginia have coffee in the living room.

VIRGINIA: The house is so clean!

LANE: Thanks.

VIRGINIA: It's working out—with your maid? What's her name?

LANE: (*American pronunciation.*) Matilde.

VIRGINIA: That's right. Mathilda. (*American pronunciation.*)
Don't they say Matilde (*Brazilian pronunciation.*) in Brazil?

LANE: I don't know.

VIRGINIA: I think they do.

LANE: How would you know?

> *Virginia shrugs.*

VIRGINIA: Mm…

LANE: Well, I'm sure she would tell me if I were saying her name
wrong. Anyway. She seems much better. How are you?

VIRGINIA: Oh, fine.
How's Charles?

LANE: Why do you ask?

VIRGINIA: No reason.

LANE: He's fine.

VIRGINIA: That's good. The last time I saw Charles was Christmas.
You both work so hard.

LANE: He's been doing nine surgeries a day—we hardly see each
other. I mean, of course we see each other, but, you know how it is.
More coffee?

VIRGINIA: No, thanks.

LANE: Matilde! Could you clear these, please?

Matilde enters from the kitchen.

MATILDE: (*To Virginia.*) Your cup, miss?

VIRGINIA: Oh, I'll get it—

Matilde winks at Virginia.
Matilde clears the plates.

VIRGINIA: Thanks.

MATILDE: Did everyone enjoy their coffee?

LANE and **VIRGINIA:** Yes.

MATILDE: Good.

She exits.

LANE: Oh. That's Matilde. Sorry. That was rude. I should have introduced you. Or is it rude? Do you introduce the maid to the company?

VIRGINIA: I'm not the company. I'm your sister.

LANE: You're right.
I should have introduced you. I can't get used to having another person in the house.

VIRGINIA: Mmm. Yes. It must make you uncomfortable to—I don't know—read a magazine while someone cleans up after you.

LANE: I don't read magazines, Virginia. I go to work exhausted and I come home exhausted. That is how most of the people in this country function. At least people who have jobs.

A pause.
For a moment,
Lane and Virginia experience
a primal moment during which they
are seven and nine years old,
inside the mind, respectively.
They are mad.
Then they return quite naturally

to language, as adults do.

LANE: Sorry—I didn't mean—

VIRGINIA: I know.

At the same time:

VIRGINIA: Are you—?   **LANE:** I keep meaning to—

VIRGINIA: What?

LANE: Oh—it's just—I keep meaning to have you two over for dinner. It's ridiculous—living so close and never seeing each other.

VIRGINIA: You're right. Maybe next week?

LANE: Next week is crazy. But soon.

Virginia nods.

12. Lane and Matilde.

Night.
Matilde is trying to think up a joke.
Matilde looks straight ahead,
in the dark, in the living room.
She thinks.
Lane comes home from work.
She turns a light on.

LANE: Oh! You startled me.

MATILDE: You startled me too.

LANE: What are you doing in the dark?

MATILDE: I was trying to think up a joke.
I almost had one.
Now it's gone.

LANE: Oh—well—can you get it back again?

MATILDE: I doubt it.

LANE: Oh.
Is Charles home?

MATILDE: No.

LANE: Did he call?

MATILDE: No.

LANE: Oh, well, he's probably just sleeping at the hospital.

> *Matilde is silent.*

LANE: Sometimes there's no time to call home from the hospital. You're going from patient to patient, and it's—you know—crazy. When we were younger—Charles and I—if we had a crazy night at the hospital —we would page each other, we had this signal—two for good-night —and three for—well, I don't know why I'm thinking about this right now. The point is—when you get older, you just *know* that a person is thinking of you, and working hard, and thinking of you, and you don't need them to call anymore. Since Charles and I are both doctors we both—understand—how it is.

MATILDE: Mmm.

> *A silence.*

LANE: Well, good-night.

MATILDE: Good-night.

LANE: Are you going to—just—sit here in the dark?

MATILDE: I might stay up a little longer to—what's the word?—tidy up.

LANE: Oh. Great. Just shut the light off when you—

> *Matilde turns the light off.*

LANE: Oh. Good-night.

MATILDE: Good-night.

Lane exits.
Matilde, alone.

MATILDE: (*To the audience.*)

This is how I imagine my parents.
I cannot fall asleep.
They are sitting outside in the summer, laughing in the dark.
They hear me in my bed, practicing a joke.
They say, sleep, Matilde. Sleep.
They sing me a song, through the windows,
to make me fall asleep.

> *Matilde's mother and father appear,*
> *bringing with them the sensation of summer,*
> *paper lanterns, hammocks, fireflies.*
> *[They sing her a fragment from a Brazilian lullaby.]*
> *Matilde closes her eyes.*
> *Night turns to day.*

13. Virginia and Matilde. Then Lane.

> *Virginia irons.*
> *Matilde watches.*

MATILDE: I have a really good joke coming.

VIRGINIA: That's good.

MATILDE: You know how most jokes go in threes? Like this: Da da DA. I'm making up one that goes in sixes: Da da Da da da DA.

VIRGINIA: I didn't know jokes had time signatures.

MATILDE: Oh, they do. Ask me what my profession is then ask me what my greatest problem is.

VIRGINIA: What's your profession?

MATILDE: I'm a comedian.

VIRGINIA: What's your—

MATILDE: Timing.

VIRGINIA: That's good.

MATILDE: But you're not laughing.

VIRGINIA: I'm laughing on the inside.

MATILDE: Oh. I like it better when people laugh on the outside. I'm looking for the perfect joke, but I'm afraid if I found it, it would kill me.

> *Virginia comes upon a pair of women's red underwear.*

VIRGINIA: My God!

MATILDE: Oh…
No—
(*As in—he wouldn't dare.*)

VIRGINIA: No.

MATILDE: But—
(*As in—he might dare.*)

VIRGINIA: Do you think—here—in the house?

MATILDE: Maybe a park. I bet he puts them in his pocket, afterwards, and forgets, because he's so happy. And then she's walking around for the day, with no underwear, and you know what? She probably likes it.

VIRGINIA: I hope it's not a nurse. It's such a cliché.

MATILDE: If she's a nurse, they would pass each other in the hospital, and she would say, hello doctor. And she knows, and he knows: no underwear.

VIRGINIA: No underwear in a *hospital*? It's unsanitary.

MATILDE: Or—maybe he just *likes* women's underwear. He might try them on.

VIRGINIA: Charles? No!

MATILDE: It's possible. You don't like to think about it, because he's your brother-in-law, but these things happen, Virginia. They do.

> *Lane enters.*
> *Virginia quickly puts down the iron and sits down.*
> *Matilde stands and begins to iron.*
> *Virginia hides the red underwear.*

LANE: (*To Virginia.*) What are you doing here?

VIRGINIA: Nothing.
How was work?

> *Lane doesn't say anything.*
> *She moves to the kitchen.*

VIRGINIA: Where are you going?

LANE: I'm going in the other room to shoot myself.

VIRGINIA: You're joking, right?

LANE: (*From the kitchen.*) Right.

> *Matilde and Virginia look at each other.*
> *Matilde irons underwear.*
> *Virginia sits.*
> *Virginia stands.*
> *Virginia sits.*
> *Virginia stands.*
> *Virginia has a deep impulse to order the universe.*
> *Virginia arranges objects on the coffee table.*
> *Lane enters.*
> *Her left hand is bleeding.*
> *She holds it with a dish towel.*

VIRGINIA: Lane—what—are you—?

LANE: I'm disguising myself as a patient.

VIRGINIA: That's not funny.

LANE: I cut myself.

> *They look at her, alarmed.*

LANE: Don't worry. Even my wounds are superficial.

VIRGINIA: Lane?

LANE: Can opener. I was making a martini.

VIRGINIA: Why do you need a can opener to make a martini?

LANE: I didn't have the right kind of fucking olives, okay?
I only have black olives! In a can.

VIRGINIA: Lane?

LANE: He's gone off with a patient.

VIRGINIA: What?

LANE: His patient.

MATILDE: Oh…

LANE: Yes.

> *Virginia and Matilde glance towards the underwear and look away.*

VIRGINIA: Was it a—?

LANE: Mastectomy. Yes.

VIRGINIA: Wow. That's very—

LANE: Generous of him?

MATILDE: A mastectomy?

> *Virginia gestures towards her breast.*
> *Matilde nods.*

VIRGINIA: How old is she?

LANE: Sixty-seven.

VIRGINIA and **MATILDE:** Oh!

LANE: What?

VIRGINIA: Not what I expected.

LANE: A young nurse? The maid? No. He's in love.

VIRGINIA: But—with an older woman?

LANE: Yes.

VIRGINIA: I'm almost—impressed. She must have—substance.

LANE: She's not a doctor.

VIRGINIA: Well, most men in his position…he's still—so—good-looking…

LANE: Virginia!

VIRGINIA: Sorry.

LANE: I've never been jealous, I've never been suspicious. I've never thought any other woman was my equal. I'm the best doctor. I'm the smartest, the most well-loved by my patients. I'm athletic. I have poise. I've aged well. I can talk to anyone and be on equal footing. How, I thought, could he even look at anyone else. It would be absurd.

VIRGINIA: Wow. You really are—confident.

LANE: I was blind. He didn't want a doctor. He wanted a housewife.

> *A pause.*
> *Lane looks around the house.*
> *She sees the objects on the coffee-table—*
> *a vase, some magazines, forcefully arranged.*
> *Matilde irons, badly.*

LANE: (*To Virginia.*) Have you been cleaning my house?

> *Virginia and Matilde look at each other.*

VIRGINIA: No, I haven't been cleaning your house.

LANE: These objects on the coffee-table—this is how you arrange objects.

Virginia looks at the coffee table.

VIRGINIA: I don't know what you mean.

LANE: Matilde—has Virginia been cleaning the house?

VIRGINIA: I said no.

LANE: I asked Matilde.
Has Virginia been cleaning the house?

MATILDE: Yes.

LANE: For how long?

MATILDE: Two weeks.

LANE: You're fired.
You're both fired.

VIRGINIA: You can't do that.
This is my fault.

LANE: I'm *paying* her to clean my house!

VIRGINIA: And your house is clean!

LANE: This has nothing to do with you, Virginia.

VIRGINIA: This has *everything* to do with me.

LANE: Matilde—do you have enough money saved for a plane ticket back home?

MATILDE: No.

LANE: You can stay one more week. I will buy you a plane ticket.

VIRGINIA: Lane. Your husband left you today.

LANE: I'm aware of that.

VIRGINIA: You're not capable of making a rational decision.

LANE: I'm always capable of making a rational decision!

MATILDE: You don't need to buy me a plane ticket. I'm moving to New York, to become a comedian. I only need a bus ticket.

VIRGINIA: (*To Lane.*) You can't do this!

LANE: I will not have you cleaning my house, just because the maid is depressed—

VIRGINIA: She's not depressed. She doesn't like to clean! It makes her sad.

     Lane looks at Matilde.

LANE: Is that true?

MATILDE: Yes.

LANE: So—
then—
why? (*To Virginia.*)

VIRGINIA: I don't know.

LANE: You looked through my things.

VIRGINIA: Not really.

LANE: I find this—incomprehensible.

VIRGINIA: Can't I do a nice thing for you without having a *motive*?

LANE: No.

VIRGINIA: That's—

LANE: You have better things to do than clean my house.

VIRGINIA: Like what?

LANE: I—

VIRGINIA: Like what?

LANE: I don't know.

VIRGINIA: No, you don't know.

I wake up in the morning, and I wish that I could sleep through the whole day because it is too painful, but there I am, I'm awake.

So I get out of bed. I make eggs for my husband. I throw the egg-shells in the disposal. I listen to the sound of delicate eggshells being ground by an indelicate machine. I clean the sink. I sweep the floor. I wipe coffee grounds from the counter.

I might have done something different with my life. I might have been a scholar. I might have described one particular ruin with the cold-blooded poetry of which only a first-rate scholar is capable. Why didn't I?

LANE: I don't know.

VIRGINIA: I wanted something—big. I didn't know how to ask for it. Don't blame Matilde. Blame me. I wanted—a task.

LANE: I'm sorry.
I don't know what to say.
Except:
(*To Matilde.*)
you're fired.

VIRGINIA: It's not her fault! You can't do this.

LANE: (*To Virginia.*) What would you like me to do?

VIRGINIA: Let me…take care of you.

LANE: I don't need to be taken care of.

VIRGINIA: Everybody needs to be taken care of.

LANE: Virginia. I'm all grown up. I DO NOT WANT TO BE TAKEN CARE OF.

VIRGINIA: WHY NOT?

LANE: I don't want my sister to clean my house. I want a stranger to clean my house.

Virginia and Lane look at Matilde.

MATILDE: It's all right. I'll go.
I'll pack my things.
Good-bye Virginia.
Good luck finding a task.

> *She embraces Virginia.*

Good-bye, doctor.
Good luck finding your husband.

> *She exits.*
> *Lane and Virginia look at each other.*

14. Lane. Then Matilde. Then Virginia.

> *Lane, to the audience.*

LANE: This is how I imagine my husband and his new wife.

> *Charles and Ana appear.*
> *Charles undoes Ana's gown.*
> *Is it a hospital gown or a ball gown?*

LANE: My husband undoes her gown.
He is very gentle.
He kisses her right breast.

> *Charles kisses Ana's right breast.*

He kisses the side of it.
He kisses the shadow.
He kisses her left torso.

> *He kisses her left torso.*

He kisses the scar,

> *He kisses the scar.*

the one he made.
It's a good scar.
He's a good surgeon.
He kisses her mouth.
He kisses her forehead.
It's a sacred ritual, and
I hate him.

> *Matilde enters with her suitcase.*
> *The lovers remain.*
> *They continue to kiss one another*
> *on different body parts, a ritual.*

MATILDE: Is there anything else before I go?

LANE: No. Thank you.

MATILDE: Who are they?

LANE: My husband and the woman he loves. Don't worry. It's only my imagination.

MATILDE: They look happy.

LANE: Yes.

MATILDE: People imagine that people who are in love are happy.

LANE: Yes.

MATILDE: That is why, in your country, people kill themselves on Valentine's Day.

LANE: Yes.

> *Charles and Ana disappear.*

MATILDE: Love isn't clean like that. It's dirty. Like a good joke. Do you want to hear a joke?

LANE: Sure.

> *Matilde tells a joke in Portuguese.*

LANE: Is that the end?

MATILDE: Yes.

LANE: Was it funny?

MATILDE: Yes. It's not funny in translation.

LANE: I suppose I should laugh then.

MATILDE: Yes.

> *Lane tries to laugh.*
> *She cries.*

MATILDE: You're crying.

LANE: No, I'm not.

MATILDE: I think that you're crying.

LANE: Well—yes. I think I am.

> *Lane cries.*
> *She laughs.*
> *She cries.*
> *And this goes on for some time.*
>
> *Virginia enters.*

VIRGINIA: Charles is at the door.

LANE: What?

VIRGINIA: Charles. In the hall.

MATILDE: Oh…

LANE: You let him in?

VIRGINIA: What could I do?

And—there's a woman with him.

LANE: In the *house*?

VIRGINIA: Yes.

LANE: What does she look like?
Is she pretty?

VIRGINIA: No.
(*With apology.*) She's beautiful.

LANE: Oh.

CHARLES: (*From offstage.*) Lane?

> *The women turn to look at each other.*
> *Black-out.*

END OF ACT ONE

ACT TWO

The white living room has become a hospital.
Or the idea of a hospital.
There is a balcony above the white living room.

1. Charles Performs Surgery on the Woman He Loves.

Ana lies under a sheet.
Beautiful music.
A subtitle flashes:
Charles Performs Surgery on the Woman He Loves.
Charles takes out surgical equipment.
He does surgery on Ana.
It is an act of love.
If the actor who plays Charles is a good singer,
it would be nice if he could sing
an ethereal medieval love song in Latin
about being medically cured by love.
He sings acappella as he does the surgery.
If the actress who plays Ana is a good singer,
it would be nice if she recovered from the surgery
and slowly sat up and sang a contrapuntal melody.
When the surgery is over,
Charles takes off Ana's sheet.
Underneath the sheet,
she is dressed in a lovely dress.
They kiss.

2. Ana.

> *Ana, to the audience.*

ANA: I have avoided doctors my whole life.

I don't like how they smell. I don't like how they talk. I don't admire their emotional lives. I don't like how they walk. They walk very fast to get somewhere—tac tac tac—I am walking somewhere important. I don't like that. I like a man who saunters. Like this.

> *Ana saunters across the stage like a man.*

But with Charles, it was like: BLAM!
My mind was going: you're a doctor, I hate you.
But the rest of me was gone, walking out the door, with him.
When he performed surgery on me,
we were already in love.
I was under general anesthetic but I could sense him there.
I think he put something extra in—during the surgery.
Into the missing place.
There are stories of surgeons who leave things inside the body by mistake: rubber gloves, sponges, clamps—
But—you know—I think Charles left his soul inside me.
Into the missing place.

> *She touches her left breast.*

3. Charles.

> *Charles, to the audience:*

CHARLES: There are jokes about breast surgeons.
You know—something like—I've seen more breasts in this city than—
I don't know the punch line.

There must be a punch line.

I'm not a man who falls in love easily. I've been faithful to my wife. We fell in love when we were twenty-two. We had plans. There was justice in the world. There was justice in love. If a person was good enough, an equally good person would fall in love with that person. And then I met—Ana. Justice had nothing to do with it.

There once was a very great American surgeon named Halsted. He was married to a nurse. He loved her—immeasurably. One day Halsted noticed that his wife's hands were chapped and red when she came back from surgery. And so he invented rubber gloves. For her. It is one of the great love stories in medicine. The difference between inspired medicine and uninspired medicine is love.

When I met Ana, I knew:
I loved her to the point of invention.

4. Charles and Ana.

CHARLES: I'm afraid that you have breast cancer.

ANA: If you think I'm going to cry, I'm not going to cry.

CHARLES: It's normal to cry—

ANA: I don't cry when I'm supposed to cry.
Are you going to cut it off?

CHARLES: You must need some time—to digest—

ANA: No. I don't need time. Tell me everything.

CHARLES: You have a variety of options. Many women don't opt for a mastectomy. A lumpectomy and radiation can be just as effective as—

ANA: I want you to cut it off.

CHARLES: You might want to talk with family members—with a husband—are you married?—or with—

ANA: Tomorrow.

CHARLES: Tomorrow?

ANA: Tomorrow.

CHARLES: I'm not sure I have any appointments open tomorrow—

ANA: I'd like you to do it tomorrow.

CHARLES: Then we'll do it tomorrow.

> *They look at each other.*
> *They fall in love.*

ANA: Then I'll see you tomorrow, at the surgery.

CHARLES: Good-bye, Ana.

ANA: Good-bye.

> *They look at each other.*
> *They fall in love some more.*
> *She turns to go. She turns back.*

ANA: Am I going to die?

CHARLES: No. You're not going to die.
I won't let you die.

> *They fall in love completely.*
> *They kiss wildly.*

CHARLES: What's happening?

ANA: I don't know.

CHARLES: This doesn't happen to me.

ANA: Me neither.

CHARLES: Ana, Ana, Ana, Ana…your name goes backwards and forwards…I love you…

ANA: And I love you.
Take off your white coat.

> *They kiss.*

5. Lane, Virginia, Matilde, Charles, and Ana.

> *We are back in the white living room.*
> *We are deposited at the end of the last scene from the first act.*
> *Charles is at the door, with Ana.*

CHARLES: Lane?

LANE: Charles.

CHARLES: Lane. I want us all to know each other. I want to do things right, from the beginning. Lane: this is Ana. Ana, this is my wife, Lane.

ANA: Nice to meet you. I've heard wonderful things about you. I've heard that you are a wonderful doctor.

LANE: Thank you.

> *Ana holds out her hand to Lane.*
> *Lane looks around in disbelief.*
> *Then Lane shakes Ana's hand.*

CHARLES: This is my sister-in-law, Virginia.

ANA: Hello.

VIRGINIA: How do you do.

MATILDE: You look like my mother.

LANE: This is the maid. Matilde. (*To Ana.*)
I fired her this morning. (*To Charles.*)

ANA: Encantada, Matilde.(*Nice to meet you, Matilde.*)

MATILDE: Encantada. Sou do Brasil. (*Nice to meet you. I'm from Brazil.*)

ANA: Eu falo um pouco de portugues, mas que eu falo, falo mal. (*I know a little bit of Portuguese, but it's bad.*)

MATILDE: Eh! boa tentativa! 'ta chegando la!
Es usted de Argentina?
(*Ah! Good try! Not bad.
You're from Argentina?*)

ANA: ¿Cómo lo sabe?
(*How did you know?*)

MATILDE: (*Imitating Ana's accent.*) ¿Cómo lo sabe?
(*How did you know?*)

> They laugh.

LANE: We've all met. You can leave now, Charles.

CHARLES: What happened to your wrist?

LANE: Can opener.

CHARLES: Oh.

> Charles examines the bandage on Lane's wrist.
> She pulls her hand away.

MATILDE: ¿Ha usted estado alguna vez en Brasil?
(*Have you ever been to Brazil?*)

ANA: Una vez, para estudiar rocas.
(*Once to study rocks, in Spanish.*)

MATILDE: Rocas?

ANA: Sí, rocas.

MATILDE: Ah, rochas!
(*Ah, rocks! in Portuguese, pronounced "hochas."*)

ANA: Sí!

They laugh.

VIRGINIA: Should we sit down?

They all sit down.

LANE: Virginia!—Could you get us something to drink.

VIRGINIA: What would you like?

MATILDE: I would like a coffee.

ANA: That sounds nice. I'll have coffee too.

VIRGINIA: Charles?

CHARLES: Nothing for me, thanks.

VIRGINIA: Lane?

LANE: I would like some hard alcohol in a glass with ice. Thank you.

Virginia exits.

LANE: So.

CHARLES: Lane. I know this is unorthodox. But I want us to know each other.

ANA: You are very generous to have me in your home.

LANE: Not at all.

ANA: Yes, you are very generous. I wanted to meet you. I am not a home-wrecker. The last time I fell in love it was with my husband, a long time ago. He was a geologist and a very wild man, an alcoholic. But so fun! So crazy! He peed on lawns and did everything bad and I loved it. But I did not want to have children with him because he was too wild, too crazy. I said you have to stop drinking and then he did stop drinking and then he died of cancer when he was thirty-one.

Matilde murmurs with sympathy.

My heart was broken and I said to myself: I will never love again. And I didn't. I thought I was going to meet my husband —eventually—in some kind of afterlife with fabulous rocks. Blue and green rocks.

And then I met Charles. When Charles said he was married I said Charles we should stop but then Charles referred to Jewish law and I had to say that I agreed and that was that. I wanted you to understand.

LANE: Well, I don't understand. What about Jewish law.

CHARLES: In Jewish law you are legally obligated to break off relations with your wife or husband if you find what is called your *bashert*.

ANA: Your soul-mate.

CHARLES: You are *obligated* to do this. Legally bound. There's something—metaphysically—objective about it.

LANE: You're not Jewish.

CHARLES: I know. But I heard about the *bashert*—on a radio program. And it always stuck with me. When I saw Ana I knew that was it. I knew she was my bashert.

ANA: There is a *midrash* that says when a baby is forty days old, inside the mother's stomach, God picks out its soulmate, and people have to spend the rest of their lives running around to find each other.

CHARLES: Lane. Something very objective happened to me. It's as though I suddenly tested positive for a genetic disease that I've had all along. *Ana has been in my genetic code.*

ANA: Yes. It is strange. We didn't feel guilty because it was so *objective*. And yet both of us are moral people. I don't know Charles very well but I think he is moral but to tell you the truth even if he were immoral I would love him because the love I feel for your husband is so overpowering.

LANE: And this is what you've come to tell me. That you're both innocent according to Jewish law.

ANA and **CHARLES:** Yes.

> *Virginia enters with the drinks.*

MATILDE: Thank you.

> *Lane takes the glass from Virginia.*

LANE: (*To Virginia.*) Charles has come to tell me that according to Jewish law, he has found his soul-mate, and so our marriage is dissolved. He doesn't even need to feel guilty. How about that.

VIRGINIA: You have found your *bashert*.

LANE: How the hell do you know about a *bashert*?

VIRGINIA: I heard it on public radio.

CHARLES: I'm sorry that it happened to you, Lane. It could just as well have happened the other way. You might have met your *bashert*, and I would have been forced to make way. There are things—big invisible things—that come unannounced—they walk in, and we have to give way. I would even congratulate you. Because I have always loved you.

LANE: Well. Congratulations.

A silence. A cold one.

MATILDE: Would anyone like to hear a joke?

ANA: I would.

Matilde tells a joke in Portuguese.
Ana laughs. No one else laughs.

ANA: ¡Qué bueno! ¡Qué chiste más bueno!
(*What a good joke!*)

You are firing Matilde? (*To Lane.*)

LANE: Yes.

ANA: Then we'll hire her to clean our house. I hate to clean. And Charles likes things to be clean. At least I think he does. Charles? Do you like things to be clean?

CHARLES: Sure. I like things to be clean.

ANA: Matilde? Would you like to work for us?

MATILDE: There is something you should know.
I don't like to clean so much.

ANA: Of course you don't. Do you have any other skills?

MATILDE: I can tell jokes.

ANA: Perfect. She's coming to live with us.

LANE: My God! You can't just walk into my home and take everything away from me.

ANA: I thought you fired this young woman.

LANE: Yes. I did.

ANA: Have you changed your mind?

LANE: I don't know. Maybe.

ANA: Matilde, do you have a place to live?

MATILDE: No.

ANA: So she'll come live with us.

VIRGINIA: Matilde is like family.

MATILDE: What?

VIRGINIA: Matilde is like a sister to me.

ANA: Is this true?

MATILDE: I don't know. I never had a sister.

VIRGINIA: We clean together. We talk, and fold laundry, as women used to do. They would gather at the public fountains and wash their clothes and tell stories. Now we are alone in our separate houses and it is terrible.

ANA: So it is Virginia who wants you to stay. Not Lane.

LANE: We both want her to stay. We love Matilde. (*An attempt at the Brazilian pronunciation of Matilde.*)

ANA: Matilde?

MATILDE: I am confused.

LANE: I depend on Matilde. I couldn't stand to replace her. Matilde— are you unhappy here with us?

MATILDE: I—

LANE: Is it the money? You could have a raise.

ANA: Matilde—you should do as you wish. My house is easy to clean. I own hardly anything. I own one table, two chairs, a bed, one painting and I have a little fish whose water needs to be changed. I don't have rugs so there is no vacuuming. But you would have to do Charles' laundry. I will not be his washerwoman.

VIRGINIA: Excuse me. But I think that people who are in love—really in love—would like to clean up after each other. If I were in love with Charles I would enjoy folding his laundry.

> *Lane looks at Virginia.*

ANA: Matilde—what do you think? Would you like to work for us?

VIRGINIA: Please don't leave us, Matilde.

MATILDE: I will split my time. Half with Lane and Virginia, half with Ana and Charles. How is that?

ANA: Lane?

LANE: Matilde is a free agent.

ANA: Of course she is.

CHARLES: Well.
That's settled.

LANE: Are you leaving now?

CHARLES: Do you want me to leave?

> *A pause.*

LANE: Yes.

CHARLES: Okay. Then we'll leave.
Ana and I are going apple-picking this afternoon.
She's never been apple-picking.
Would anyone like to join us?

MATILDE: I've never been apple-picking.

CHARLES: So Matilde will come. Virginia?

VIRGINIA: I love apple-picking.

LANE: Virginia!

CHARLES: Lane?

LANE: You must be insane! Apple-picking! My god! I'M SORRY! But apple-picking? This is not a foreign film! We don't have an *arrangement*! You don't even *like* foreign films! Maybe you'll pretend to like foreign films, for *Ana*, but I can tell you now Ana, he doesn't like them! He doesn't like reading the little subtitles! It gives him a head-ache!

CHARLES: Lane. I don't expect you to—understand this—immediately. But since this thing—has happened to me—I want to live life to the fullest. I know—what it must sound like. But it's different. I want to go apple-picking. I want to go to Machu Picchu. You can be part of that. I want to share my happiness with you.

LANE: I don't want your happiness.

MATILDE: (*To Ana.*) Es cómo una telenovela. Tan triste. (*It's like a soap opera. So sad.*)

CHARLES: Lane—I—

LANE: What.

CHARLES: I hope that you'll forgive me one day.

LANE: Go pick some apples.
Good-bye.

CHARLES: Good-bye.

ANA: Good-bye.

MATILDE: Good-bye.

VIRGINIA: I'll stay.

    Ana, Matilde, and Charles exit.

LANE: I want to be alone.

VIRGINIA: No, you don't.

LANE: Yes, I do.

VIRGINIA: No, you don't.

> *Lane sits on the couch.*
> *Virginia pats her shoulder, awkward.*

VIRGINIA: Do you want—I don't know—a hot water bottle?

LANE: No, I don't want a hot water bottle, Virginia.

VIRGINIA: I just thought—

LANE: —That I'm nine years old with a cold?

VIRGINIA: I don't know what else to do.

> *A pause.*

LANE: You know, actually, I think I'd like one. It sounds nice.

6. Ana and Matilde. Then Charles.

> *Ana and Matilde are up on Ana's balcony.*
> *It is high above the white living room.*
> *It is a small perch, overlooking the sea.*
> *Through French doors,*
> *one can enter or exit the balcony.*
> *A room leading to the balcony is suggested but unseen.*
> *Matilde and Ana wear sunglasses and sun-hats.*
> *They are surrounded by apples.*
> *The following dialogue may be spoken in a*
> *combination of Portuguese and Spanish*
> *and subtitled in English.*
>
> *Underneath the balcony,*
> *Lane is in her living room.*
> *She lies down with a hot water bottle.*

Ana polishes an apple.
They look around at all of the apples.

ANA: Nunca nos vamos a comer todas estas malditas manzanas.
(*We're never going to eat all of these damn apples.*)

MATILDE: Mas é legal ter um monte.
Tantas que é uma loucura ter tantas assim.
Porque você nunca pode comer todas elas.
(*But it's nice to have so many.*
So many that it's crazy to have so many
Because you can never eat them all.)

ANA: Si.

Ana picks out an apple and eats it.

MATILDE: Eu gusto das verdes.
De quais você gosta?
(*I like the green ones.*
Which ones do you like?)

ANA: Las amarillas. Son más dulces. (*The yellow ones. They're sweeter.*)

MATILDE: We could take one bite of each and if it's not a really, really good apple we can throw it into the sea.

ANA: Ahora vos estás hablando como una Norte Americana.
(*Now you're talking like a North American.*)

MATILDE: Vai ser engraçado.
(*It will be fun.*)

ANA: Okay.

They start taking bites of each apple
and if they don't think it's a perfect apple they throw it into the sea.
The sea is also Lane's living room.
Lane sees the apples fall into her living room.
She looks at them.

MATILDE: Eu inventei uma piada nova hoje.

(*I made up a new joke today.*)

ANA: Ah! Bueno!

MATILDE: I made up eighty-four new jokes since I started working for you. I only made up one at the other house. Mas era uma boa. (*It was a good one though.*) Sometimes you have to suffer for the really good ones.

ANA: Why don't you tell jokes for a job?

MATILDE: Algum dia.
(*Someday.*)

> Matilde throws an apple core into the living room.

ANA: Por qué algun día? Por qué no ahora?
(*Why someday? Why not now?*)

MATILDE: I'm looking for the perfect joke. But I am afraid if I found it, it would kill me.

ANA: Por qué?
(*Why?*)

MATILDE: Minha mãe morreu rindo. (*My mother died laughing.*)

ANA: Lo siento.
(*I'm sorry.*)

MATILDE: Obrigada. (*Thank you.*)
She was laughing at one of my father's jokes.

ANA: What was the joke?

MATILDE: Eu nunca vou saber. (*I'll never know.*) Let's not talk about sad things.

> Matilde finds a really really good apple.

MATILDE: Prove essa.
(*Try this one.*)

> Matilde tries it.

ANA: Mmmm. Perfecta.

Charles enters.
From offstage:

CHARLES: Ana!

ANA: We're on the balcony!

> *Charles rushes in wearing scrubs and*
> *carrying an enormous bouquet of flowers.*
> *He goes to Ana and kisses her all over*
> *and continues to kiss her all over.*

ANA: My love! We were just eating apples.

CHARLES: Aren't they delicious?

ANA: Here is the very best one.

> *Charles takes a bite of the best apple.*

CHARLES: Divine!
Excuse me, Matilde.
I need to borrow this woman.

> *He kisses Ana.*
> *He picks up Ana and carries her off into the bedroom.*

MATILDE: Have fun.

ANA and **CHARLES:** Thank you! We will!

> *They exit.*

MATILDE: *(To the audience.)*

The perfect joke happens by accident. The perfect joke is the perfect
music. You want to hear it only once in your life, and then, never again.

> *A subtitle projects:*
> *Matilde tries to think up the perfect joke.*
> *She looks out at the sea.*
> *She thinks.*

7. Matilde, Virginia and Lane.

Virginia is cleaning.
Lane shuffles cards.

LANE: (*Shouting to Matilde who is offstage.*)
Matilde! Your deal.

> *Matilde leaves the balcony.*
> *Lane shuffles the cards.*

VIRGINIA: Lane—your couch is filthy. Wouldn't it be nice to have a fresh clean slip-cover? I could sew you one.

LANE: That would be nice. It would give you a project.

> *Matilde enters.*

LANE: Your deal.

> *Matilde sits.*
> *Above them, on the balcony,*
> *Ana and Charles dance a slow dance.*

LANE: So. Are you happy there? At the other house?

MATILDE: Yes.

LANE: What's her house like?

MATILDE: It's little. She has a balcony that overlooks the sea.

LANE: What's her furniture like?

MATILDE: A table from one place—a chair from another place. It doesn't go together. But it's nice.

LANE: What does she cook?

MATILDE: I'm not a spy!

LANE: I'm sorry.

> *They play cards.*
> *On the balcony,*

> *Charles and Ana finish their dance.*
> *They exit, into the bedroom.*
> *Lane puts down a card.*

LANE: Do they seem like they are very much in love?

MATILDE: Yes—they are very in love.

LANE: How can you—tell?

MATILDE: They stay in bed half the day. Charles doesn't go to work. He cancels half his patients. He wants to spend all his time with Ana.

LANE: Oh.

> *A pause.*

MATILDE: Because Ana is dying again.

LANE: What?

MATILDE: Her disease came back.
She says she won't take any medicine.
She says it's poison.
He says:

CHARLES: You have to go to the hospital!

MATILDE: And she says:

ANA: I won't go to the hospital!

MATILDE: Then they really fight.
It's like a soap opera.
Charles yells and throws things at the wall.

LANE: Charles never yells.

MATILDE: Oh, he yells.
And Ana yells and throws things at him.
They broke all the condiments and spices yesterday.
There was this yellow spice—
and it got in their hair and on their faces
until they were all yellow.

From the balcony:

ANA: I don't want a doctor!
I want a man!

> *A spice jar goes flying.*
> *A cloud of yellow spice lands in Lane's living room.*

ANA: NO HOSPITALS!

LANE: She won't go to the hospital?

MATILDE: No.
I might have to spend more time—you know—at the other house.
To help.

VIRGINIA: Poor Charles.

LANE: Poor Charles?
Poor Ana.
Poor me!
Poor sounds funny if you say it lots of times in a row: poor poor poor
poor poor…Poor. Poor. Poor. Doesn't it sound funny?

VIRGINIA: Lane? Are you all right?

LANE: Oh, me? I'm fine.

8. Ana and Charles. Then, Matilde.

> *Ana and Charles sit on the balcony.*
> *Ana is dressed in a bathrobe.*
> *Ana and Charles try to read one another's mind.*
> *Below the balcony, in the living room,*
> *Lane and Virginia fold laundry together.*

CHARLES: Eight.

ANA: No, seven. You were very close.

CHARLES: I'll go again.

ANA: Okay.

CHARLES: Four.

ANA: Yes!

CHARLES: I knew it! I could see four apples. Now, colors.

ANA: Okay.

CHARLES: I'll start.

ANA: Red.

CHARLES: No.

ANA: Blue.

CHARLES: No.

ANA: I give up.

CHARLES: Purple.
We have to concentrate harder. Like this. Ready? You go.

ANA: I'm tired.

CHARLES: I'm sorry. I'll stop.

> *Charles rubs Ana's head.*

ANA: Why all these guessing games?

CHARLES: You know Houdini?

ANA: The magician?

CHARLES: Yes. Houdini and his wife practiced reading each other's minds. So that—if one of them died—they'd be able to talk to each other—you know, after.

ANA: Did it work?

CHARLES: No.

ANA: Oh.

CHARLES: But I love you more than Houdini loved his wife. He was distracted—by his magic. I'm not distracted. Ana. Let's go to the hospital.

ANA: I told you.
No hospitals!

> *Charles is sad.*

ANA: Don't be sad, Charles.

CHARLES: Don't be sad! My God!

ANA: I can't take this.
I'm going for a swim.
Matilde!
Come look after Charles.
I'm going swimming.

> *Ana exits.*
> *Charles looks out over the balcony,*
> *watching Ana run out to the water.*

CHARLES: (*To Ana.*) Ana! Think of a country under the water! I'll guess it from the balcony!

MATILDE: She can't hear you.

> *Charles disrobes to his underwear.*
> *He throws his clothes into Lane's living room.*

CHARLES: Excuse me, Matilde. I'm going for a swim.

MATILDA: I thought you can't swim.

CHARLES: I'll learn to swim.

> *Underneath the balcony, in Lane's living room,*
> *Lane comes across Charles' sweater.*
> *She breathes it in.*
> *She weeps.*
> *Charles finishes disrobing and leans over the balcony.*

CHARLES: Ana! What's the country? I think it's a very small country! Is it Luxembourg? Ana!

He runs off.
Matilde looks out over the water.
A pause.
Matilde is startled.
Suddenly, with great clarity,
Matilde thinks up the perfect joke.

MATILDE: My God.
Oh no.
My God.
It's the perfect joke.
Am I dead?
No.

9. Lane, Virginia. Then Matilde.

Lane sits with Charles' sweater in her hands.
Virginia enters, vacuuming.

LANE: Stop it!

VIRGINIA: What?

LANE: Stop cleaning!

VIRGINIA: Why?

LANE: *(Over the vacuum.)* I DON'T WANT ANYTHING IN MY HOUSE TO BE CLEAN EVER AGAIN! I WANT THERE TO BE DIRT AND PIGS IN THE CORNER AND LOTS OF DIRTY FUCKING SOCKS—AND NONE OF THEM MATCH—NONE OF THEM— BECAUSE YOU KNOW WHAT—THAT IS HOW I FEEL.

Lane unplugs the vacuum.

VIRGINIA: Wow. I'm sorry.

LANE: AND YOU KNOW WHAT? I WILL NOT LET MY HOUSE BE A BREEDING GROUND FOR YOUR WEIRD OBSESSIVE DIRT

FETISH. I WILL NOT PERMIT YOU TO FEEL LIKE A BETTER PERSON JUST BECAUSE YOU PUSH DIRT AROUND ALL DAY ON MY BEHALF.

VIRGINIA: I was just trying to help.

LANE: Well, it's not helping.

VIRGINIA: I wonder—when it was—that you became—such a bitch? Oh, yes, I remember. Since the day you were born, you thought that anyone with a *problem* had a defect of the will. Well, you know what? You're wrong about that. Some people have problems, real problems—

LANE: Yes. I see people with *real problems* all day long. At the hospital.

VIRGINIA: I think—there's a small part of me—that's enjoyed watching your life fall apart. To see you lose your composure. For once. I thought—we could be sisters. Real sisters who tell each other real things. But I was wrong. Well, fine. I'm not picking up your dry cleaning anymore. I'm going to get a job.

LANE: What job?

VIRGINIA: Any job!

LANE: What are you qualified to do at this point?

VIRGINIA: No wonder Charles left. You have no compassion.

LANE: (*overlapping*)	**VIRGINIA:**
I do so have compassion.	Ana is a woman with
I do so have compassion!	compassion.

VIRGINIA: Really. How so.

LANE: I traded my whole life to help people who are sick! What do you do?

> *Virginia and Lane breathe.*
> *Virginia and Lane are in a state of silent animal warfare,*
> *a brand of warfare particular to sisters.*

LANE: I'm going to splash some water on my face.

VIRGINIA: Good.

> *Lane exits.*
> *From the balcony, the strains of an aria.*
> *Ana listens to opera on the balcony, looking out over the sea.*
> *Virginia dumps a plant on the ground and the dirt spills onto the floor.*
> *She realizes with some surprise that she enjoys this.*
> *Virginia makes a giant operatic mess in the living room.*
> *Matilde enters.*

MATILDE: What are you doing?
Virginia?

> *Virginia finishes making her operatic mess.*
> *The aria ends.*
> *Ana leaves the balcony.*

MATILDE: (*To Virginia.*) You are okay?

VIRGINIA: Actually. I feel fabulous.

> *Matilde sits down.*
> *Matilde puts her head in her arms.*
> *Lane enters.*

LANE: What the hell happened here?

VIRGINIA: I was mad. Sorry.

> *Virginia flicks a piece of dirt across the room.*
> *Lane looks at Matilde.*
> *Matilde continues to bury her head in her arms.*

LANE: (*To Virginia.*) What's wrong with her?

> *Virginia shrugs.*

MATILDE: It's a mess.

VIRGINIA: I'll clean it up.

MATILDE: Not this. Ana. Charles. It's a mess.

LANE: Have they—fallen out of love?

MATILDE: No.

VIRGINIA: Is she very sick?

MATILDE: Yes.

LANE: Oh.

VIRGINIA: How terrible.

MATILDE: Yes.
And now Charles has gone away.

LANE: What?

MATILDE: (*To Lane.*) To Alaska.

VIRGINIA: What?

MATILDE: (*To Virginia.*) To Alaska.

LANE: But—why?

MATILDE: He says he's going to chop down a tree for Ana.

VIRGINIA: What?

MATILDE: A "you" tree.
He called it a you tree.

     Matilde points: you.

VIRGINIA: A you tree?

MATILDE: A you tree. He says he's going to invent a new "you medicine."

VIRGINIA: My, God. He's gone crazy with love!

LANE: He's not crazy. It's a yew tree. Y-E-W. (*Spelling it out.*) A Pacific Yew tree. The bark was made into Taxol. The compound prevents microtubules from decomposing. Cancer cells become so clogged with microtubules that they are slower to grow and divide.

MATILDE: He said it was a special tree.

LANE: Yes. It is a special tree.

MATILDE: He wants to plant it in the middle of Ana's courtyard.

So she can smell the tree, while she's on her balcony. She won't go to the hospital. So he said he would bring the hospital to her.

VIRGINIA: That's beautiful.

LANE: It's not beautiful, Virginia. There is a woman dying, alone, while Charles chops down a fucking tree. How heroic.

VIRGINIA: Does she need a doctor?

MATILDE: Yes. She needs a doctor.
But she won't go to the hospital.
So I thought I would ask.
Do you know any doctors who go to the house?

VIRGINIA: You mean house calls?

MATILDE: Yes, house calls.

> *Virginia and Matilde look at Lane.*

LANE: Why are you looking at me?

> *They continue to look at Lane.*

LANE: You want me to take care of my husband's soul mate.

VIRGINIA: Look at her as a patient. Not a person.
You can do that.

LANE: If she wanted to see a doctor, she'd go to the hospital. I am *not* going to her house. It would be totally inappropriate.

> *They look at Lane.*
> *In the distance, Charles walks slowly across the stage dressed in a parka,*
> *looking for his tree.*
> *A great freezing wind.*

10. Lane Makes a House Call to her Husband's Soul Mate.

On Ana's balcony.
Lane listens to Ana's heart with a stethoscope.

LANE: Breathe in.
Breathe in again.

Lane takes off her stethoscope.

LANE: Are you having any trouble breathing?

ANA: No. But sometimes it hurts when I breathe.

LANE: Where?

ANA: Here.

LANE: Do you have pain when you're at rest?

ANA: Yes.

LANE: Where?

ANA: In my spine.

LANE: Is the pain sharp, or dull?

ANA: Sharp.

LANE: Does it radiate?

ANA: Like light?

LANE: I mean—does it move? Does it move from one place to another?

ANA: Yes. From here to there.

LANE: How's your appetite?

ANA: Not great.
You must hate me.

LANE: Look— I'm being a doctor right now. That's all.

Lane palpates Ana's spine.

LANE: Does that hurt?

ANA: It hurts already.

LANE: I can't know anything without doing tests.

ANA: I know.

LANE: And you won't go to the hospital.

ANA: No.

LANE: All right.

ANA: Do you think I'm crazy?

LANE: No.

ANA: Well. Can I get you anything to drink? I have some iced tea.

LANE: Sure. Thank you.

> *Ana goes to get some iced tea.*
> *Lane looks over the balcony at the sea.*
> *She starts weeping.*
> *Ana comes back with the iced tea.*

ANA: Lane?

LANE: Oh, God! I'm *not* going to cry in front of you.

ANA: It's okay. You can cry. You must hate me.

LANE: I don't hate you.

ANA: Why are you crying?

LANE: Okay! I hate you! You—glow—with some kind of—thing—
I can't *acquire* that—this thing—sort of glows off you—like a veil—in
reverse—you're like *anyone's* soul mate—

You have a balcony—I don't have a balcony—Charles looks at you—
and he glows too—you're like two glow-worms—he never looked at
me like that.

ANA: Lane.

LANE: I looked at our wedding pictures to see—maybe—he looked at me that way—back then—and no—he didn't—he looked at me with *admiration*—I didn't know there was another way to be looked at—how could I know—I didn't know his face was capable of *doing that*— the way he looked at you—in my living room.

>   *Pause.*

ANA: I'm sorry.

LANE: No you're not. If you were really sorry, you wouldn't have done it.
We do as we please, and then we say we're sorry. But we're not sorry. We're just—uncomfortable—watching other people in pain.

>   *A pause.*
>   *Ana hands Lane an iced tea.*

LANE: Thank you.

>   *They sit for a while.*
>   *They breathe.*
>   *Lane drinks her iced tea.*
>   *They both look at the fish in the bowl.*

LANE: What kind of fish is that?

ANA: A fighting fish.

LANE: How old is it?

ANA: Twelve.

LANE: That's old for a fish.

ANA: I know. I keep expecting it to die. But it doesn't.

>   *Lane taps on the bowl.*
>   *The fish wriggles.*

ANA: How did you and Charles fall in love?

LANE: He didn't tell you?

ANA: No.

LANE: Oh. Well, we were in medical school together. We were anatomy partners. We fell in love over a dead body.

> *They look at each other.*
> *Lane forgives Ana.*

ANA: Want an apple?

LANE: Sure.

> *Ana gives Lane an apple.*
> *Lane takes a bite and stops.*

LANE: Did Charles pick this apple?

ANA: I don't know who picked it.

> *Lane eats the apple.*

LANE: It's good.

> *In the distance,*
> *Charles walks across the stage in a heavy parka.*
> *He carries a pickaxe.*
> *In the living room, it is snowing.*

11. Lane calls Virginia.

> *Lane and Virginia on the telephone.*

LANE: I saw Ana.

VIRGINIA: And?

LANE: She's coming to live with me.

VIRGINIA: What?

LANE: She can't be alone. She's too sick. I invited her.

VIRGINIA: That's generous. I'm impressed.

LANE: So will you be around—during the day—to help Matilde look after her?

VIRGINIA: Oh, me? No. I got a job.

LANE: What?

VIRGINIA: I got a job.

LANE: Doing what?

VIRGINIA: I'm a check out girl. At the grocery store.

LANE: You're not.

VIRGINIA: I am. I had my first day. I liked it. I liked using the cash register. I liked watching the vegetables go by on the conveyor belt. Purple, orange, red, green, yellow. My colleagues were nice. They didn't care if I went to Bryn Mawr. There was fellow feeling among the workers. Solidarity. And I liked it.

LANE: Wow.

VIRGINIA: So, I'm sorry. But I'll be too busy to help you.

    Pause.

LANE: Wait. You made that story up.

VIRGINIA: Fine.

LANE: So you'll help me.

VIRGINIA: You want my help?

LANE: Yes.

VIRGINIA: Are you sure?

LANE: Yes.

VIRGINIA: Say: I want your help.

LANE: I want your help.

VIRGINIA: Then I'll help you.

12. Ana and Virginia. Then Matilde. Then Lane.

> *All of Ana's possessions have been moved into Lane's living room.*
> *Ana's fish is in a bowl on the coffee table.*
> *There are bags of apples on the carpet.*
> *And luggage. With clothes spilling out of a bag.*
> *Virginia is delivering a special tray of food for Ana.*

ANA: People talk about *cancer* like it's this special thing you have a *relationship* with. And it becomes blood count, biopsy, chemotherapy, radiation, bone marrow, blah blah blah blah blah. As long as I live I want to retain my own language.

Mientras tenga vida, quiero aferrarme mi propio idioma.

No extra hospital words. I don't want a relationship with a disease. I want to have a relationship with death. That's important. But to have a relationship with a *disease*—that's some kind of bourgeois invention. And I hate it.

> *Virginia gives Ana the tray.*

ANA: Thank you.

> *Ana eats a bite.*

VIRGINIA: Do you like it?

ANA: It's delicious. What is it?

VIRGINIA: It's a casserole. No one makes casserole anymore. I thought it might be—comforting.

ANA: What's in it?

VIRGINIA: Things you wouldn't want to know about.

ANA: Well, it's good. Thank you for taking care of me, Virginia.

> *Virginia is moved.*

ANA: What's wrong?

VIRGINIA: I'm not used to people thanking me.

Matilde enters, holding a telegram.
She hands it to Ana.

MATILDE: There is a telegram. From Charles.

In the distance, Charles appears
wearing a heavy parka. Snow falls.

CHARLES: Dear Ana. Stop. I have cut down the tree. Stop. Cannot get on plane with tree. Stop. Must learn to fly plane. Stop. Wait for me. Stop. Your beloved, Charles.

He exits.

ANA: I want him to be a nurse and he wants to be an explorer. Asi es la vida.
(That's life.)

Lane enters.

LANE: Hi.

ANA: Hello!

An awkward moment.

VIRGINIA: Would anyone like ice cream? I made some ice cream.

LANE: You *made* it?

VIRGINIA: It was no trouble.

ANA: I love ice cream.

VIRGINIA: Do you like chocolate?

ANA: Who doesn't like chocolate. Crazy people,

VIRGINIA: I'll get it.

MATILDE: I'll help you.

Matilde and Virginia exit.
Ana and Lane sit on the couch.
Lane taps on the fish-bowl.

LANE: He made it all right.

ANA: He's a strong fish.

>*Lane taps the bowl.*
>*The fish wriggles.*
>*Matilde and Virginia come back with spoons.*
>*They all eat ice cream out of the same container.*

ANA: Mmmm! Amazing!

MATILDE: It must be what God eats when he is tired.

ANA: So soft.

MATILDE: Sometimes ice cream in this country is so hard.

ANA: Si.

LANE: I like ice cream.

>*They all eat ice cream.*

ANA: Can you imagine a time before ice cream? When they couldn't keep things frozen? There was once a ship filled with ice—it sailed from Europe to South America. The ice melted by the time it got to South America. And the captain of the ship was bankrupt. All he had to sell when he got there was water.

VIRGINIA: A ship full of water.

MATILDE: A ship full of water.

>*Lane finishes the container of ice cream.*
>*No one cleans up.*

VIRGINIA: (*To Ana.*) You look feverish. Are you warm?

ANA: I'm cold.

VIRGINIA: I'll get a thermometer.

ANA: No thermometers!

LANE: How about a blanket?

ANA: Okay. I'd like a blanket.

LANE: (*To Virginia.*) Where do I keep blankets?

VIRGINIA: I'll show you.

> *They exit.*

ANA: Matilde. My bones hurt.

> *Matilde stays.*

MATILDE: I know they do.

ANA: Do you know what it feels like when your bones hurt?

MATILDE: No.

ANA: I hope you never know.
Matilde. You once told me that your father killed your mother with a joke.

MATILDE: Yes.

ANA: I would like you to kill me with a joke.

MATILDE: I don't want to kill you. I like you.

ANA: If you like me, help me.

MATILDE: What about Charles? Will you wait for him?

ANA: No.

MATILDE: Why?

ANA: I would lose all my bravery.

MATILDE: I understand.

ANA: You'll do it then?

> *A pause.*

MATILDE: Okay.

ANA: When?

MATILDE: When you want me to.

ANA: You don't need time to make up a joke?

MATILDE: I made it up on your balcony.

ANA: Tomorrow, then.

MATILDE: Tomorrow.

> *Lane enters with a blanket.*
> *She hands it to Ana.*

LANE: I hope it's warm enough.

ANA: Thank you.
(*To Matilde.*) Good-night.

MATILDE: (*To Ana.*) Good-night.

> *Ana puts her head on the pillow, closing her eyes.*

MATILDE: (*Whispering to Lane.*) Are you coming?

LANE: In a minute.

> *Matilde exits.*
> *Lane sits on the floor and watches Ana sleep.*
> *Lane guards Ana the way a dog would guard a rival dog,*
> *if her rival were sick.*

13. Matilde tells Ana a joke.

> *The lights turn from night to day.*
> *The next day.*
> *Lane, Virginia, and Matilde are gathered around Ana.*

ANA: I want to say good-bye to everyone before Matilde tells me a joke.

LANE: Can't I give you anything for the pain?

ANA: Good-bye, Lane.

LANE: Good-bye, Ana.

> *They embrace.*

ANA: Take care of Charles.

LANE: You think I'll be taking care of him?

ANA: Of course.

LANE: Why?

ANA: You love him.
Good-bye Virginia.

> *Virginia weeps.*

ANA: Don't cry.
Thank you for taking care of me, Virginia.

> *Virginia weeps.*

ANA: Oh—see? That makes it worse. Oh, Virginia. I can't take it. Matilde.
Let's have the joke.

MATILDE: Are you ready?

ANA: Yes.
Everyone's always dying lying down.
I want to die standing up.

> *Ana stands.*

ANA: The two of you had better leave the room.
I don't want you dying before your time.

> *They nod.*
> *They leave.*

ANA: Matilde.
Deseo el chiste ahora.
(I want the joke now.)

> *The lights change.*
> *Music.*
> *Matilde whispers a cosmic joke in Ana's ear.*
> *We don't hear it.*
> *We hear sublime music instead.*

A subtitle projects:

The funniest joke in the world.

Ana laughs and laughs.
Ana collapses.
Matilde kneels beside her.
Matilde wails.

MATILDE: Ohh—

Lane and Virginia rush in.
Lane checks Ana's pulse.
The women look at one another.

VIRGINIA: What do we do?

LANE: I don't know.

VIRGINIA: You're the doctor!

LANE: I've never seen someone die in a house before.
Only in a hospital.
Where they clean everything up.

VIRGINIA: What do the nurses do?

MATILDE: They close the eyes.

LANE: That's right.

Matilde closes Ana's eyes.

MATILDE: And they wash the body.

LANE: I'll wash her.

Lane goes to get a towel and a bowl of water.

VIRGINIA: Should we say a prayer?

MATILDE: You say a prayer, Virginia. A prayer cleans the air the way water cleans the dirt.

VIRGINIA: Ana. I hope you are apple picking.

Lane enters with a bowl of water.
She washes Ana's body.
Time slows down.
Suddenly, from offstage:

CHARLES: Ana!

Charles pounds on the door.

CHARLES: Ana! Ana!

The women look at one another.
Charles walks in carrying an enormous tree.
The tree reaches all the way up to the balcony.
Charles is sweating and breathing as though
he has carried his tree great distances.
Lane goes to Charles.

CHARLES: I brought back this tree.
I went to the other house—but no one was—
It won't help?

LANE: No.

CHARLES: Why?

LANE: Charles.

CHARLES: You were here?

LANE: Yes.

CHARLES: Can I see her?

Lane nods.

LANE: Charles?

Lane kisses Charles on the forehead.

CHARLES: Thank you. Will you hold my tree?

LANE: Yes.

Lane holds the tree.

> *The light changes.*
> *Charles moves towards Ana's body*
> *As the lights come up on Matilde.*

14. Matilde.

> *Matilde, to the audience.*

MATILDE: This is how I imagine my parents.
My mother is about to give birth to me.
The hospital is too far away.
My mother runs up a hill in December and says: *now!*
My mother is lying down under a tree.
My father is telling her a joke to try and keep her calm.

> *Ana and Charles become Matilde's mother and father.*
> *Matilde's father whispers a joke in Portuguese to her mother.*

My mother laughed. She laughed so hard that I popped out.
My mother said I was the only baby who laughed when I came into
the world.
She said I was laughing at my father's joke.
I laughed to take in the air.
I took in some air, and then I cried.
They sang me a song to make me stop crying.
It goes like this:

> *[Matilde's parents sing a fragment of a Brazilian lullaby to her].*
> *A moment of completion between Matilde and her parents.*

MATILDE: I think maybe heaven is a sea of untranslatable jokes.
Only everyone is laughing.

END OF PLAY

NOTES ON HELEN
by Ellen McLaughlin

This play is hugely indebted to Liz Engelman, who organized the Hedgebrook Women Playwrights Festival at ACT Theatre in Seattle in 2000. Four playwrights were invited to submit new work for readings at the theatre, followed by a retreat at Hedgebrook. Liz invited me in the winter of '99, when I was licking my wounds after a bruising critical reception for my play *Tongue of a Bird* in New York. I had been severely blocked for months—the syrup wasn't pouring—and I was dubious as to whether I'd ever be able to write again. Indeed week after week went by as I stared at my relentlessly blank computer screen. I eventually had to confess to Liz that not only did I not have a play, I didn't even have an idea for a play. Perhaps they should give this opportunity to some, well, writer? Liz told me that whatever I could come up with in the remaining weeks, they'd do a reading of it. If not for her unaccountable confidence I would never have written this play, but I would also have missed out on the extraordinary experience of Hedgebrook, where I spent a week in Oak cottage, writing in that good solitude (when not doing errands for my beloved woodstove) and waking at night to listen to the intricate silence of the woods. The company of other playwrights and dramaturgs at the farmhouse table was one of the great joys of that time. I remember a lot of laughter, but also long conversations with colleagues about craft and our lives as writers. I will always be grateful.

Happily, the syrup, as it were, poured.

What happened was that I remembered a suggestion from Brian Kulick, who was associate director at the Public Theater when *Tongue of a Bird* was produced there. He thought I should take a look at Euripides' play, *Helen*, wherein Helen never goes to Troy at all, having been replaced by a simulacrum, made by the gods, who is taken to Troy in her place while the real Helen spends the entire war in Egypt, waiting for Meneleus to come pick her up after the war is over. Most peculiar. Euripides wrote it, as far as we can make out, in 412 B.C., which was when the first reports were just coming back to Athens concerning the calamitous outcome of their expedition against Sicily. The city was in shock, reeling with grief over what had become of their imperial venture. (Not a single boat came back. One in four Athenians died and a large number of those who weren't killed ended up working as slaves in the quarries in Sicily.) Rather than write something along the lines of *The Trojan Women*, an outright *cri de coeur* against war and its horrors—of which the Athenians were all too aware at the moment —he wrote *Helen*, which is unlike anything else we have in the canon of classic plays.

Helen is what might be called a tragicomedy and the feeling of it is somewhat surreal, at least to modern ears. The basic premise seems absurd and slightly amusing at the same time that there is something terrifically disturbing about the whole thing. Early on in the play, Helen is confronted by a Greek soldier who, after finally being convinced that she is who she seems to be (the play is filled with recognition scenes, as one might expect), lets out a howl of disbelief and horror at the thought that so many should have died for a mere phantom—for nothing, in fact. That moment interested me. And I'm sure it had a dark piquancy for its original audience. To find that a ghastly war was fought under false pretenses makes the war almost unthinkably obscene —a truth Americans are all too familiar with at this moment in our history. Euripides' *Helen* is one of the greatest, if strangest, antiwar plays anyone ever wrote and it is born of a despair and disorientation we are sadly coming to know for ourselves.

I take huge liberties with Euripides' text, as anyone familiar with the original will no doubt notice. But I hope my version is faithful in tone to the disquieting hybrid creature that inspired it.

— **Ellen McLaughlin**

BIOGRAPHY

Ellen McLaughlin's plays include *Days and Nights Within, A Narrow Bed, Infinity's House, Iphigenia and Other Daughters, Tongue of a Bird, The Trojan Women, Helen, The Persians, Oedipus, Ajax in Iraq, Kissing the Floor,* and *Penelope.*

Producers include Actors Theatre of Louisville, the Actors' Gang, Classic Stage Company, Intiman Theatre, Almeida Theater (London), the Mark Taper Forum, the Public Theater, Oregon Shakespeare Festival, National Actors Theater, the Getty Villa, and the Guthrie Theater, among others.

Grants and awards include the Great American Play Contest, the Susan Smith Blackburn Prize, National Endowment for the Arts, the Writer's Award (Lila Wallace-Reader's Digest Fund), the Berilla Kerr Award for Playwriting, and a TCG/Fox Residency Grant (for *Ajax in Iraq,* written for the American Repertory Theater Institute).

She has taught playwriting at Barnard College since 1995. Other teaching posts include Breadloaf School of English, Yale Drama School, and Princeton University, among others.

McLaughlin is also an actor. She is most well known for having originated the part of the Angel in Tony Kushner's *Angels in America,* appearing in every U.S. production from its earliest workshops through its Broadway run.

Publications include *The Greek Plays,* published by Theatre Communications Group and publications of seven of her plays by Playscripts.com. Recent Off-Broadway productions include *Ajax in Iraq* (Flux Theater) and *Septimus and Clarissa,* an adaptation of Woolf's *Mrs. Dalloway,* with Ripe Time at Baruch Center for the Performing Arts.

ACKNOWLEDGMENTS

Helen premiered at the Public Theater (George C. Wolfe, Producer; Michael Hurst, Managing Director) in New York City on April 3, 2002. The director was Tony Kushner. The set design was by Michael Yeargan, costume design by Susan Hilferty, lighting design by Scott Zielinski, and sound design by Gina Leishman. The production stage manager was C.A. Clark. The cast included Johanna Day, Donna Murphy, Denis O'Hare, Phylicia Rashad, and Marian Seldes.

HELEN
by Ellen McLaughlin

CHARACTERS

HELEN, impossible to tell how old she is. Suffice it to say that seventeen years ago, she was in her prime.

SERVANT, about a decade older than Helen, hard to say.

IO, about a decade younger than Helen.

ATHENA, a goddess. Yet Helen's age.

MENELAUS, a veteran. Middle-aged.

TIME AND PLACE

Egypt, about seven years after the end of the Trojan War.
Yet Helen gets some cable.

The play takes place in a hotel room in Egypt. It's a fairly upscale hotel, perhaps with a dash of colonial Victorian detail, but there can be some slightly kitschy elements in the decor as well as several touches that clue us into the fact that we are indeed in Egypt. There is a large television set of the boxy, glowing, sixties type, complete with rabbit ears. It's pointed away from the audience and toward the glum if attractive woman sitting on the bed. She is surrounded by a certain amount of feminine debris: make-up, nail polish, clumps of Kleenex, a waxing kit, that sort of thing. There might be a number of aging bouquets of flowers. Helen's hair is down. She is wearing a beautiful undergarment, a gown of some kind, covered by a stunning robe. She holds a large, ornate fly-swatter in readiness. She stares out at the audience, listening.

HELEN: It's just a matter of time. It starts with one and then the next… I spend the whole day killing them. One by one. Until they're all dead. And then night comes. And it's finally silent. And that's my doing. But then every morning it starts all over again when the first one makes itself known. (*She listens.*) This is the nature of my existence. (*She turns her attention to us.*) It's not…it's not a *punishment* exactly, I mean I'm not in Hades…You know, that poor sap Sisyphus, with the *rock*? No. For one thing, I'm not *dead*, and this is…the whole set-up (*she gestures around*), it's all very…mean, I have nothing to *complain* about, it's just… it's just that nothing ever happens, I mean NOTHING EVER HAPPENS. No one comes, no one goes, except the help, if you could even call her that—these Egyptian help, they need a lot of help, if you know what I mean…And then there are flies. Not a lot. Just enough. Enough to make you want to rip your face off, if you could, and I can't, of course. If I could have done *that*…(*A moment of depression. She shakes it off.*) I've actually gotten rather good at it. I mean, it's not *surprising* that you might excel at something when it's the *only thing you do all day every day for seventeen years.* But see, here's the thing, each slaughter is remarkably like…an event. It makes the day, um, occur somehow. Here in my sanctuary from all that (*she gestures outside*), I kill flies.

> *She hears a fly. She smiles and puts up a finger. Expertly she stalks her prey and then—thwack—swats the night table. She lifts the swatter to inspect the body, then darts the swatter beneath it and carries it off stage left, as if transporting a flapjack on a spatula. We hear a toilet flush. She reenters.*

Ah, the first little death of the day. I often think it's the best. Except, of course, for the last.

Surprising isn't it? In this hotsy totsy hotel. But that's Egypt for you. Positively teeming with life. All that muck. River ooze.

Suddenly, she is seized by a fragment of poetry. This poetic mode always seems to come out of nowhere and when it's over, she doesn't quite know what to make of what's happened to her.

"As when flies in swarming myriads animate the spring air—haunting the herdsman's stalls and spinning in buzzing circles over the pails of new milk—in such vast multitudes mustered the long-haired Greeks upon the plain." (*A slightly perplexed moment.*)

The war. Every now and then these snatches of poetry go through my head. I can't explain it, and I never know when it's going to happen. Maybe I make them up. Or maybe my unconscious mind is tuned to some frequency—WGR EEK, or something, who knows? But it's the only news of the war I get. God knows there's nothing worthwhile on *this* piece of crap. (*She smacks the television with her fly swatter.*) It's hardly worth bothering. (*She turns the television on.*) I mean, look at this. Barbarian nursery rhymes, cooking shows, bowling, endless foreign soap operas with tinny music and shiny polyester costumes. It's maddening. *I have no idea what's going on.* You go looking for something with *relevance*, a larger sense of what is happening and the best you can do is the Weather Channel, which…It's the only network with anything like *global concern* and yet…Look at it! Record highs, record lows. Spiral clouds of color graphics that spin bumpily toward a coast and stop, spin and stop…and there they are, there they always are… those amiable people in sports jackets standing in front of a livid map of some place you can't…quite…make…out…and yes, they're gesturing with their pointers and they're presumably talking about some sort of *front*, cold or hot, wet or dry or… (*She screams in frustration.*)

IS THIS *NEWS*?

THIS IS ALL SO *UNHELPFUL*!

She bangs the top of the set with the flyswatter.

There's a war going on, people, right underneath those cumulus clouds! Could we maybe get a graphic of that? (*She changes the channel.*)

MORE MAKE-UP TIPS. WHO WATCHES THIS SHIT?

> *A servant enters.*

NO, I DON'T WANT A FACIAL. NO, I DON'T WANT ANOTHER MANICURE. MY FINGERTIPS ACHE AND THEY'RE TOO SHINY.

SERVANT: Cow to see you, Madam.

HELEN: A what?

SERVANT: A cow. Anxious for an interview.

> *Helen lifts an eyebrow.*

She's Greek.

HELEN: Send her up.

> *Servant exits.*

First time in *years*. I mean (what am I talking about?) EVER. FIRST TIME EVER anyone other than, you know, the *help*, has entered this room…Oh, fabulous. (*She futzes with her clothing happily.*) A CONVERSATION. And with a *Greek*! Albeit a Greek *cow*, but apparently a talking one. (*She puts a hand to her heart.*) I really must get a grip. Remember who I am, and all that, but oh, maybe she can tell me *what the heck has been going on!*

> *She hears and then sees a fly. She swats it efficiently and carries it off to the toilet. We hear a flush. Io enters. She is not in fact a cow anymore, though she has retained the white ears. Other than that, she is quite human, attractive and a bit hyper. She wears a plush white hotel robe—hieroglyphs indicating the hotel name on the pocket—and hotel slippers. Helen enters.*

IO: Sorry to barge in like this. I just got to town and, my God, when I heard there was someone on the top floor who spoke Greek, I mean, I just *had* to talk to *someone*. I haven't talked to anyone in ages, I mean I literally haven't talked to anyone in ages. I was until recently a cow.

HELEN: You were a cow.

IO: Yeah. Four legs, tail, moo, milkable, the whole bit. Years like that. Awful. But since I arrived in Egypt I've just been feeling so much better.

Practically back to normal. Except for the ears.

HELEN: I kind of like them.

IO: Some slight glitch. They keep telling me they'll work it out

HELEN: They do nice things for your face.

IO: You really think so? Thanks. I'll be glad to get rid of them though. I've been working with such a limited color palette. I mean I have been a SLAVE to white for years now. And you know how white spots. It's just impossible to keep clean when you're on the road. (*Pause.*) You know who you look like?

HELEN: Yes.

IO: (*Dawning realization.*) No, really, it's uncanny.

HELEN: Yes. I do.

IO: Oh my GOD. DO YOU KNOW WHO YOU ARE?

HELEN: Pretty much, yeah.

IO: What are you doing here? You're the Queen! Of Sparta! Shouldn't you be in…Sparta?

HELEN: I'm actually supposed to be in Troy at the moment.

IO: Troy?

HELEN: (*Unsettled that she needs to explain this.*) There was a whole kerfuffle with a sort of contest between the major goddesses, it was a big deal. And the upshot is that there's been this *huge*…'cause everybody *thinks* that I'm in… (*Io is still clueless.*) Gosh, you are out of touch…What happened was that this prince of Troy named Paris was for some reason the judge of the contest and Aphrodite promised me to him as a bribe so that he'd choose her as the most beautiful goddess. I guess it just kind of *slipped her mind* that I was already married. But hey, she's a goddess, what does she care? So Paris sails over to Sparta pronto for a visit and we just knock ourselves out for him. Endless banquets every night, tours of the capital, state functions, dances. House guests. You know the deal.

IO: Was he cute?

HELEN: Pretty dreamy. Coffee colored skin, lots of hair, a way of sort of *taking you in* when he looked at you, like he was sort of *dying*. Real style—you know how foreign men are—top notch fabrics, nice drape, no pockets, just…but not too…I mean, he had *taste* but he didn't make a big *thing* of it.

IO: Uh huh.

HELEN: (*Trying to remember.*) And he smelled like oranges…and… and crushed rosemary.

IO: Yummy.

HELEN: That's what I thought. Of course my husband, Menelaus, was just completely clueless. Told one hunting story after another while the two of us were playing footsie under the table. I'm not *proud* of what I did, I'm just *saying*…The guy was a charmer, you know, and I'd been doing the wife-of-the-great-man bit for, like, *years*, nothing but Chanel suits and sensible shoes day in day out. And as for the sex, it had been strictly missionary position since the git-go—years of staring at the ceiling while he went at it. And, and, he HUMMED.

IO: Hummed?

HELEN: Yeah, all the time. I mean ALL the time. His eyes would glaze over and he'd just…(*She hums tonelessly.*)

IO: Yow.

HELEN: This is what I was up against. So when Menelaus leaves us alone for a few days while he goes to visit his mother or something, well…

IO: So, what? You eloped? Vanished into the night?

HELEN: So the story goes. One of the stories anyway.

IO: Weren't you, like, *there*?

HELEN: Well. No. Hera gets this bee in her bonnet about the whole thing—says I'm the reason she lost the contest basically, and she decides to replace me with some *copy* of me, I mean she looks just like me except that she isn't, you know…*me*. She's made out of *cloud* or something… So anyway she gets this *copy* to go to Troy with Paris and cause all this trouble while she spirits me, the *real* me, here. To Egypt. Where nobody knows me. And the TV reception stinks and the front desk will just NOT listen to my special needs and there doesn't seem to be a dry cleaner on the entire CONTINENT who can press a simple PLEAT to save his LIFE, for Pete's sake.

IO: Why did she do that?

HELEN: Hera? Who knows? It was probably all about preserving my virtue, whatever *that* means.

IO: Yeah, she's really into that.

HELEN: I just wish she could have let *me* make the call on that one.

IO: So, would you have done it? Gone with him? (*Slightly melodramatic.*) Betrayed your husband, your people, your country for love?

HELEN: I honestly can't remember. It's been so long since I felt like I could make a decision of any kind…Who knows? I might have just made out with him for awhile. He was pretty hot. It wouldn't have hurt anyone. It's not like I wanted anybody to *die* because of it, for Goodness' sake.

IO: Of course not.

HELEN: It would have been something my *own*. A little mistake, or a little dalliance, something I could maybe *learn from*, you know? In a personal-growth kind of way. *But they just don't give you a chance.* It's, like, you are not *allowed* a private life, you know?

IO: Oh, I *know*. How long have you been here?

HELEN: Seventeen years, three months, nine days.

IO: (*Slightly stunned, but covering.*) Huh. OK So how long is this supposed to go on?

HELEN: Well, the way the story is *supposed* to go, last I heard, is that I wait out the war—

IO: The war?

HELEN: There's a war out there, there *should* be a…See, the way my father set the whole thing up was that whichever suitor married me— I had *loads* of suitors—

IO: —Like *thousands*—

HELEN: —Exactly. The deal was that the other suitors had to agree to join an alliance with the winner if anyone, you know, *abducted* me, or—

IO: —Oh, I remember this—

HELEN: —So, I'm basically assuming that—

IO: —(*Suddenly getting it.*) There's a WAR, being fought in YOUR NAME—

HELEN: —Precisely. Between the Trojans and the Greeks.

IO: Wow. No wonder you bailed.

HELEN: Bailed? Excuse me, darling, I was replicated and… dematerialized.

IO: Not before playing footsie for awhile.

HELEN: (*Slightly thrown.*) Oh, that was nothing. I was just bored and… it wouldn't have…(*Regaining focus.*) So the idea is that I wait out this war and Menelaus swings by and picks me up after it's over. That's of course if the Greeks *win* it. And if Menelaus isn't killed, or doesn't die on the journey home. And then, on top of *that*, it's got to occur to him that the woman he's got in the boat with him isn't me. And of course, the whole thing depends on if he manages to stumble into this particular Egyptian hotel.

IO: That's a lot of ifs.

HELEN: Tell me about it.

IO: In fact, the whole thing seems, excuse me for saying so, a little unlikely. Have you ever tried leaving?

HELEN: What do you mean?

IO: You know, getting in the elevator and...(*She makes the gesture of descending.*)

HELEN: (*Slightly put off.*) I don't think that would work.

IO: But the elevator's great, I just came up in it, no problem—

HELEN: —That's not what I mean. I mean I'm supposed to wait here, in this room, until he comes. And he's supposed to take me home. That's the way it works.

IO: And if he doesn't?

HELEN: I...It's...He has to come, eventually, it's just...(*Pause.*) He'll be here. It's just a matter of time.

IO: (*Unconvinced.*) Uh huh. (*Pause.*) Well, this is a cushy set-up, I have to say. Even if the reception's crummy. I mean, I'll trade you the last seventeen years of my life, no problem.

HELEN: It must have been awful.

IO: Crazy awful. (*She shudders.*) Oh, that poor cow. Years and years, I was just—

HELEN: —Excuse me, before you...I mean, I do want to hear your whole, you know, *saga* and everything, but I'm sorry I just have to ask—You mean you've heard *nothing* about a war?

IO: Um...I have to admit I kind of tuned everything out there for awhile. It's not like I could *ask*...And people don't tend to talk to cows, as a rule. (*She tries to think.*) I guess I knew there was a war. But then there always seems to be a war, because there are always refugees. There were so many of us. I wasn't alone. And they're mostly women. I mean look. There we are.

HELEN: (*Confused.*) That's just the Weather Channel.

IO: (*Mesmerized by the image.*) No, it's us. It's the spinning masses of refugees, swarming the globe like clouds of bees—swirling in a twisting wash across the face of the earth, trying to achieve invisibility. That is our great goal. It took me years. I don't even know how I did it. I guess I just lasted long enough to cease to be of interest. The gods looked elsewhere and gradually forgot me. I still don't understand why it happened in the first place. There I was, a vaguely happy shepherdess, minding my own business, when suddenly a whirlwind descended and lifted me from the lip of the hill. I felt myself being kneaded like dough, like mud under a chariot wheel, and all the while the wind sighed in my ear speaking to me in some warm language I couldn't understand.

HELEN: (*Nodding.*) The ravishment of Zeus. Mother told me all about it.

IO: But before whatever was about to happen could happen, everything stopped for a sickening moment and I could hear the approach of something else, a screaming, sliding descent from a vast distance. It sounded like an enormous bird, sharp beak open, talons spread.

HELEN: Hera, of course. Breaking down the door. Trying to keep Zeus's wick clean.

IO: You could feel the suck of air as she rushed down upon us. But in the second before she arrived I lost my body…He took it from me. Or really, it was more like being jammed into the casing of another body, stuffed like rags into an urn or something. I looked down and saw my new self—a cow. This tent of a body heaving and echoing like a drum. And all the while I could sense the goddess hovering above me as an eagle hovers over its prey. I tried to scream and that was when I realized the worst of it. That I was mute now as well. All thought, all feeling locked now in my wide swinging head. A cow. It's been a hell of a thing.

HELEN: That's a terrible story.

IO: Yeah. And the strangest part is…It made a kind of awful sense. Even then. Because I had only just arrived at the moment when my body didn't seem to belong to me anymore. Like it wasn't just *mine*. I could feel this distinct…I don't know…like when I walked past a group of men…Suddenly there was this girl, this other girl, the one they were looking at, who was…well, *me*, I guess, but also, I mean she was, I was looking at her, at me, *with* them and I felt what they felt for her which was a kind of…(*She is disoriented and disturbed.*) I don't know. (*Pause.*) You know?

HELEN: Yes.

IO: It's not that I wanted to be a cow. That was horrible. But it did relieve me of the particular confusion of being a girl. Having to live inside a body which was so desired and yet so detested.

HELEN: But that's what it is to be beautiful.

IO: Boy, they must really loathe you.

HELEN: (*Flattered.*) That's a sweet thing to say. As it happens they do. I've heard I'm the most hated woman in history.

IO: Really? Well done. Must be lonely. Being her.

HELEN: (*Poetic mode.*) "She is the dream to which we cling
That shining, shifting, darting thing
Her face is blinding as the sun
Her depths are sounded by no one
So we drift on her legend and drown there."

IO: Sad. Pretty though.

HELEN: Well, that's me all over. I wonder what that's from.

IO: Gee, I don't know. I haven't been able to keep up, you know, with the whole poetry scene…

HELEN: Maybe it's the gods. Messing with my head. Because they can. (*Pause.*) What do you think they want from us?

IO: The gods? All I know about the gods is what I learned from the suffering of my own body. Hera set a gadfly on me and he drove me in a dance of anguish across the face of the earth. He was my halo, that gadfly, circling above me before landing, time and again, to bow his sharpness to the tortured white. I was never free of him. Oh, the landscapes we saw together. The length and breadth of the known world. We crossed it all. There was one night when I kicked and howled, prancing unwilling down the Persian coast. The moon was twinned like a double cherry in its own reflection on the glassy sea. I watched it extract itself from itself and leave its ghost behind to stare up at it as it made its stately arc up the sky. (*Pause.*) He showed me the world, my gadfly—and I finally learned to see it for what it is—just another hide stretched on pain. No different from my own tortured landscape of welts and weals. Every one of them a site of misery. My poor body, it was a terrible place and we made it together, my gadfly and I. It took years. Maybe we made it for god.

HELEN: For god?

IO: I don't know. I guess I have to believe my misery was sacred. After all, it's the only gift they ever gave me. (*Pause.*) I'm sorry, it's just that I haven't spoken in so long—

HELEN: —I haven't either. Really talked to anyone. It seems we've both been subject to…peculiar existences.

IO: I do think sometimes about the life I might have led if I'd never been noticed. If I'd lived out my days safe in the hollow of the one mountain, never out of earshot of the dull bells of my own herd.

HELEN: You could go home. Now that it's over.

IO: No. It isn't over. I'm still one of the refugees. We can never go home. We wouldn't recognize it. It wouldn't recognize us. That girl's life was not to happen.

HELEN: (*Pause. Then, abruptly.*) So what's up for you now? Off to the tourist attractions? Maybe do some shopping? See the sights?

IO: I don't know. I might just head back to my room and stretch out. I'm still a little zonked from all the traveling. I love my room. It has a door. And a lock. And hippopotami *everywhere*, even the bidet has these little *ears*…Do you use yours? I'm a little flummoxed as to how one is supposed to—

HELEN: —My what?

IO: Your bidet?

HELEN: Oh, I don't use anything. Well, I mean, I use the toilet to flush the flies, but that's pretty much it.

IO: You don't use it to—? I'm sorry, I don't understand.

HELEN: I don't seem to have any bodily needs.

IO: (*Flabbergasted.*) *What?* Like you don't eat or…you don't eat?

HELEN: No, I haven't eaten anything in years. Not even in the old days. I was always on a diet and I guess it just…*stuck.*

IO: God, you must be starving.

HELEN: I wouldn't know. It's hard to say what's going on in there. (*They both look at her body.*) I'm probably exhausted too, but who knows?

IO: Wow. I wish I could do that. It's always been such a struggle for me to control my desire for, you know, food and stuff, I've just been such a—

HELEN: —Cow?

IO: Exactly. (*They laugh.*)

HELEN: No, you don't.

IO: What?

HELEN: Wish for this. It's terrible. Once you abandon your body you can never return and that means you can never really feel anything again. Hunger, fear, anger, delight, each is played on the only instrument you have, the body, your body, and if you can't hear it, feel it, you've lost a hold of your very self. What is yours.

IO: Could you go back?

HELEN: What? Back inside my body somehow? At this late date?

IO: Might be worth a try. It's done wonders for me, I gotta say.

HELEN: (*A little panicky.*) I don't think it's possible, I think, you know, the gods might—

IO: —Well, it's up to you. (*Pause.*) It's a nice room. I guess you could stay here…indefinitely.

HELEN: Do you know what they have in store for you?

IO: The gods? Not much, I hope. I mean, after the last few decades, just the idea of a Do Not Disturb sign brings tears to the eyes.

HELEN: Oh, not to worry, you will be left alone for years and years. Enjoy. (*Io exits. To the heavens.*) OK What was *that* about? (*To us.*) Of course that makes no sense. That was Io. Io was way before my time. I've heard that story since I was a kid. I was raised on that story. She was one of the first of the endless host of Zeus' unwitting, unwilling amours. My mother was one of them, and she was long after Io. I mean, Io's part of a myth so old I know like nine versions of it. And despite what she wishes, Zeus hasn't forgotten her, even if Hera has. He's just biding his time. And of course he *will* impregnate her soon enough, but this time he does it by touching her gently—a ravishment so uncharacteristically sweet she names the child born of it Epaphus, "light touch of a hand." (*It just gets stranger and stranger the more she puts it together.*) And he becomes the king…of Egypt…ages ago. There are monuments all over the place. (*This is quite disturbing.*) I don't understand. (*She attempts to shake it off.*) But then (*she shrugs.*) that's Egypt for you. Everybody ends up here sooner or later. Even the dead. Even the fictitious. And they all carry their stories with them, like balls of wool they wind and rewind over and over. Telling themselves and all their variations, as if they'd never come to an end. As if the echoes were never too faint to hear. (*Pause. Mounting anxiety.*) This is impossible. And still no word of the war.

> *Servant enters, wheeling a garment rack of several identical gowns.*

Any telegrams? (*Servant shakes her head.*)

Any letters? (*Servant shakes her head.*)

Phone messages? (*Servant shakes her head.*)

SERVANT: Are there ever?

HELEN: No. But I thought perhaps today…(*Servant shakes her head then gestures toward the rack ala Vanna White.*) I can't decide. You pick. (*The servant performs a little drama of deliberation then yanks one of the dresses off the rack and begins to put it on Helen.*) Well, she was intelligent. For a cow. If uninformative. I mean, here she's traveled the entirety of the known world and she has absolutely bupkis to say about the biggest war that's ever taken place. Ever. (*Poetic mode.*) "Two mighty armies poised in deadlock on the bitter stones of Ilium. They hold between them the pride of the world and their clangor will wake the woe of the ages." Does that ring a bell?

SERVANT: (*Shrugging cryptically.*) Greek poetry.

HELEN: (*Noticing the dress she's wearing for the first time.*) Oh, why did you pick this one? I hate this one! (*The servant rolls her eyes.*) Do my hair.

> The servant begins to arrange an elaborate coif.

You're sure there was nothing?

SERVANT: I was just at the front desk. There's nothing for you. Nothing at all.

HELEN: Tell me a story.

SERVANT: Let's see. Once upon a time there was an incident. What shall we call it? An abduction? An elopement? The beginning of the end of the world? (*Pause.*) An incident. And forty-six household servants— staff, secretaries, and security personnel flooded the local police station. Quite a scene. And every one of them had a story to tell. One maid clutched a ring she said had been pressed into her hand by the lady of the house as she'd been dragged weeping down the hallway. "Tell my husband I love him," the lady had gasped through her sobs, "and tell him he must find me!" Touching. Yet the gardener said he'd heard the lady and the visiting gentleman giggling together in the gazebo where they had camped out like children, with a blanket and graham crackers stolen from the scullery. In the spill of light from the full moon, he could see them slapping each other's naked buttocks and playing sordid games with their flashlights. On the other hand, a secretary said that she'd seen her mistress, mink coat shrugged over a negligee, run silently across the library to throw open the French doors. The smell of freshly cut grass flooded in as she ran barefoot down the long lawn that ended at the harbor and a waiting ship. There were as many stories as there were people to tell them. Each one patiently taken down by nodding tired men. The night wore on. Then the real fun began. Because then the detective sketch artists were brought in to do their work. Forty-six remarkably similar renderings of an abductor were brought forth but when it came to the abductee, well…There was no consensus on any single detail, from the color of the eyes to the length or even color of the hair. The sketch artists were wild with frustration. They'd never done such insipid work; none of the pictures satisfied them. They grew pettish, ripping up their sketches and stalking out to the water cooler, such that the witnesses themselves could be seen in the hallways, murmuring encouragement, coaxing them to go back in and try again. Face after face they drew but each was strangely disappointing. Just one more vapid beauty. Each one lovely to be sure but hardly unique, hardly, well, what was it one expected of that face? Something. Something no one had yet found a way of describing. The police chief finally calls it a night and sends everyone home. He rubs his aching eyes and yawns. He walks between the desks, each one stacked high with conflicting narratives. All he can hear is the sound of the sketch artists. They refuse to go home. In the breaking dawn he listens to the swoop of the pencils, the slough of the erasers, the low cursing, the quiet agony as they work and rework, portrait after portrait, not one of which will ever satisfy them. (*The hairdressing is complete.*)

HELEN: (*Quietly disturbed.*) I do worry about the world. This splitting of image from being never bodes well. The first knock-off only begs for another. Copy spews forth copy, an infinite proliferation, like a nuclear reaction. Each replication spawning yet another generation of duplicates until she moves like a virus through a city, facing you at every turn. Her name spelled out in the night sky. Her pictures blown like debris to be tread underfoot and washed into gutters. She is everywhere.

SERVANT: Hard to believe there ever was an actual Helen. Just some woman. With breasts that swell or sag, hair that grows, menstrual cycles—

HELEN: —THOUGHTS! THOUGHTS! SHE HAS AN INTERIOR LIFE! SHE'S NOT JUST A BODY!

SERVANT: (*Unfazed by Helen's outburst.*) Someone who belongs to herself and not to the world. See, there is the *image* of Helen and that does not belong to her. It's ours. She is part of us, like our dreams, that Helen. Something we see on the back of our closed eyelids when someone says, for instance, "the most beautiful woman in the world." We possess, it turns out, so much of her. Images of her crying at state funerals, sleek in black, the mist of a veil only adding to her beauty. Or she see her sitting on some podium, looking attentively at the back of her husband's head as he stands there pontificating, unheard. He knows she is there, blazing behind him. He knows no one is looking at him. Except her, of course. And that is enough. We have tracked the nature of our times on her body. Eras of greed are displayed for us in her cycles of embarrassing weight gain, her mortifying battle with her demons. We pored over the least flattering shots, those furtive, ungainly escapes into limousines, her skirt rucked up over her thick haunches. Or there were the times she starved herself like a saint for us, when her dresses hung limp on her and her eyes sunk like bright stones in her bony face. Then we clucked our disapproval and shook our heads, feeling something we couldn't name—was it pity? (*She considers this, then rejects it.*) No. Just revulsion, really. I mean look at her. She never knew when to stop. Thank goodness. Because still we hungered for her. Image after image. We couldn't get enough. We made her sleep with the lights on, her window shades up, so that we could press our noses against the windowpane and watch her dreams slide over her face.

Helen shudders, as if shaking off a nightmare.

HELEN: I'll tell you the one I hated most. The simpering vulnerable one. With skin like spun sugar so soft and sweet your jaws ached when you looked at her. Those wet eyes. That high breathy voice. The head always cocked to the side like a not-too-bright cocker spaniel who has to be told everything twice. (*She puts out a hand to have her nails buffed.*) But that was only one role in an infinite repertoire. She was... spectacularly accommodating.

SERVANT: She was a child, and yet a whore.

HELEN: An angel, and yet a goddess of sex.

SERVANT: She slices, she dices…

HELEN: She walks, she talks, she's remarkable.

SERVANT: She was remarkable. How did she do all those things at once?

HELEN: Oh, I don't know. Sometimes I think it is impossible to pull it off, embody all those contradictions and still be so…vacant. No wonder she…disappeared. How could anyone keep it up? You just get worn out, sick to death of trying to slot into everybody's personal fantasies. Having to be so *visible* all the time…She never had a minute to herself. It was consuming her. It was terrible, it was— (*Pause.*) That's enough! My cuticles are throbbing! Leave me alone!

> *Servant leaves, taking the clothes rack with her.*

OH MY GOD, I CAN'T STAND IT ANYMORE. I NEED SOME INFORMATION. SOMETHING TO LIVE ON. IT'S LIKE SWALLOWING DUST FOR SEVENTEEN YEARS.(*To the heavens.*) IF I DON'T GET TO GO TO TROY COULD YOU AT LEAST SEND SOMEONE OVER HERE WHO CAN *TELL* ME ABOUT IT?

> *Suddenly, amidst great fanfare, Athena enters in complete regalia, looking pissy.*

ATHENA: Would you simmer down, for goodness sake? They can hear you clear back to the ice machine.

HELEN: Athena? What are you doing here? You hate me.

ATHENA: Well, who doesn't, if it comes to that?

HELEN: Have you come to tell me about the war?

ATHENA: The war? Oh, that's been over for ages.

HELEN: Over? Who won?

ATHENA: We did.

HELEN: We did?

ATHENA: OK, so when you say "we," you mean who exactly? Your big buddies the Greeks, whom you betrayed? Or your dear friends the Trojans whose civilization you're responsible for destroying?

HELEN: Um. Both I guess.

ATHENA: Well, then you won. And you lost. Horribly. But that's true of everyone. It was a very long war.

HELEN: Has the house of Priam fallen?

ATHENA: Oh, gosh yes. A smoldering ruin.

HELEN: Is everyone in the royal family gone?

ATHENA: (*Trying to remember.*) Ummmmm, nnnnnnnnyes. Yup. Not a soul left.

HELEN: All dead? Even the women?

ATHENA: As good as. Last I saw they were lining them up on the beach, assigning them to various warriors as slaves.

HELEN: What about the Queen?

ATHENA: Hecuba? Oh, she was given to Odysseus, not that he really wanted the old bag. She was quite upset. Straw that broke the camel's back kind of thing. It was the end of a really bad week for her. Legendary bad. Oh, they'll be talking about her for years. I think she threw herself off the boat or something. Or maybe they stoned her on the beach. I can't remember. Anyway, she's dead.

HELEN: I'm…that's terrible. Queen Hecuba. I've been thinking about her all these years, imagining her. It's like I knew her, though I never… I loved her, I think.

ATHENA: Well, she was never exactly over the moon about you, I can tell you that.

HELEN: No, I suppose she wouldn't have been.

ATHENA: She called you "the gift that keeps taking."

HELEN: I see.

ATHENA: Tough old bitch. I liked her.

HELEN: What about the Greeks? Did many die?

ATHENA: Oh, yes. Thousands. The best of them. (*Yawns.*)
It was a nightmare, really.

HELEN: You sound like you're bearing up pretty well.

ATHENA: Well, it's not like it wasn't very *sad* and *tragic* and *momentous* and everything, it's just that it *took so long. Ten years.* I mean, really, who can stay interested? Of course the first few weeks were just plain thrilling. We could see waves of soldiers skidding across the landscape —it was delirious, like watching a sheet being flapped in the wind, lines of men curving and snapping. And, oh, the horses, glorious. None of the gods could get anything done. We just dropped everything. We'd be down on the mountains, cheering them on, or leaning on the clouds, propped up for the show. Marvelous stuff. What a disappointment when everything bogged down and all the boys went underground. For months all you could hear was the sound of spades, the rasp of miles of barbed wire being uncoiled. There was really nothing much of interest after that. You'd catch yourself nodding off, head lolling on the clouds, even during the long bombardments. Very little entertainment value in a siege. Pretty soon, we were stifling yawns and slinking back to our hobbies: archery, jewelry-making, trying to train birds. And still the war went on, unnoticed. For nothing and no one.

HELEN: For me.

ATHENA: Not even for you. For some *idea* of you. Whole populations, whole cities wiped out, and all for a *concept*. Not even a good concept. Some chick. A *rumor* of a chick. A rumor of a chick pretty much everyone despised, including the husband who was trying to get her back, including the guy who took her in the first place. All that mayhem in the name of *what*? I mean, look at you. You're just some blonde. And the big joke of course is that *you* weren't even there.

HELEN: What was the point?

ATHENA: Oh, it seemed like a good idea at the time. Something about glory. You know we've been around for awhile, watching you people. The interest was beginning to wear thin. After awhile we just wanted something truly epic. All those piddling little sacrifices, a bull here, a deer there. No, no, we wanted you. The human race itself on the altar, twisting like worms on pavement after a rainstorm.

HELEN: You *wanted* that?

ATHENA: We thought we did. But I began to have my doubts. I remember looking down at the pocked mud—the burnt daggers that once were trees, the dun colored creatures struggling about, tanks tipped and lodged in mud, horses screaming—you could almost hear them—I remember thinking: Perhaps there was little in the way of glory to be gleaned from this.

They lapse into silence, staring out.

I notice you haven't asked.

HELEN: About what?

ATHENA: Your hubby.

HELEN: Ah, yes. Him. Is he all right?

ATHENA: Just fabulous. Got through the whole thing without a scratch.

HELEN: (*Without enthusiasm.*) Great. (*Pause.*) So where is he?

ATHENA: Oh, he's wandering in circles around the Aegean. Honestly, that guy, he couldn't find his prick if you gave him a map.

HELEN: You know, for a goddess who is supposedly staunchly pro Greek—

ATHENA: —Well, of course I am. I was. But they pissed me off at the end of the war. Poseidon and I decided to make their journey home *really* interesting. We blew them all over the fucking place. Menelaus has spent seven years tacking against the wind and puking over the side of his boat only to be blown back to the wrong coast time after time. It's been fun, what can I say?

HELEN: Does he know he's looking for me?

ATHENA: Are you kidding? The *Hummer*? We could have put a dress on a dog's squeaky chew toy and he would have bought it. Really.

HELEN: What's she like?

ATHENA: Who? You?

HELEN: Yeah. Her.

ATHENA: Sweet, really. If you like that sort of thing. All melting looks and breathless giggles. Good tempered but not saintly. Knowing but innocent.

HELEN: Sounds familiar. So she did her perfectly.

ATHENA: (*A concession.*) There was a kind of perfection involved.

HELEN: I remember. Once I stood at the center of history. It roared around me, whipping at my clothes, howling and breathing its terrible breath on me. But I would turn a face like marble to the world. A face unmarred by thought, serene and closed up tight as a vault. A face that could hold itself still and unblinking as it was battered by the gazes of the millions. Nothing animated it. It was a mask of perfection. Shining and reflective as a pond. So that when they peered into me, I showed them their own dream of themselves staring back at them, lips parted, inaccessible and spellbound. Beauty. It's a hell of a thing.

ATHENA: You couldn't have kept it up. That's why we had to replace you. You were losing your edge.

HELEN: (*Incensed.*) What are you talking about? I never slipped up for a second. I could walk through a crowd of screaming fans and hear nothing. They could claw at me, each one trying to get a fistful of me, and I would merely smile and keep moving. I was beyond good. They would look at me and, no, I wasn't there. I had retreated back from my eyes, curled my entire soul into the size of something unremarkable and tiny, like a walnut. I would lodge in my throat and stay there for days, safe in my own darkness, far from view.

ATHENA: I'm not saying you weren't good. I'm just saying you were losing it. Your eyes. There was something you started betraying. A distinctness of feeling. Your own. Nobody wanted that.

HELEN: OF COURSE THEY DID! They LOVED my feeling! They couldn't get enough of it! One time I got some grit under a contact lens when I was sitting in the theater and I teared up a little. The paparazzi were on me like piranhas, blinding me with flashbulbs. The next day every supermarket tabloid was screaming HELEN: WEEPS FOR HERAKLES! It was pathetic.

ATHENA: They wanted you *weeping*. They didn't want you *feeling*. Not you. Personally. Feeling. Not at all. Feeling your own feelings, thinking your own thoughts? Absolutely not. It's all supposed to be written on the body. Right out front where they can see it and own it. Otherwise you're no use to them. You're just another woman, full to the brim with tediously idiosyncratic and impenetrable secrets and needs. You think you were "loved"? Please. They just endowed you with whatever qualities they were hankering for at the moment and made up everything else. Nobody was ever particularly interested in you. Human love. What a joke.

HELEN: What do you want from us?

ATHENA: The gods? (*Helen nods.*) What do the *gods* want from you? (*She laughs.*) You guys. You crack us up. I swear. (*Pause while she chuckles.*)

HELEN: Well?

ATHENA: You're too much, kid. (*She pinches Helen's cheek.*) You know what we love about you people? You die. And that means you've all got stories. That's why we came up with you. Even the dullest mortal life has a beginning, middle and an end. It's so fucking poignant. It could be that the whole Trojan War was just a big fat dramaturgical mistake on our parts. Way too tidy. Our desire to wrap everything up with a single enormous blow-out just ended up diluting all the stories down to one unsatisfying truncated shrug of a narrative. I mean, it's not like it's your *fault*, but we lost respect for you guys. You just looked like so many panicked beetles scrambling around on that dung hill. Or maybe it was the monotony of the deaths that got to us. Not that there wasn't a lot of *variety*—we could watch people get blown to bits by bombs, cut down like wheat by machine gun fire slicing across rows of stumbling men, or of course there were those endless agonizing deaths, all the boys lined up in their cots, oozing through their swaddling in the tent hospitals—oh, there were *variations*...But really when all was said and done, it was just a whole heck of a lot of death. And it turns out that death makes human *life* interesting. But that death *itself* isn't particularly interesting. Because you all die the same way. Looking surprised. It's amazing. Here you are the only creature on earth who knows you're going to die—it colors your entire existence from your earliest moments of consciousness. You can even spend years on a battlefield, watching *other* people die left and right of you, but when your *own* death comes, *as you always knew it would*, you're still, like, "What? ME? Surely you don't mean ME!" (*Amused.*) It kills us.

HELEN: You know, sometimes I think we came up with you.

ATHENA: (*Ominously calm.*) Is that right? And why would you do that?

HELEN: So that we could have someone to blame for everything that goes wrong, some way to explain everything we don't understand.

ATHENA: You watch yourself, Missy. I think you've had a bit too much time on your hands. It just makes you brood. Why don't you take up weaving or something? It passes the time. While you wait.

HELEN: What exactly am I waiting *for* do you think?

ATHENA: (*Smiles.*) The end of the story, Doll. If nothing else, there will be your death. And I, for one, am *really* looking forward to that

HELEN: But I'm a story now. I'll never die.

ATHENA: Oh, don't kid yourself, honey. You'll die. Your story will go on and on. But it'll have precious little to do with you. Not that it ever did. I mean, you're *pretty* and everything, but let's face it, *nobody's* that pretty. I gotta run. (*Starts to exit.*) Give my regards to that hubby of yours when you see him.

HELEN: Wait! (*Athena turns.*) Do you think he'll find me?

ATHENA: Stranger things have happened. You of all people should know.

> *Athena exits, with appropriate fanfare. Possible act break with intermission.*

HELEN: (*Profoundly disoriented.*) It's over. It's been over all this time. I missed everything.

> *Servant enters, dragging a bouquet of racetrack magnitude.*

SERVANT: More flowers.

HELEN: Who are they from?

SERVANT: Who are they ever from?

HELEN: No card? No telegram?

SERVANT: Just the flowers.

HELEN: It *reeks*. God, my allergies. Get it out of here.

SERVANT: And take it where?

HELEN: I don't know! Dump it in the nearest pyramid, I don't care! My sinuses are going bonkers!

> *The servant drags the flowers out as Helen reflexively and futilely lifts the receiver of the ornate little bedside phone for the umpteenth time.*

AND I STILL DON'T HAVE A DIAL TONE!

> *She dumps the phone on the floor then grabs the remote and begins to channel surf agitatedly. We hear a ping from the elevator in the hall and the Servant reenters.*

SERVANT: I left them on the elevator. Going down.

HELEN: That's nice. (*They watch television.*) Maybe they'll get all the way down to the underworld. Make some dead person's day. I wouldn't be at all surprised if Egyptian elevators had a direct line to Hades. Your whole country just seems to be mad for dead people. (*Cruising from channel to channel.*) Arts 'n Crafts With Pampas Grass, the Sideways Sex Station, Painting Landscapes Without Looking At Landscapes, The Make Your Own Mummy Show…Why am I even watching this anymore? (*She turns off the television.*) Nothing I thought I was looking for was ever there for me to find. My war. I lost it. (*Poetic mode.*) "For ten years, 'twixt the black ships and the river of Xanthus, the watch fires of the armies glitter through the nights. As if the countless stars, burning above in fathomless space, were mirrored below in a sea gone glass-still, so many and so bright were the multitudes of those great armies."

That war is lost.

Tell me a story.

SERVANT: There's a girl who is imprisoned in a high tower, or a ring of fire, or she's chained to a rock above the thrashing sea, or she sleeps in a glass box, a coffin made of ice in the center of a forest of thorns. She is frozen. Stranded in the perpetual stillness of her most beautiful moment. There is no animation there where she waits because life cannot continue in the face of such perfection. It's a spell she casts, such a girl, such a beauty, and we skirt death when we look at her. She stops the breath. Nature shudders to a halt to gaze upon her and the world freezes slowly around her, like a lake around its coldest island.

HELEN: Is she dead?

SERVANT: Almost. The next best thing. She's perfect. Meaning symmetrical, as nothing in this rocking asymmetrical mess of a world is. She waits in a kind of impossible balance, straddling the two worlds, between life and death. Completely alone.

HELEN: It's awful. What is it about beauty that is so. . . killing?

SERVANT: It shames the world. This slovenly, pulsing world, limping toward its own ruin, charging around some hot star like a dog chasing its tail. Perfection is an affront in such a place.

HELEN: She's cold.

SERVANT: You think?

HELEN: No, worse. She's numb. She's fallen asleep in blankness and she'll never wake up.

SERVANT: We'll see.

HELEN: Does anyone know she's there?

SERVANT: Oh, there's someone looking for her. A man. There always is.

HELEN: Will he find her?

SERVANT: That's certainly the idea. Someday.

HELEN: What if he doesn't?

SERVANT: Then I guess it's up to her.

HELEN: But how can she do anything? She's practically dead.

SERVANT: Not quite.

HELEN: But she doesn't even know who she is!

SERVANT: Oh, really? But this was all her idea.

HELEN: It was not! It was done to her! She couldn't help what they did to her!

SERVANT: Nobody had a gun to her head.

HELEN: It was that old witch with an apple! I remember this. Some old lady poisoned her.

SERVANT: Far as I can tell she climbed into that coffin all by herself—

HELEN: —There was a witch!—

SERVANT: —without any help from anyone—

HELEN: —You're telling it wrong!—

SERVANT: —and she pulled the lid down after her—

HELEN: —You know that's not what happened!—

SERVANT: And that's where she's been for a long time now, pretending to sleep.

HELEN: You're lying! I hate this story. This is a terrible story.

SERVANT: Yes it is.

> *A nasty pause. Helen hears a fly and begins swatting about her ferociously yet unsuccessfully.*

SERVANT: Did it ever occur to you that you might have a choice where the flies are concerned?

HELEN: (*Distracted, still whacking away.*) What are you blathering about now?

SERVANT: Yes, you can kill them, of course. But they are in fact only creatures desperate to escape this place. (And who can blame them?) They're not *trying* to irritate you. They're screaming, that's all. They're begging you (*she does a fly voice*), "Let me, out! Let me out! Let me out!"

HELEN: (*Still flailing.*) SO? What are proposing?

SERVANT: You could pity them.

> *Helen turns on the servant and glares at her.*

HELEN: I really loathe you at the moment.

SERVANT: Foot massage?

HELEN: (*Defeated.*) Oh…why not?

> *The Servant sits on the bed. Helen lies on the floor and puts her feet in the Servant's lap. The Servant massages her feet.*

Seven years. Seven years since all the fires burned down to embers. Seven years since the first vultures circled the ruins of the city, wobbling in the smoky air, dizzy with the feast of death beneath them. Seven years it's been over.

SERVANT: Oh, it's far from over. They're still sorting everything out on the banks of the river which courses through the basement of the world. The whole operation has been backed up for ever so long. One can hear the complaints of Charon, the harried ferry man of the dead. Even up here, at the top of the elevator shaft. The size of the slaughter was awesome. Men in every uniform imaginable line the bank as far as the eye can see. Waiting to cross. This is so familiar, they think. Yet another riverbank, yet another maneuver gone wrong. Countless men to be shifted and not enough boats. It must be the usual idiocy: some git in the rear must have failed to fill out a form. And here they all are, crammed together on the muddy bank, waiting for a single boat, manned by a wheezing old coot, to carry every mother's son of them to the opposite shore. It will take forever. But happily, forever is exactly what they have now; their only remaining possession. They settle and wait, scratch themselves, write letters with blunt pencils or pop the white lice eggs which are strung like tiny pearls along the seams of their pants. Or they simply stare open mouthed into a middle distance where the fog leans down to meet the iron silence of the river water. Boat after boat he loads with them, each shipload packing itself with an admirable efficiency. Charon never has to say a word. They are so used to making themselves small, these men. They hug their knees to their tight chests and array themselves snugly as teeth in a jawbone along the long swag of the gunwale. The boat fills silently again and again. Charon turns it around and grunts as he stamps the pole once more on the silty river bottom and heaves his weight against it. The tin helmets chime against each other with every push. But other than that the boat is silent. Even Charon is unnerved by such quiet docility. He shivers in the stillness, lonely in the midst of countless men. He finds his only solace in watching each boy shed his brief history in the crossing. He sees the mist rise off the water and wreath itself around the faces of these ancient children. In the course of the slow journey across he can see the coils of each life story loosen and fall, leaving the creases smooth and the fists unclenched as forgetfulness washes over them like a summer rain. The blessing is so complete that by the time the boat nudges the opposite shore, they dazedly tumble out, often leaving their guns and jangling kits behind. No more organized than skittering sea birds, their heads lift as they wander up the dim shore. Lit by a vague curiosity, they patter aimlessly into the next world.

Helen lifts her feet off the Servant's lap and rolls on her side.

HELEN: (*She stares out.*) I wonder where he is

SERVANT: He's just lost.

HELEN: Just lost. The poor dope. Are you sure there wasn't a telegram? A phone message? A letter?

SERVANT: I'll go down and check again.

The Servant leaves.

HELEN: Perhaps I've been unkind. It's been so easy to be cruel about him in the abstract. It's just been such a long time. And he had the great misfortune of playing the fool. Someone had to. I never thought about what it must have cost him. It must have been awful. Coming into that empty room, the rumpled bed, the traces of hurried packing, a jumble of shoes strewn on the floor, a perfume bottle shattered in the bathroom sink. I see him standing in the wake of our flight, window open to the dark. He blinks, his head is heavy, his mind is blank. He is staring at the pattern of the bedroom rug. He's like a bull in the bullring as the afternoon closes in and his death approaches. He's trying—it's terrible, his head is buzzing—he's trying to make sense of it all. There are two wives, he thinks. The one he loved and the one who could do this. Or perhaps there never was the one he thought he loved, only the second one, or perhaps…But the more he tries to figure it out the less it makes sense. All he knows for certain is the hollow roar of shame at the center of his chest. And this is only the beginning. There are humiliations unimaginable in store. News cameras and microphones jammed in his face, the cool silence followed by the audible contempt as he passes a crowd, any crowd, he has never been more famous. Famous for this. A cuckold, a rube, a chump. He walks the empty house at night, muttering to himself, snapping with rage, but then, exhausted, he winds himself in my dressing gown, which is still hanging where I left it. He stands there, a blind cylinder, anchored to the closet door, smelling the wife who left him and weeping for the love of her.

I think he did love me. And perhaps I loved him.

I try to remember sometimes. But it was so long ago.

What he must think of me now…I can only imagine.

The door to the hallway slowly opens and Menelaus slides to the floor. It is as if he had fallen asleep in the act of knocking.

HELEN: Well, what do you know.

She goes to where he lies and reaches out to touch him, but he scares her off by plunging suddenly into a nightmare.

MENELAUS: (*Still unconscious.*) Heads down, boys! Heads down! She's coming in, she's…Oh, God…Where's my whistle? Where's my…?

He braces, curling himself into a ball in anticipation of a bomb. It "hits" but he is unharmed and he relaxes a bit. Helen touches his face gently.

HELEN: (*Poetic mode.*) "Ah, but the happy gods did not forget you after all, long suffering warrior. Even she, the iron goddess, pitied you, and waved the darting arrow from your heart as a mother waves a fly away from her dearly sleeping child."

Menelaus's eyes snap open and though he doesn't see Helen yet, he sees the room. He is disturbed.

MENELAUS: This isn't my suite.

HELEN: Isn't it?

MENELAUS: I must be on the wrong floor. (*Pause.*) Literally. (*He begins to get up and sees Helen for the first time. He is shocked and attempts to cover.*) I'm so sorry.

He scrambles to get up and pull himself together, utterly disoriented.

HELEN: It's all right. It's confusing.

MENELAUS: I was shipwrecked. I haven't had much sleep.

HELEN: It's all right.

MENELAUS: Is it?

HELEN: Yes. You've had a bad time. I can tell.

MENELAUS: It's only the last in a long sequence of…You don't want to know.

HELEN: I do though.

MENELAUS: No, I don't think I could even begin to…It's too…I'd be…(*Pause.*) Do you know my wife?

HELEN: Yes.

MENELAUS: It's funny. From the moment…And you speak Greek. I can't tell you what a…Huh.

HELEN: Where is she?

MENELAUS: Who?

HELEN: Your wife.

MENELAUS: She's already…You're… (*A monumental effort to understand this thing.*) Hang on, is this 28B?

HELEN: 29B.

MENELAUS: Ah. The difference of a story.

HELEN: Exactly. Where is your wife?

MENELAUS: (*Slight hesitation as he tries to remember.*) I killed her.

HELEN: Did you?

MENELAUS: Yyyes.

HELEN: Just now?

MENELAUS: No, no, years ago. The sack of Troy.

HELEN: You didn't though.

MENELAUS: Didn't I?

HELEN: It just felt like it.

MENELAUS: (*He slaps his forehead in a gesture of remembrance.*) No, of course, of course. You're right. Of course. She's…she's *here*, right *here*…

HELEN: Yes, she is.

MENELAUS: She went straight up. Something about a hot bath, she's ...she's fine. She's always fine. She's quite...remarkable.

HELEN: So I've heard.

MENELAUS: (*Exhausted and disbelieving, he looks at her.*) She's... something else.

HELEN: You hate her.

> *He shrugs.*

You wanted to kill her.

> *He nods without much passion.*

Why?

MENELAUS: I could take it, everything, everything she did to me, until the horse.

HELEN: The horse?

MENELAUS: The Trojan Horse. Odysseus's crazy idea. It was our last ditch to break the siege. We pretend to sail away, the whole army, like we just gave up, but we leave this enormous wooden horse on wheels outside the city, just looking at the gates, like a pet dog waiting to be let in. I was inside it with the others. We spent the whole day in there, wearing all our armor, trying to hold still so we don't clank, you know? We're in there from dawn to dusk listening to everybody trying to decide what to do with this thing. Somebody wants to *burn* it, somebody wants to stab *javelins* into the belly, we're *worried*, OK? But lucky for us, it's a beautiful piece of work, this thing, and nobody wants to nick it up. Somebody, thank you God, has the bright idea to drag it into the city and after that, we're pretty much home free if we can just wait it out until everybody goes to sleep. But that's, like, *a long time.* First they *dance* around us, then they *sing* for awhile, then there's a substantial amount of like *drinking*, but it's finally dying down around two in the morning. We're actually beginning to relax. It really looks like we're going to manage to get out of the fucking thing, and I know I am not alone in saying that I personally would have risked death at that point just to take a whiz, fuck the sacking of the city. You know?

HELEN: Then what happened?

MENELAUS: She comes up. You can hear the little jingling of the bangles around her ankles. She's really quiet. But you just knew. There she was. And then she starts stroking the side of the horse and sort of, um, *chuckling*. I don't know how to describe it. But it was like she was making love to it, us, *all of us*. And she was *good*, you know? These guys, we hadn't seen our wives for ten years, and you can practically *feel* her hands stroking, just sooo…But that wasn't the worst of it. Then she starts calling our names, not *loud*, but like the way you call a lover back to bed, you know, each name of us. And this is the thing— she calls each man using his *wife's voice*—I don't know how she—but it's worse than that even, she's calling them by the pet names the wives used. Names they haven't heard in all this time. It was unbearable. These guys, they are, like, losing it, grown men weeping, trying not to make sound, but tears are just streaming down their faces and everybody's sort of shaking, clanking a little bit. And then she does this thing. She calls to Antichus, this one kid, sweetest guy in the world, right? He'd left for Troy only a week after getting married. His wife is this skinny girl he's known since they were kids together and he's just like totally nuts about her, talks about her all the time, dreams about her every night. He's just so homesick for her he's going crazy. Then Helen, she puts her mouth right underneath where Antichus is sitting and she says, "Darling Bear, why did you never come home to me?" How she knew that's what his wife called him, I have no idea, but he's just freaking out at this point. Odysseus is sitting behind him and he puts his fist in Antichus' mouth to try to stifle the sound of his crying and he might have made it but she says, "If you don't tell me you love me now, I'll hang myself." Antichus is making little animal sounds like a dog dying, he can't help it. "Do you love me? Tell me! Tell me!" And that's when he tries to throw off Odysseus and call to her. But Odysseus is too quick for that, he can see it coming. So he strangles the guy. Right there. This sweetheart of a kid. We all listen to the air choking out of him and then watch as Odysseus rests the body against his chest, then tips the head back so he can close the eyes, which are popping out of his face. That's when you could hear the little jingle of her, her bare feet running away across the city square. But that's not all you could hear. You could also hear her laughing. Then dead quiet. So we came out of the horse like bees swarming out of a hollow oak. And we went to work. There was no mercy.

HELEN: So why didn't you kill her?

MENELAUS: Because it wouldn't work. It'd be like slashing a movie screen to kill the film star. From the first time I saw her, I knew I'd never be free of her. If I killed her, it wouldn't make any difference at all. And I never lost her to Troy. She's plastered all over the walls on the inside of my head. I close my eyes and I see her. I look up at the sky at night and her face knits the stars up. I spent ten years trying to get a woman back I never lost and when I finally got her back I still didn't have her. Not really. I can hold her naked body next to me all night long but she's still. . . it's not. . . I've never really been with her. Not once since the beginning. But I've never been without her. Not once since the beginning. (*He looks at her.*) It's a hell of a thing.

    Long pause.

HELEN: Where is your wife?

MENELAUS: I don't know anymore.

HELEN: Who is your wife?

MENELAUS: I don't know anymore.

HELEN: Do you know who I am?

MENELAUS: Yes.

HELEN: Who am I?

MENELAUS: (*Trying not to answer, begging her.*) Please...don't make me...

HELEN: Who am I?

MENELAUS: It doesn't make sense.

HELEN: No, it doesn't. But who am I?

MENELAUS: It can't be.

HELEN: But it is. I've been here all this time.

MENELAUS: See, I used to dream of this. Because I hated you so much but I couldn't stop loving you. Years went by. I would walk the beaches all night long. I would look up at the high walls and see the yellow lights coming from the windows of the palace and I'd torture myself. I'd try to pick out which one of those rooms might be yours, which one of them was where he was pawing you, where you were straddling him, riding his hips and laughing the way you did. I drove myself crazy. Until the only way I could put the pain to rest was to think the whole thing must be some sort of hoax. Just another cruel joke of the gods. That maybe you weren't even there at all. That there was some phantom in your place, some girl tricked up to look like you and all the while you were safe somewhere, waiting for me to come get you.

HELEN: But that's the truth!

MENELAUS: But don't you see, it's too late.

HELEN: Of course it's not! It's what you wanted! You just said—

MENELAUS: —It's too late.

HELEN: —But you just said!

MENELAUS: TOO MANY PEOPLE HAVE DIED.

HELEN: What does that have to do with me?

MENELAUS: They died in your name!

HELEN: BUT I WASN'T THERE.

MENELAUS: IT DOESN'T MATTER. THEY DIED FOR YOU.

> *Long pause.*

HELEN: But you took her, you took me back. You didn't kill me. Her.

MENELAUS: I couldn't do it. We'd fought a war for her. You. I had to take her home. That was the whole point.

HELEN: Take me back.

MENELAUS: It's not you they want. They want her.

HELEN: I've been waiting seventeen years. I want to go home.

MENELAUS: I can't. It's not fair.

HELEN: What? To her?

MENELAUS: TO THEM! TO THEM! CAN'T YOU GET IT THROUGH YOUR HEAD WHAT'S HAPPENED? A generation of men threw down their lives in that hellhole for the sake of you. My God, the dead. They rise up in terrible armies every night in my dreams. They stalk around my bed on their hacked limbs, moaning of homesickness, the families they never saw again. They carry their severed heads in their arms and the heads scream and scream. They died for you.

HELEN: They died for the idea of me. The gods did this. Not me. It's not my fault.

MENELAUS: IT DOESN'T MATTER WHETHER IT'S YOUR FAULT OR NOT.

HELEN: How can that not matter?

MENELAUS: IF YOU WEREN'T THERE, THEY DIED FOR NOTHING.

HELEN: BUT THEY DID!

MENELAUS: *(His hands to his ears.)* It's unbearable.

HELEN: THEY DIED FOR NOTHING. IT'S THE TRUTH.

MENELAUS: It's unbearable. *(He is in agony.)* All those boys. I must have written ten thousand letters. Ten thousand reorderings of the same tepid lies. "He left this world shining in the wake of his glory," not, "Your son died as he was trying to stuff his entrails back into his belly." Or, "He gave up his body with characteristic nobility of spirit," not, "His head was shattered like a pumpkin under the wheels of his own chariot." All for some schmuck of a husband whose whore of a wife threw her dress up over her head for a house guest.

HELEN: But that didn't happen.

MENELAUS: What does it matter when everything else did?

Pause.

HELEN: Take me home.

MENELAUS: I can't. You're not the woman all those people died for. You're not the woman a city fell for. She is.

HELEN: Let me be her then. Leave her here. I'll play her.

MENELAUS: But don't you see? You'd never be able to stop performing her. Not once for the rest of your life would you be able to retreat into the privacy of the truth. There would be no end to lying. You couldn't manage it. No one could.

HELEN: I'm good. Don't you remember how good I am?

MENELAUS: (*With tenderness and finality.*) That was a long time ago. We're old now. You couldn't keep it up. She can.

HELEN: Look at me.

He does.

Do you feel love for me anymore?

He shakes his head. Pause. He nods. Pause. He shakes his head.

Do you love her?

He nods. Pause. He shakes his head. Pause. He nods.

I see.

MENELAUS: I should go.

HELEN: Yes.

He leaves.

I shall die having accomplished nothing.
I saw nothing. I heard nothing.
My single achievement: I did nothing wrong. I was saved from that.
I made no mistakes. I was perfect.

Servant enters.

SERVANT: Time for bed.

HELEN: Yes.

The servant begins undoing Helen's elaborate coif and then brushing out her hair.

Tell me a story.

SERVANT: Once upon a time there was a woman. She was loved, if you can call it that, or at any rate considered so extraordinary that thousands of copies are made of her, every one of them more durable than the original. Some are put in museums in good or mottled light. Some are in village squares, where dogs lift their legs at them or women dance around them. Some are sold to investors who keep them in their dens and do God knows what to them. With every copy comes another rumor, another narrative spawned. The most famous copy goes on a long voyage and animates a city. She breeds herself there and her image is simultaneously in several places: cat walking the battlements in an iridescent dress to make the soldiers below sick with lust and hatred. Or moving like smoke through the streets at night, tumbling from bed to bed, house to house, slipping into the dreams of men and women alike. She is impartial and pervasive, this cipher, this phantom. And the strange thing is that all this time, the copy has been thinking of her original self, the real Helen, who has lived in seclusion, protected from everything, even narrative. Literally nothing has happened to that woman. Except that she's aged. As her replicas have not. And during all the years she spent waiting to meet herself, her own story, on its long way home, what has she done?

She has dreamed. She has dreamed of a war. A great epic. And a terrible one. A war fought for nothing and costing everything. A war that churned around an emptiness, a hollow like the navel at the center of the world. Battles reeled and spun, treading centuries of civilization under their bloody wheels. Like corn under a millstone they are all ground to dust. Until at last all beauty vanishes from the earth and only that emptiness remains, perfumed by death.

What can she do with the awesome weight of this story?

Her own story.

She has a choice, it turns out. She can do one of two things:

Either she can maintain her costumes and that body she never knew, keep herself in readiness as best she can for some distant day, almost unimaginable now, when she might tread the boards again in the guise of that sex goddess she has been impersonating since time immemorial. Or she could eschew all that, leave it to the other girls, the copies, who do that kind of work so much better than she could ever manage it, being objects to begin with and thus immortal, if dead. Because she might instead do something quite surprising. Something no one sees her do. She might open her eyes. She might lift the lid of her own casket and climb out, then slip through the thicket of thorns in the dead of night into utter invisibility.

And no one would ever hear from her again.

Years go by and though her image in all its unearthly beauty still breeds and transfixes on billboards and movie screens, prolific as ever, the world loses track of the woman herself. There are rumors, of course, sightings in the oddest places, though the figure glimpsed is always silent. Tramps say they met her hopping freights up north, sleeping with her shoes on, a newspaper shielding her eyes. Some woman says she sees her every Wednesday walking the empty seashore and tossing saltines to the gulls. Some physicist claims she attended his lecture, sitting in the back with her knitting, nodding and chuckling when he got to the tricky stuff.

But this is what I think:

There's a diner in the high desert. It's winter and she is sitting at the counter one afternoon when the blind old man on the stool next to her starts to tell her about himself. (Everyone she meets tells her about themselves, she notices.) He's a story-teller, you see, has been doing it all his life. He can memorize anything he's told after hearing it only once. It's a gift, you see. "Everybody's got a story", he says, "did you ever notice that?" She's smiling now, this ancient woman, crumbling crackers in the old man's soup for him. He can't see her, of course, but he can tell she was probably beautiful once; it's like a scent that comes off her. But they're so old, these two, that they look like twins. It's hard to say who's the woman and who's the man, that's how ancient they are.

A silence comes over the place. It's late in the afternoon, no one's in there but the two of them, sitting at the counter. It's snowing outside and the steam rises from their bowls and makes her eyes shine. And then as she hands him his spoon, he catches her hand, the blind poet, and he says the thing she's been waiting all her life to hear. He says, "Tell me a story."

And she opens her mouth at last. And she does.

> *Helen's hair is down. The women stare out together. The door opens. Sound of crickets. Long pause in stillness.*

END OF PLAY

NOTES ON MEMORY HOUSE
by Kathleen Tolan

Some years ago I met a woman who had adopted a child from Eastern Europe. She talked about the urge she had felt to raise a child and her circuitous and fraught search that ended up in an orphanage in a small town in Bulgaria, where the tallest building was two stories. She told of the arrival of the six-year-old girl to her apartment in Manhattan and the difficulties of that relationship over the years, the expectations, the complicated love.

I'd been drawn to the subject of having/not having a child, and a few of my plays explore this territory. I was intrigued by the woman's story, of the complexity of the act—that she was taking and saving this child—and of the child's response, of gratitude and anger, relief and loss. And it resonated for me, with questions about the larger world that many of us continue to ask about our country's foreign policy: when are we helping and when damaging, what is the nature of our interest, who are we in the world?

I decided my fictional daughter would come from Russia. I interviewed adoptive parents, children, and agents that arranged adoptions of Russian children. I interviewed a pediatrician who specialized in internationally adopted children, a sociologist who had worked in Eastern Europe and Russia helping create support systems for families who didn't want to have to give up their children and programs to get orphans off the street. I read about the culture and politics of Russia in the 1990s and the state of Russian orphanages. I read books that likened international adoption to imperialist plunder of a poor country and others that celebrated it as a way to save children from a miserable life.

For a while I thought the play would span a number of years and a couple of continents, and I'd still like to write that play, but finally I decided to write it with two characters, the mother and daughter, in real time. When I told a colleague I was doing that, he said "No! Don't do a two-character play! There will be no place to hide!" And that was challenge enough.

I decided to set the action when the daughter was up against her college application deadline. (Having recently been in a house with a daughter who sent in her applications at the very last moment, it was territory I didn't need to read a book about.) I imagined that the pressure to write a personal essay about one's origins, combined with the anticipation of leaving home, could force an eruption of the stuff that had been put away years before: questions about the adoption, identity, and one's place in the world.

I didn't need to read a book about what a mother of a teenager might feel, anticipating her daughter leaving home, or the worry she might have for the safety and happiness of that child, or of her own fear of being alone. I didn't have to read a book about a teenage girl who made hairpin turns from confidence to uncertainty, from eloquence to babble, from optimism to an uncertainty about whether life was worth it. And I didn't have to read a book about the challenge of staying in the room with a teenager who needs you to be there and needs you to leave, or about the parent who can be a support and a burden to her child.

During a time when I was wanted and not wanted by my teenager and I was trying to figure out how to be present but occupied, I decided to make a pie. I got advice on how to bake it from a couple of my more competent friends, and it turned out to be quite successful, as a strategy and as a dessert. And so I decided my character, Maggie, would have that project as she tried to be there and not there while her daughter suffered her college essay. And I realized that, just like a gun in the first act that must go off in the third, if she puts a pie in the oven on page thirty-eight, it better come out at the end.

I am wary of the process of play development that can flatten a new play, and I accepted Hedgebrook's invitation with a certain amount of trepidation. We spent the first week in rehearsal for staged readings at Seattle Repertory Theatre, and I was immediately thrown in with a group of playwrights—Sarah Ruhl, Julia Cho, and Karen Zacarías—who became fast friends and cherished colleagues. The engagement and delight in each other's work, and the stories that they shared with me about their relationships with their mothers when they were teenagers were gold. Christine Sumption was my dramaturg, and her insights and support were crucial, and when we went off to

Hedgebrook after that first week, Mame Hunt and Kristin Newbom joined us around the dinner table and in the sitting room at night where we read aloud the pages we'd written in our cottages that day. It was joyful, and it went deep. It was the perfect place to make a play.

— **Kathleen Tolan**

BIOGRAPHY

Kathleen Tolan's plays include *A Weekend Near Madison* (Actors Theatre of Louisville, Astor Place Theatre in NYC), *Kate's Diary* (Playwrights Horizons, Public Theater), *Approximating Mother* (Women's Project), *A Girl's Life* (Trinity Repertory Company), *The Wax* (Playwrights Horizons), *False Servant*, an adaptation from Marivaux (Classic Stage Company). As an actor, she has worked in Andre Gregory's company the Manhattan Project, Off- and Off-Off-Broadway, and in regional theatre, TV, and film.

Tolan has received the McKnight Fellowship, a NYFA Fellowship, several MacDowell residencies, the Stanford Calderwood Fellowship, the Thornton Wilder Fellowship, the Revson Fellowship, and a couple of Sundance Playwrights residencies. She has had numerous commissions from various theatres. She is the Chair of the Dramatic Writing Program Conservatory of Theatre Arts and Film at Purchase College where she teaches playwriting.

ACKNOWLEDGMENTS

Memory House was originally commissioned by Trinity Repertory Company, Providence, Rhode Island. It had its first reading at Seattle Repertory Theatre as part of the Hedgebrook Women Playwrights Festival. The play premiered at Actors Theatre of Louisville (Marc Masterson, Artistic Director; Jennifer Bielstein, Managing Director) in Louisville, Kentucky. The director was Sandy Shinner. The scenic design was by Paul Owen, costume design by Lorraine Venberg, lighting design by Deb Sullivan, sound design by Lindsay Jones, and video design by Jason Czaja. The play has subsequently been produced at Playwrights Horizons, Victory Gardens Theatre in Chicago, Seattle Repertory Theatre, and Trinity Repertory Company, among others.

MEMORY HOUSE
by Kathleen Tolan

CHARACTERS

MAGGIE, in her 50s.

KATIA, 18.

SETTING

New Year's Eve, New York City, now.

A video screen. A tape is played.

A shot of a bare institutional room, going in and out of focus, and the sound of conversation off-camera. The conversation is in Russian. The voices sound like they are giving directions, cajoling, admonishing. A girl, age six, walks stiffly into frame. She is wearing a new dress and has a bow in her hair. She carries a large ball. The off-camera voices call to her, cheerfully give her orders. She throws the ball to someone off-camera. It bounces back, she catches it. The voices say something else. She begins to sing a folk song in Russian. The tape goes off. Black.

A living room/kitchen in an NYC apartment. Eminem blaring. Katia sits on the couch. Her coat has been flung beside her, her knapsack is

*open with papers and envelopes falling out, a laptop computer open
on the coffee table in front of her. Books and boxes and stuff has been
pulled from the shelves in the apartment. Katia sits, types, stops,
agitated, staring at the screen and then off into space. Maggie
comes in from outside with a couple of bags of groceries.*

MAGGIE: Would you turn that down?

Katia, surprised, covers, grabs the remote and turns down the music.

KATIA: What?

MAGGIE: Or off. You could even turn it off.

Katia turns off the music.

MAGGIE: (*Referring to the mess.*) What happened? Was there a break-in?

KATIA: I'll clean it up.

MAGGIE: Did you finish?

KATIA: No.

MAGGIE: Katia.

KATIA: What?

MAGGIE: Why aren't you at your Dad's? He was going to help you,
with his big brain.

KATIA: I thought you were going out.

MAGGIE: I did. Now I'm back. (*Referring to the computer screen.*)
What's this?

KATIA: My masterpiece.

Maggie reads aloud.

MAGGIE: I want to go to college to get a hunk o' knowledge." Nice
whatsit, lead sentence.

KATIA: Thanks.

MAGGIE: "Cuz my ma no finished school so she set down the rule, if I ain't got a degree I is up a bare tree, cuz she was fancy free, but the man he done gone—" You're taking liberties here. I have many men.

KATIA: I mean the central man.

MAGGIE: Central to you.

KATIA: Where are your men?

MAGGIE: They go out for a smoke when you come over.

KATIA: So they'll have the run of the place when I'm gone.

MAGGIE: They'll still need to smoke. When you're gone? You mean, to college?

KATIA: Or the street. Who knows?

MAGGIE: Who does know? May I share this with my bridge club?

KATIA: You don't have a bridge club.

MAGGIE: But I want to start one so I can share these fantastic lyrics.

KATIA: Okay.

MAGGIE: What do you have left?

KATIA: I have to print it out.

MAGGIE: That's it?

KATIA: Yes.

MAGGIE: You're using the rap?

KATIA: No.

MAGGIE: You've written a pop version?

KATIA: Yeah.

MAGGIE: Why did you say it wasn't done?

KATIA: It's done.

MAGGIE: That's wonderful.

KATIA: It is.

MAGGIE: Congratulations.

KATIA: Thank you.

MAGGIE: Do you want me to read it?

KATIA: No, thanks.

MAGGIE: Just to proof it.

KATIA: No, thanks.

MAGGIE: Even professional writers have their articles proofread.

KATIA: How do you know?

MAGGIE: I read it. In an article.

KATIA: It's all good.

MAGGIE: Did Daddy read it?

KATIA: No.

MAGGIE: Was he helpful?

KATIA: In his way.

MAGGIE: Good. So are you going to mail it?

KATIA: Yes.

MAGGIE: You have to take it to the post office.

KATIA: Really?

MAGGIE: Why can't you just click it and send?

KATIA: Beats me.

MAGGIE: But you did the others.
Beat.

Right?

Beat.

That you could just click and send?
Beat.

Hello?

KATIA: Don't worry Mom.

MAGGIE: I'm not worried. Just wondered. Just curious. If you sent in the others. On the internet. The magic of the web.

KATIA: I'm not into that.

MAGGIE: Into what? The magic of the internet?

KATIA: Safety in numbers. Second choices.

MAGGIE: Honey. Just. Click and send, it's done.

KATIA: Would you not?

MAGGIE: (*Grim, restraining herself.*)

Yes. I can not.

      Beat.

How do you feel?

KATIA: Great.

MAGGIE: That's wonderful.

KATIA: It's a milestone.

MAGGIE: Do you want me to…?

KATIA: You do your thing, I'll do mine.

MAGGIE: Okay. I'll just…This shouldn't take long. I could go with you to the post office if you want.

KATIA: Thanks, Mom.

MAGGIE: Okay, you do your thing, I'll do mine.

Maggie turns her attention to the cookbooks.

KATIA: It's New Year's Eve. I thought you were going out.

MAGGIE: I am.

KATIA: No you're not.

MAGGIE: I will.

KATIA: You never go out.

MAGGIE: Of course I do.

KATIA: You stay at home and weep at the wall.

MAGGIE: Well, somebody has to do it. We each have our special calling. I try to be humble.

Maggie reads.

KATIA: What're you doing?

MAGGIE: I need to remember how to bake a pie.

KATIA: (*Skeptical.*) Remember?

MAGGIE: Huh?

KATIA: You've never baked a pie.

MAGGIE: Have too.

KATIA: I think I would know.

MAGGIE: How?

KATIA: I'm your daughter.

MAGGIE: You have been at your father's from time to time. I might have made pies then.

KATIA: Not so likely.

MAGGIE: Why?

KATIA: I would've smelled them when I got back.

MAGGIE: Not necessarily.

> *Cell phone rings. Katia reaches over, picks it up, looks at it, puts it back down.*

MAGGIE: Phone's ringing.

KATIA: Thanks, Mom.

> *The phone stops ringing. Maggie turns on the oven.*

You printing it out?

KATIA: I'm taking a break.

MAGGIE: Been doing some heavy lifting?

KATIA: Yeah.

MAGGIE: (*Reading cookbook.*)

Oh!

KATIA: What?

MAGGIE: Why don't you print out your thing?

KATIA: What?

MAGGIE: "Skill in pastry making has been regarded worldwide as a passport to matrimony."

KATIA: Go Mom.

MAGGIE: Had I known…

KATIA: What?

MAGGIE: Well…

KATIA: You wouldn't have settled for Dad?

MAGGIE: Oh, no, your dad was a prize. He must have thought I was a pastry maker. I must have lied to him. Can't think of another explanation.

KATIA: This is the problem with middle-aged women.

MAGGIE: Oh, how thrilling. You are going to illuminate this shadowy subject for me.

KATIA: You should've stayed with Dad.

MAGGIE: Where did that come from?

KATIA: Next year I'll be gone. He's still here.

MAGGIE: He's not here. He's across town with the springy mattress.

KATIA: She's not a springy mattress. She's a nice person. You should be nice to her.

MAGGIE: I am nice to her.

KATIA: No you're not.

MAGGIE: Fifty percent of all marriages in this country are across town with new mattresses. Or anyway not in the original, sagging beds. Are you blaming me for that failure?

KATIA: No.

MAGGIE: Say no, look yes. And anyway, human relationships need not be the central thing. Work, thought, experience, the sun in the morning, the moon at night. These are the things.

    Pause. Maggie reads.

Wow.

KATIA: What?

MAGGIE: Okay, this is important. "In Hungarian villages, no girl was considered eligible until her strudel dough had become so translucent that her beloved could read the newspaper through it." No wonder I can't comprehend the news. My pie dough is too thick.

KATIA: That must be it.

MAGGIE: We better set up some sessions.

KATIA: Huh?

Hedgebrook Plays · Volume One

MAGGIE: How are you gonna snag a boy, how can I call myself a mother if I let you out into the world with thick crust?

KATIA: I'm not into boys.

MAGGIE: You're not?

KATIA: No.

MAGGIE: What about Jake?

KATIA: Jake's not a guy.

MAGGIE: Oh, okay.

KATIA: He's the exception that proves the rule.

MAGGIE: I get it. Is he done with his essays?

KATIA: I don't want to talk about it.

MAGGIE: Me neither.

> *Maggie takes blueberries, pours them into a colander, continues washing and picking through.*

Gosh. Blueberries in winter. How extravagant. I could have bought a gown. Paid the mortgage. What was I thinking?

> *Maggie eats one.*

Mmm. Want one?

KATIA: No thanks, Mom.

> *Maggie dumps the blueberries into the pan.*

MAGGIE: Ok. So. I need my trusty cup…and my trusty half cup…Salt.

> *Maggie measures flour, salt, and sugar into a sifter and then sifts into a bowl.*

> *Katia seems lost in thought.*

MAGGIE: It really is a revelation.

KATIA: Is it?

155

MAGGIE: This is what people do. It's taken me half a century to get it.

KATIA: Okay.

MAGGIE: You work a job, then you have hobbies!

KATIA: That's big.

MAGGIE: The work makes you feel productive and tires you, and the hobbies gratify and amuse, and you make something, and it isn't too taxing, anyone really can do it. Hobbies I always put off, thought they would pull me from my art or something, but now I see how brilliant the whole concept is.

KATIA: It isn't a concept.

MAGGIE: Well, whatever.

KATIA: You should get a better job.

MAGGIE: I love my job.

KATIA: You do not.

MAGGIE: I do. You don't understand that's part of the deal with an office job, you go home and complain. That's the deal.

KATIA: Oh.

MAGGIE: And I just read about a survey of workers in England, that those who are paid less wages are happier! So if that's true here, I must be among the happiest in the population.

KATIA: Had me fooled.

MAGGIE: I'm happy.

>   *Maggie cuts the butter into pads.*

I'm 'appy. (*Beat.*) Just a bit a butter for your royal slice of bread.

>   *She unwraps a bar of shortening.*

MAGGIE: Lard. But do they mean real lard or fake lard?

>   *She reads the label, then reads cookbook in silence.*

Irma doesn't say. She's silent. Uncharacteristically silent. Well, we must buck up, carry on.

> *Maggie takes butter and vegetable shortening and mushes them together.*

MAGGIE: Ooo.

KATIA: What?

MAGGIE: Feels wonderful…want to try?

KATIA: No thanks. I think this baking thing is increasing the momentum of brain-unraveling.

MAGGIE: No, each instruction, each ingredient will act as an anchor, a pin to keep the brain strands in place.

> *Katia's cell phone rings. Katia ignores it.*

MAGGIE: Phone ringing.

KATIA: Thanks.

> *The phone stops ringing. Maggie picks up the butter cutter and examines it.*

MAGGIE: Okay.

> *She checks the cookbook.*

(*Pleased with the tool.*) How clever this is. And Irma kindly includes a helpful illustration to act as a guide as we cut the fat into the flour.

> *She has begun to cut the fat into the flour.*
> *The apartment phone rings.*

MAGGIE: Hon?

> *Katia doesn't respond. The phone continues to ring.*

MAGGIE: Want to get it?

KATIA: No.

MAGGIE: Go on.

KATIA: Why?

MAGGIE: I'm busy.

KATIA: So am I.

MAGGIE: With what?

KATIA: I have to finish my thing.

MAGGIE: I thought you finished it.

KATIA: I did.

MAGGIE: So finish it.

KATIA: I did.

> *The phone stops ringing. Maggie takes a long breath, lets it out.*
>
> *Maggie checks the cookbook, goes and gets ice from the freezer, plops it into a bowl of water.*

MAGGIE: Want some ice?

KATIA: No.

MAGGIE: Some water?

KATIA: No.

MAGGIE: A drink?

KATIA: No.

> *Maggie adds spoonfuls of water to the dough, mixes with a fork, begins to shape the dough into a ball.*

MAGGIE: Okay. If it's crumbly, sprinkle with a few extra drops of water. Then we shape it into a tidy ball. How charming. Remember play dough? I loved the smell, and the feel of it…And even the taste, remember the salty taste? I would sneak little bits and hold them on my tongue… Gosh, it's so cool that grownups get to do this…When you were really into art projects and the house was filled with all that stuff, I went to tea with an old friend Bill who had gone back to school and was reading

Plato.* I thought he said "play dough." "You're reading play dough?"

KATIA: That's funny.

MAGGIE: Well, it was, at the time.

> *Phone rings. Maggie moves to get it.*

KATIA: I'm not here.

MAGGIE: I noticed.

MAGGIE: (*Into phone.*) Joe's bar…Oh…Hi. I was being funny… She's here. (*To Katia.*) Your father.

> *Katia gestures furiously.*

(*Into phone.*) Sorry, she's not here…She doesn't want to talk to you.

KATIA: I'm working.

MAGGIE: (*Into phone.*) She's working…

(*To Katia.*) Are you mad at him?

> *Katia doesn't respond.*

Did you get his email?

> *Katia, irritated, gestures for Maggie to stop.*

(*Into phone.*) I'm sure she did.

(*To Katia.*) Did you take the print-outs?

KATIA: Yes.

MAGGIE: She's done…She finished…

> *Maggie listens, glances over at Katia, concerned.*

(*To Katia.*) Did you find your box?

---

* When Maggie pronounces "Plato" she shouldn't emphasize the "t" but pronounce it as it's usually pronounced.

> *Katia ignores the question. Maggie looks over at the mess with a new understanding.*

(*Into phone.*) She needs a context?…Sorry? Tag, I think it's a little late for a context. Maybe she could get that for her graduate school applications. You do know she's applying to *one college*?

KATIA: (*Forceful.*) Bye.

MAGGIE: (*Into phone.*) I'll talk to you later.

> *Maggie hangs up.*

KATIA: If you and Daddy want to get off on discussing my life why don't you rent a hotel room.

MAGGIE: You still have an essay to write?

KATIA: (*Glances at the clock.*) I have time.

MAGGIE: Katia.

KATIA: What?

MAGGIE: I'm not a conventional person.

KATIA: Really?

MAGGIE: I mean, I'm not an *anarchist*. I believe in, like, *voting*…

KATIA: Mom…

MAGGIE: You have to do this.

KATIA: I am.

MAGGIE: Really.

KATIA: I have to write about a *memory house* and how the crap can I do that if I don't remember anything?

MAGGIE: What are you talking about?

KATIA: This complete butt-hole essay for this butt-juice stupid school.

MAGGIE: Is the stupid school your first choice?

KATIA: Was.

MAGGIE: What don't you remember?

KATIA: Gee, let me think about that.

MAGGIE: What's a memory house?

> Katia doesn't respond.

Just give me a clue. Sounds like…

KATIA: Where you store your memories.

MAGGIE: You're supposed to have a house for your memories?

KATIA: Guess so.

MAGGIE: I would have a storage locker. More practical. Don't have to mow the lawn.

KATIA: Good point.

MAGGIE: But—this is so queer I guess—I store them in my head.

KATIA: Hey, why don't you write it? Maybe you could go to college, finish up, make something of your life.

MAGGIE: Yes. Let's see, well, it's more like a memory garage and there have been quite a number of garage sales so there are some gaps and it's a mess, can't get in with a shovel, have to park in the driveway. But it works for me.

KATIA: Good.

MAGGIE: Did you write anything?

KATIA: Yes.

MAGGIE: Where is it?

KATIA: Gone.

MAGGIE: It's your favorite school.

KATIA: So?

MAGGIE: So you should send in the thing.

KATIA: Why?

MAGGIE: Because it's due. It has to be postmarked today. Make it up. Memories are never accurate anyway. And it gets worse.

KATIA: Thanks for the tip.

MAGGIE: You did the others though really, right? You don't have to say. Just, don't look at me, just a slight imperceptible nod. You clicked and sent the others, right?

KATIA: I gotta go.

MAGGIE: You have to go?

KATIA: Yes.

MAGGIE: Where? To reserve a place on the street?

KATIA: Yeah.

MAGGIE: You have three hours.

KATIA: I know, Mom.

MAGGIE: To get it *postmarked*.

KATIA: I know.

MAGGIE: And then—poof—it's over. It's a new day, a new year, and you've *blown it*.

KATIA: What's the point if the world is going to explode anyway?

MAGGIE: It is? That's big.

KATIA: I hate this country.

MAGGIE: Don't say that. You do not.

KATIA: I do. It's the pig of the world. Daddy agrees.

MAGGIE: Well good for Daddy.

KATIA: He wants to help me.

MAGGIE: So let him. What's the problem?

KATIA: I'm going over there.

MAGGIE: Where? To Daddy's? Fine. Just one question: You need a context?

KATIA: Dad-speak.

MAGGIE: He gave you some print-outs? What do they say?

KATIA: Nothing.

MAGGIE: What's this mess?

KATIA: I said I'd clean it up.

MAGGIE: Were you looking for something?

KATIA: No.

MAGGIE: Your box? Of stuff?

KATIA: No.

MAGGIE: For your memory locker.

KATIA: House. No.

MAGGIE: I haven't seen it in years. It must be somewhere.

KATIA: Thanks, Mom.

MAGGIE: Did you look in your room?

KATIA: It's not there.

MAGGIE: Is it over at your dad's?

KATIA: No.

MAGGIE: Do you need it?

KATIA: (*Forceful.*) No.

MAGGIE: Katia.

KATIA: What?

MAGGIE: I realize that I may not have won any prizes as an essay writer, but maybe my ignorance could be of use. I could ask you, for instance, how do you write an essay? And you could show me.

KATIA: Don't.

MAGGIE: Okay. Fine. You do your thing, I'll do mine.

> *Maggie returns to the counter.*

KATIA: Daddy thinks I should go to Russia.

MAGGIE: In order to write the essay due in three hours? What a practical suggestion.

KATIA: Vlad is going back.

MAGGIE: Vlad? Is going back? How do you know?

KATIA: He emailed me.

MAGGIE: You could write about Vlad. He's in your memory locker, the picnics in New Jersey, the blintzes, the samovar, the music. I didn't know you stayed in touch with him.

KATIA: He's going to Russia to look for his real mother.

MAGGIE: Thanks, hon.

KATIA: For what?

MAGGIE: For sticking it to me so effectively.

KATIA: What?

MAGGIE: His "real" mother?

KATIA: First mother. Birth mother. Didn't use the right term, sorry.

MAGGIE: Oh, right, just a little semantical glitch, I understand, don't take it personally and anyway who said you're my "real" daughter.

KATIA: I would say this is an over-reaction. Did you go off your medication?

MAGGIE: I'm not on medication.

KATIA: That was a joke. Did you ever hear of "joke?"

MAGGIE: Vaguely.

KATIA: He wants me to go with him.

MAGGIE: Who?

KATIA: Vlad.

MAGGIE: To Russia? How perfect.

KATIA: What?

MAGGIE: After all these years of refusing to retain the language, the customs—

KATIA: (*Fierce.*) They're not my customs. It's not my language.

MAGGIE: Oh. Okay.

KATIA: They're not my dolls, painted eggs, songs. And you, with that man, reading to me that old Russian book—

MAGGIE: When?

KATIA: When you took me here.

MAGGIE: You've been visiting your memory house. That's good.

>   *Not able to deal with this, Maggie reads the cookbook.*

Fuck.

KATIA: What?

MAGGIE: *Twelve hours?* How incredibly annoying.

KATIA: What?

MAGGIE: I have to chill the dough.

KATIA: You can pick up a pie. This is New York. There are pies on every street corner.

MAGGIE: Don't diminish my work.

KATIA: I don't.

MAGGIE: (*Reads.*) Oh, thank god.

KATIA: You're saved.

MAGGIE: *Up to* twelve hours.

KATIA: Whew.

MAGGIE: Why can't I read?

KATIA: Maybe you need glasses.

MAGGIE: I have glasses.

KATIA: Good point.

MAGGIE: Maybe a remedial reading course.

KATIA: You'll be in the cafes reading the paper through your dough.

MAGGIE: Yes, and all the suitors will see. Plus I'll comprehend the news, finally. Who says life stops for a gal after fifty?

KATIA: Not me.

MAGGIE: Nor me.

> *Maggie begins to roll out the dough.*

Okay. Cut it in half, roll it out. Carefully. From the center, lift.

KATIA: Who will eat the pies you bake?

MAGGIE: After you're gone? (*Sings.*) And left me cryin'? After you're gone? There's no denying...

KATIA: Stop.

MAGGIE: I will eat them, after you're gone. And little orphans on the street, I'll invite them up for tea and pie.

> *Maggie finishes rolling out the dough and begins to peel it off the board.*

This may not be perfect. But is that what we're striving for?
No, no, no.

She plops it into the pan and considers it.

It may require a few patches. But cleverly, the berries will cover the thing, so as long as there aren't big leaks. *Maggie checks the cookbook and then adds sugar and cornstarch to the blueberries.*

Okay. Sucre. And starch of corn. And lemon.

She cuts a piece of lemon and smells it.

Mmm.

Maggie squeezes the lemon juice into the blueberry mix, then puts the pot onto the stove.

Okay, according to Irma it helps that the berry stuff be very hot.

Maggie turns on the burner under the pot, then returns to the dough and considers the pie dough in its pan.

How finite, how satisfying.

Maggie trims the dough.

Shall we trim it? I think we shall. Just a wee bit. Do you want to see?

KATIA: No thanks.

MAGGIE: Still on your break?

KATIA: Yes.

MAGGIE: Gosh, you must have a great union.

KATIA: Yeah. But the dues are high.

MAGGIE: Make you pay through your teeth, eh?

KATIA: Yeah.

MAGGIE: I hate that.

Beat.

How are you going to afford this trip to Russia?

KATIA: I have money saved up.

MAGGIE: That's for college expenses.

KATIA: If I decide to go to college.

MAGGIE: Oh, yeah, why not trash your life?

KATIA: You never got a degree.

MAGGIE: That should propel you to college. Like a rocket.

KATIA: If I get in.

MAGGIE: You'll get in.

KATIA: So you say.

MAGGIE: I do say. Though having a few options. Not that I have an opinion about that.

> *Maggie rolls out the rest of the dough.*

KATIA: Daddy said he could take me.

MAGGIE: To Russia? He just got a chair at the university. He has to stay in town and sit on his chair.

KATIA: Not in the summers, or vacations.

MAGGIE: They let him out of his chair on vacations? What are the print-outs?

KATIA: Nothing.

MAGGIE: Nothing? Wow, that's intense.

KATIA: Context, meaning.

MAGGIE: So what does it mean? I would like some print-outs to explain my life.

KATIA: I can explain your life.

MAGGIE: But I want print-outs. What do they say?

KATIA: Stuff about the debate on international adoption.

MAGGIE: There's a debate?

KATIA: There are a few political issues.

MAGGIE: No joke.

KATIA: Basically it's about ripping children off from their bleeding countries.

MAGGIE: Really? How interesting. That's not quite how I experienced it. But I am often repressed, delusional, yes, maybe I was lying to myself, I'd convinced myself that *Daddy* and I adopted you because—

KATIA: Because you couldn't get knocked up by Dad.

MAGGIE: Oh, yeah, that was it.

KATIA: And you were terrified that if you adopted in the States the birth mother would come to get you.

MAGGIE: Right.

KATIA: So you realized that you could go to Russia, the land of Tolstoy, your love, and pick up an orphan there.

MAGGIE: Is this your essay?

KATIA: Was.

MAGGIE: Be sure to mark it fiction.

KATIA: You wish.

MAGGIE: I know. And tell your father to go take a ride on the Reading. Where the sun don't shine.

KATIA: I'll do that.

MAGGIE: Why would he say that?

KATIA: Because I asked.

MAGGIE: What did you ask?

KATIA: How can I write anything if I don't know who I am?

MAGGIE: But guess what? We told you what we knew.

KATIA: It was a story.

MAGGIE: It was true.

KATIA: It was to make me feel good about myself.

MAGGIE: Why is that bad?

KATIA: It's not what I need.

MAGGIE: What do you need?

KATIA: To know.

MAGGIE: To know what?

KATIA: (*Drops it, emphatic.*) Forget it.

MAGGIE: What do you need to know?

KATIA: Forget it.

> *Impasse. Katia sinks into herself.*

> *Maggie considers Katia, concerned. She then turns off the stove, takes the pan of berries and pours it in.*

MAGGIE: This may turn into blueberry soup. Baked blueberry soup, with flour and butter globs.

> *Maggie cuts the remaining dough into strips and arranges them on the pie.*

I think we'll forgo the lattice this time…just kind of plop the strips down rather than truly weave…Not that I don't believe in ambition, in going for the gold, but there's something to accepting your level and looking forward to the next step.

> *Maggie finishes assembling the pie and coats the rim with the egg mixture.*

Almost ready to go in. I wonder if I'm forgetting something crucial, something that is so obvious they didn't even think to put it in the cookbook, like, hold the pan in your hands, grip it while you walk your feet over to the oven.

Okay, I'm putting it in. Ready? Want to have a race? Paper versus pie?

    Katia doesn't respond. Maggie takes the pie and puts it in the oven.

KATIA: Why didn't you choose a kid from here?

MAGGIE: You're not serious. You're just grabbing this because it's handy and you have to hang your hat on something.

KATIA: There are many poor children right here in need of a good home.

MAGGIE: (*Fierce.*) Stop it. We chose you, exactly you. I know that your father is a brilliant man but politics can be so stupid—what did Woody Guthrie sing:

(*Sings to the tune "This Land Is Our Land."*) "When he went walking, he saw a sign there, and on the sign it said no trespassing. But on the other side, it didn't say nothing. That side was made for you and me."

No, not that one. Oh, yeah, something about they made a stew and it being so thin, (*Mimicking Woody Guthrie.*) "even a politician could see through it." Like the strudel dough. (*Beat, confused.*) I know I had a point.

    Maggie considers Katia.

What book did I read?

KATIA: When?

MAGGIE: When you came here.

KATIA: Some old Russian farming book.

MAGGIE: A farming book?

KATIA: About a farmer who strode through the fields and was in love with nature or something and wanted to be a peasant.

MAGGIE: *Anna Karenina.* It isn't a farming book. We just edited the parts about the affair.

    Beat.

I thought, if I didn't know the particulars of your heritage, wouldn't Tolstoy work—for any of us, really, what could be more wonderful…

KATIA: And you had that big farmer read it to me.

MAGGIE: What farmer? Igor. He wasn't a farmer. He fixed the door of the stove.

KATIA: He was Russian.

MAGGIE: Yes, he fixed the door, we talked about his life in Russia, his wife and children, and when we brought you home we called him and he came over and helped.

KATIA: I thought he was going to take me back.

> *Beat.*

MAGGIE: I'm sorry.

> *Beat.*

He was a nice man, I thought it would help you, to have someone familiar…

KATIA: It didn't.

MAGGIE: Sorry.

KATIA: And he would read a passage of the book, and you would read it in English and the occasional weird sort of mushed up Russian word, and I thought you were retarded.

MAGGIE: Okay, I may be a retard. And…this is good. I didn't know. But it's good.

KATIA: Did you know that our government helped to totally mess up Russia?

MAGGIE: Did it?

KATIA: It did.

MAGGIE: That was mean. I hate it when our government is mean.

KATIA: Do you know that our government and all its advisors supported Yeltsin who was a complete pig and a total criminal and got into office illegally?

MAGGIE: Gee, I can't imagine our government doing something like that. I'll have to write a letter.

KATIA: Mom.

MAGGIE: Katia.

KATIA: These things are important.

MAGGIE: I agree.

KATIA: But you feel fine about joining the big rip-off, you don't have a problem with that.

MAGGIE: Okay, I missed a beat.

KATIA: I'm your loot.

MAGGIE: No.

KATIA: Dad and I were talking about this.

MAGGIE: I had a feeling.

KATIA: Did you think you could shield me from this?

MAGGIE: What did your father say?

KATIA: This is so not about what Daddy said or didn't say. It's about what happened.

MAGGIE: You know, your father *chose* to adopt you, and in spite of his incredibly cerebral positions and his ideological rigidity—

KATIA: Mom, taking off the gloves.

MAGGIE: We explored this. We did try it the old fashioned way, yes, and I know I've told you all this, having studied extensively the manuals on how to talk to your adopted child at what age—

KATIA: And how to bullshit them.

MAGGIE: Yes, *sorry*, How to Bullshit Your Adopted Child at What Age, that was the title. We studied it carefully, followed it meticulously.

　　　Beat.

And I'm sorry it's morally superior to get knocked up. Or to pick up a baby from some teenager in Texas. But it's good, really, to know that your parents—or anyway, your mother, somehow your father continues to be Teflon Dad, I don't get it, but it's just one of the many things I don't get and anyway it's good to have at least one morally crippled— I mean disabled—morally *challenged* mother, it's good to have that, and it's classic, we all need to trash Mom, it's something to define yourself in opposition to, the charred remains of Mom, makes you a classicist, that's good, the colleges will be impressed, not that you need any definition, you are pretty defined.

KATIA: No I'm not.

MAGGIE: Yes you are.

KATIA: How would you define me?

MAGGIE: You want me to define you?

KATIA: Mom.

MAGGIE: What?

KATIA: Dad thinks about the ethics of things.

MAGGIE: Yes, he does.

KATIA: That's his job.

MAGGIE: Yes.

KATIA: And he doesn't just sit on his chair. He was there, in the field—

MAGGIE: This I know.

KATIA: —in Eastern Europe, in Russia, helping to make the welfare systems work. He's an important person.

MAGGIE: A very important person. I know that. And it's important to be important. I know that, he knows that, clearly he conveyed that to you, everybody knows that. But—I have to say—

KATIA: You do?

MAGGIE: I do. There's the idea of the thing and the thing. And sometimes the idea of the thing leads you to the thing, and sometimes it leads you away from it.

KATIA: Wow, now that's clear.

MAGGIE: You have these pages, these arguments, and you are blessed with the thing, and you have to start from, and end up there.

KATIA: At the thing.

MAGGIE: Yes.

KATIA: Be a buddha, Mom.

MAGGIE: I'm not interested in trashing your father.

KATIA: Yeah, right.

MAGGIE: But I'll say—

KATIA: Yeah?

MAGGIE: He has always been more interested in the idea of the thing than the thing.

KATIA: Daddy is interested in helping me. He wants to give me what I need in the world, a context.

MAGGIE: I don't get the ethics of telling your daughter that she's the spoils of war, that her parents ripped her off from a bleeding culture—

KATIA: He didn't say that.

MAGGIE: Well where did you get it?

KATIA: (*Emphatic, conclusive.*) I read it in a book.

    Shift.

MAGGIE: You know, I would like a context too.

KATIA: Forget it.

MAGGIE: I'm serious. I mean, culture, gosh, I mean, being a mutt from Minneapolis, being a lapsed Catholic, well, I'm so not attached to any of that, it means nothing to me.

KATIA: Well good for you. You have that luxury. You know where you came from.

MAGGIE: You came from here. From me.

KATIA: No I didn't, why do you say that?

MAGGIE: I mean, as much as anything.

KATIA: No. Stop it.

MAGGIE: What culture did we rip you from? The culture of the Russian orphanage? Gee, sorry about that. So sorry. Do you remember any of that?

KATIA: No.

MAGGIE: Well, that's good.

KATIA: No it's not. It's part of me.

MAGGIE: No it's not.

KATIA: Yes it is. You just don't want to look.

MAGGIE: At what?

KATIA: Who I am.

MAGGIE: I do. But these distinctions, what's correct and incorrect, they can freeze you, just be a way to stop action—

KATIA: Stop *action*? Are you *joking*? What's your big action—staring at the wall? Thanks, Mom, the whole world thanks you.

MAGGIE: I'm not holding myself up as an example.

KATIA: You shouldn't.

MAGGIE: I'm not. Thank god I have my baking, always a source for solace.

    Maggie checks the pie in the oven, adjusts the temperature.

KATIA: You used to be a *dancer*.

MAGGIE: Really?

KATIA: You used to have a *company*.

MAGGIE: I did?

KATIA: You used to have a *life*.

MAGGIE: I have a life.

KATIA: You used to *dance*.

MAGGIE: I still dance.

KATIA: When I'm over at Dad's?

MAGGIE: Yes. And in my head. Much more efficient. And easier on the bod. I do apologize for having succumbed to the inevitable descent and decay, I know that it's humiliating to you, mortifying, and I realize that you don't bring your friends around anymore, it's mortifying to witness the descent and decay though, just a guess, I think you'll understand, in time.

KATIA: No I won't.

MAGGIE: You know, not everybody figures out how to be a big shining star, most people find jobs and do work and have hobbies and occasionally weep at the wall because it feels sad, that's what people do. I hope you have a bright and shiny life but I doubt if you'll avoid a few little failures—

KATIA: I know that.

MAGGIE: A few disappointments and regrets—

KATIA: Disappointments maybe but not regrets. I hate that you have regrets.

MAGGIE: But I'd say that it would be helpful to get your applications in. Not that educated people are happier than uneducated people, I've read the surveys—

KATIA: Stop.

MAGGIE: (*Loses it, erupts.*) Fine. Fuck it. Crash and burn. Go for it.

I don't give a flying fuck.

    Silence.

Why are you here, anyway? Why have you parked yourself in

my living room? Why don't you go crash and burn at Daddy's? I have things to do.

KATIA: Oh. Sorry.

MAGGIE: You think I want to be here? You think I give a flying fuck about this fucking pie? I don't care. I don't care at all.

KATIA: Okay.

MAGGIE: I don't care if you blow it, okay?

KATIA: Well why the fuck are you baking the fucking pie and going on and on and on about what a fucking revelation it is as if anybody cares, why don't you leave, why don't you go?

MAGGIE: Because this is my living room.

KATIA: And it's not mine.

MAGGIE: Yes it is.

KATIA: No it's not. I don't have a home. I don't have a place. There's no place that is home. I don't belong anywhere.

MAGGIE: You belong here. You belong with me. And with your father. And your friends. And in school. And in college. This is modern life.

KATIA: Oh, god, please, not another lecture.

MAGGIE: Modern Life. A Lecture. An essay! Just write it. Just do it. Don't think about it.

KATIA: I can't.

MAGGIE: You can.

KATIA: It isn't your business.

MAGGIE: It is my business. Then my life's work will be done and I can lie down and die.

KATIA: That is what you think.

MAGGIE: You wish.

KATIA: I know.

They regroup. Maggie goes and looks in the oven.

MAGGIE: Pie is winning. *The phone rings. Maggie answers it.*

Pronto…Sorry, thought I was in Italy. Can't keep my coasts clear…I'm not making light of it…Coming along. I think she appreciates your input…

Maggie looks over at Katia. Katia gestures emphatically that she doesn't want to talk on the phone.

…Well, that's a good point…Yes I do…I think it's a very good point. Valid. Totally valid…I am not making fun of you…I am taking this seriously…She's doing it. She wants to do it. She's just finishing up. I promise. No. No. No, you go out, have fun. No, I don't think it would be helpful for you to come over. But she values your insights…Yes, Bob Dylan, "Patriotism, the last refuge to which a scoundrel clings… Steal a little." Yes, I remember. Oh, for fuck's sake.

Maggie hangs up. Katia's cell phone begins to ring. She doesn't move to get it.

MAGGIE: He's a lunatic.

KATIA: So are you.

MAGGIE: I know that.

KATIA: It isn't him anyway.

MAGGIE: Why don't you get it?

KATIA: Why don't you?

MAGGIE: It's your phone.

KATIA: It's your house.

MAGGIE: It's your house. What's mine is yours.

The phone stops ringing.

Why don't you see who it was?

KATIA: Why?

MAGGIE: Maybe it's Jake. Or one of your jolly friends. Maybe they can help you. Are they done with their essays?

Katia sinks into herself. Maggie begins to clean up the kitchen.

MAGGIE: You know, these berries, this flour, the butter and lard, you could write a book about each thing, the political context of each thing, it's been done…

KATIA: Oh my god.

MAGGIE: I'm just saying—

KATIA: Don't.

MAGGIE: This berry, where did it grow? There's a whole history, how it was cultivated, whether pesticides were used, whether the farmer was a nice man—

KATIA: A "nice man?"

MAGGIE: Yes. Whether he was nice to his farm workers, whether he was kind or at least fair to them. If that's possible in this world, to be fair.

KATIA: Oh my god.

MAGGIE: Whether the berries depleted the soil which made it hard for the people to grow their own food, or whether the berries helped to pay for their food, whether the berry company kept the money or shared it. And the man who drove the truck of berries up to New York, whether that polluted the atmosphere, whether the truck driver could only afford artery-clogging fast food on his way up, to keep down the cost of the berry so we could buy it and eat it…And if we turn our attention to the burger he ate at the fast food stand—

KATIA: But we won't.

MAGGIE: There are so *many things*. A book could be written about *this berry*. And, along with everything else, *this berry* is a miracle. And in December! Who could have imagined such a thing! I feel blessed—though I'm not a religious person, I feel blessed to have it in my kitchen and to put it in my pie.

KATIA: Mother.

MAGGIE: Yes.

KATIA: I'm a person.

MAGGIE: I know that.

KATIA: Not a *berry*.

MAGGIE: I know that.

> *Maggie goes to the oven and checks the pie.*

I can't believe I'm baking a pie. I used to be an interesting person.

KATIA: Interesting people don't bake pies?

MAGGIE: Honey, I don't know what to tell you, what you need to know.

KATIA: Well what do I write? That I'm a victim from a bleeding country?

MAGGIE: No.

KATIA: That I owe my life to the people who took advantage of the tragedy of Russia and ripped me off which was great cuz now I don't have to be a hooker on the streets of Moscow but—oops—now I'm a citizen of the country of bullies?

MAGGIE: No, honey—

KATIA: And all these other countries and people hate us because we invaded them *for no reason* and we're bombing more *countries* and invading them and messing them up and *I'm the spoils of that.*

I don't know where to go, what to do—go back to Russia? Why would I do that? Stay here? Why would I do that?

Beat.

Meanwhile my friends are all totally freaking out about their fucking stupid test scores and their totally inane application essays and jackass interviews and their parents are all flipping out and acting like their kids are trying to kill them, as if their kids are thinking about them at all, this is so totally not about them and they think it is and so they have to deal with debilitating lunatic parents on top of everything else.

Beat.

And I'm thinking, don't they get that we're the bad guys? And don't look at me like this is some teenage thing or some psychological thing or like you have to protect me and go along. And now that your hero's in office everything is going to be great because he's so handsome and so articulate and if only he weren't married so you could date him.

Beat. Maggie sighs.

There are people getting killed, people dying, this fine country that saved me from a terrible life is sending soldiers to poor countries to kill innocent people. And you know what? If I were tending my blueberries, just trying to eke out some way to feed my children, and just get the blueberry on the truck for the man with the clogged arteries to drive it up to you for your pie, and out of the big sky came a bomb that tore up my field and killed my dear children and my dear wife and friends and neighbors and I had nothing and it was because this big rich country wanted to get some guys they thought might be hiding somewhere who were lunatics or who were so angry they'd strapped a bomb to their backs and they were willing to explode their lives because they were so insane and angry and desperate. How would I feel? What would be the thing to do?

Beat.

I mean, what do I say on these things, what the fuck do I say?

MAGGIE: You could write that.

KATIA: Or I could just strap a bomb to my back and detonate.

MAGGIE: Don't even say that.

KATIA: Why not?

MAGGIE: Don't think it.

KATIA: Why not? Really, I mean it, why not?

MAGGIE: It would not be helpful to the world.

KATIA: Oh, and I do want to be helpful.

MAGGIE: Yes, you do. We all do. It's hard to know how.

KATIA: Or I could just fill my pockets with rocks, just walk into the river and drown.

MAGGIE: Katia. Don't, please.

KATIA: Or I could just go and live on the street. I think about that, I do, that's the place, maybe that is the place to be.

MAGGIE: It's hard—

KATIA: No, don't.

MAGGIE: I'm just saying that it's easy to get sunk, to feel hopeless, I do that, I lose hope, it's a challenge, and I agree it's not about being a teenager. How do we live in the world...how do we keep going?

Katia's cell phone rings. She checks phone, answers it.

KATIA: (*Into phone.*) Hi...Cool...I don't know...I don't know if I want to...No...Okay.

Katia closes the phone.

But—if there is anything of value—any thought or feeling—why put it in a college essay? Why put little secret pieces of memory in a pitch to fucking guys who couldn't figure out how to have their own lives, leeches who have to suck off our lives, and what about our strange affliction of having to learn more? What about that?

MAGGIE: Okay.

KATIA: And what business is it of anybody's, my past, and everybody's assumptions about my past, and putting it into a glass jar to look at and have theories about? And get degrees about. Let's get a degree off my dead mother. Let's write a paper about how I'm a refugee from a broken land. That's my angle—that is what Daddy thinks, gotta have an angle, an argument, why not reduce it all, I should be able to score off this as long as I don't mind using my dead mother as collateral, hey, why not, she's not going to care, right? Why not spend these little pieces of memory. Why not sell them to the highest offer?

    Shift.

You know where it is, don't you?

MAGGIE: What?

KATIA: My box of stuff.

MAGGIE: Do you want it?

KATIA: No.

MAGGIE: It was here.

    Maggie glances over at the shelves.

KATIA: You hid it.

MAGGIE: No I didn't. It just might have been buried…

    Maggie goes over to the shelves, searches through them.

KATIA: (*Losing nerve.*) Never mind.

MAGGIE: It should be here.

KATIA: Never mind.

MAGGIE: Let me just see…

    Maggie pulls out a box from behind some books, blows dust off it.

KATIA: Put it back.

MAGGIE: Let me at least wipe it off.

KATIA: Why?

MAGGIE: It's so dusty.

KATIA: I don't want to look at it.

MAGGIE: Then we won't.

KATIA: But I need to.

MAGGIE: Why?

KATIA: So I can know.

MAGGIE: Honey, you saw it many times. Year after year, I took it down from the shelf and you went through it, sat with it…looked at the video. There's a video of you the orphanage sent us, bouncing a ball and singing a song. Do you remember?

KATIA: No.

MAGGIE: You used to watch it over and over. Do you want to see it?

KATIA: No.

MAGGIE: Maybe you'd be glad to look through it. Maybe it would help. You stopped asking for it.

KATIA: You wanted me to forget it.

MAGGIE: I'm sorry. Katia, I'll do anything for you.

KATIA: (*Fierce, passionate.*) Please, don't, don't do anything for me. I already owe you my life. I hate that.

MAGGIE: Sorry.

KATIA: Don't say you're sorry. God.

> *Katia makes a sudden move: she picks up the box, opens it, takes out an audio cassette tape.*

What's this?

MAGGIE: I think I interviewed the director of the orphanage. I'm sure you listened to it.

> *Maggie looks through the box, takes out a video tape. A piece of tape hangs out of the cassette.*

The video is broken. We can get it fixed.

Katia pulls out a dress, similar to what the girl in the videotape was wearing: a girl's party dress, size about six.

You wore it when we picked you up.

She takes out a teddy bear that looks new.

It was brand new, they must have given it to you just before you left, when we got home, you didn't want it, so we put it in the box.

She takes out something small. It's a cork from a bottle.

MAGGIE: Do you remember that? A cork, you can still see, very faintly, a face, drawn on it with a pen...You would take it out and turn it over and over in your hand.

Abruptly Katia takes the audiotape, gets up, crosses to the stereo, puts it in and pushes "play." As they listen to the tape, Katia holds the cork, turns it over in her hand. A woman's voice speaking in Russian. Another woman's voice translates. There's the sound of other voices and activities in the background.

VOICE 1: Okay, she says—(*In Russian.*) The mother, not here?

VOICE 2: (*In Russian.*) The mother, not here, the grandmother, she is sick. It's too much for her...

VOICE 1: (*In English.*) The mother, not here, the grandmother, she is sick...

VOICE 2: (*Overlapping, in Russian.*)...the father is not here. He is gone. He could not do it. It is too much for him.

VOICE 1: (*In English.*) ...the father is not here... He is gone...It is better. No food, no money, it is better...

VOICE 2: (*Overlapping, in Russian.*) It is on? Can you get the reception?

VOICE 1: (*In English.*) The television is not getting the reception. (*In Russian.*) Did you turn it on? You cannot get it...(*In English.*) There is a hypnotist, very popular in Russia today, everybody watches him, he comes on T.V. and he hypnotizes us, you only think of what you want and need and this he does for everybody, one woman got an apartment, she was waiting for many years and after she was hypnotized she got the apartment.

VOICE 2: (*In Russian.*) Not on now. I don't know why…

Silence. Katia ejects the tape and throws it back into the box.

KATIA: It just is so stupid. It doesn't mean anything. It's so nothing.

Katia pulls out a bunch of papers from the box.

What is this?

MAGGIE: Let me see.

Maggie takes the papers, looks through them.

The court papers…The Civil Cases Board of Omsk Regional Court presided over by Ivolgina N.V., Lednyeva Ye.S., Yelkina T.M…

KATIA: (*Wanting to stop.*) Okay, okay.

Maggie looks through the papers. Katia seems to sink into herself.

MAGGIE: Adoption papers, some notes I made about the country… people spending their last kopecks to buy a loaf of bread, eating stray dogs…no phone service in one town, thieves stole the cables. No police…cattle gone, cow barns gutted, fields of weeds…"

The oven bell begins to ding. Maggie gets up, goes to the oven, turns off the bell, checks the pie.

MAGGIE: Oh, my goodness, how thrilling.

Maggie adjusts the timer.

Honey?

Katia looks over at her.

Time out.

KATIA: What?

Beat.

MAGGIE: Come here.

KATIA: (*She can't.*) Mom.

MAGGIE: What? It's just fun. It's so neat that the stove people put a light in the oven so you can look at it. Want to put on some music?

> *Katia sighs, picks up the remote, points it at the stereo, Eminem blares. Maggie stiffens, starts wiping the counter. Katia sits. At a particular offensive passage, Maggie breaks.*

(*Loud.*) That's enough.

> *Katia flicks it off.*

Why do you listen to this?

> *Katia erupts. This comes from a deep place.*

KATIA: You're such a fake.

MAGGIE: A fake what?

KATIA: Fine, it's your house, your life, you say it's all for me but that is a total lie.

MAGGIE: Excuse me?

KATIA: Everything has to be on your terms, reality on your terms, what's acceptable, you're so delicate, I have to tip-toe around. You just go to work in your stupid boring office and come back home to your non-life, you're just hiding out.

MAGGIE: *I'm* hiding out?

KATIA: I come home and you're sitting there on the couch or you're kind of slumped over drooling on the pillow and your face is like this old dog who looks really strange cuz he's like had a mild stroke while I was out, but he perks up anyway cuz his beloved master has come home, that's all he cares about, he's completely dependent on her for his life and his love for his master is going to eat me it's going to devour me.

MAGGIE: Huh.

KATIA: It makes me need to bark at you, get back, makes me foam at the mouth so you don't swallow me whole.

MAGGIE: I wouldn't do that.

KATIA: Daddy's happy.

MAGGIE: Well, bully for Daddy.

KATIA: He's out in the world. He's doing things. He laughs. You, you think you're clinging to some kind of moral position but really you're clinging to the couch. Your moral stand isn't being noted. Nobody's in the room with you.

MAGGIE: You are.

KATIA: Not for long.

MAGGIE: We'll see about that, won't we?

KATIA: What the hell does that mean?

Maggie erupts.

MAGGIE: *Who* has decided to put on the brakes, come to a screeching halt, oh, I was an A student, I have won awards on the debate team and I'm a wonderful musician until I crashed and burned that, I did have a ton of friends who now have stopped calling because I never call them back, last semester I barely passed a couple of courses, was supposed to finish these fucking essays in August, then September, then October—

KATIA: I know my calendar, Mom, you don't have to recite it.

MAGGIE: Who is hiding out?

Pause. The eruption has passed; momentary regrouping.

MAGGIE: You want a cup of tea or something?

KATIA: No.

MAGGIE: Let's put on something we both like. Is that such an extreme and terrible idea?

Maggie goes to the CDs, selects one, puts it on.

You used to love this one. We would play it over and over, and dance all over the apartment.

> *She puts on "Keep on the Sunnyside" by the Nitty Gritty Dirt Band. It plays, Maggie goes back to the kitchen, then as she cleans up she begins a little dance, a series of movements, playful, to get Katia to laugh. At first Katia, though guarded, seems to relax and enjoy Maggie in spite of herself. Then her face darkens. She steams. In a sudden violent move, she takes her box with the stuff in it and throws it down. Maggie stops in her tracks, stands there. Katia yells at her over the music.*

> *Maggie picks up the remote and flicks off the music as Katia continues without stopping.*

KATIA: (*Fierce.*) Oh yeah let's embrace life to its fullest. Let's do that. Let's just do that. (*Breaking down.*) But if I even try to *think* of my first mother, I mean, if you even see a flicker—Christ, you won't even let me call her mother, what a control trip, yes, ma'am, birth mother, ma'am, like she was my hired wet nurse, the carrier, a lab assistant, a Petri dish, so arrogant. And when you look at me like that, like you're going to shatter into a thousand little pieces of glass, my brain freezes, and I could care less about fucking *ancestry*, or *culture*, but some- thing—some connection to something.

MAGGIE: I'm sorry.

> *Maggie goes to Katia, touches her shoulder. Katia may first resist but finally gives in to the embrace. They sit together on the couch. Maggie holds Katia, comforts her.*

I don't know what to say.

KATIA: (*A child.*) Tell me something.

MAGGIE: I don't know...

KATIA: Just something.

> *Pause.*

MAGGIE: At night I'd tuck you in, and you would say, "Talk story."

Do you remember?

Beat.

Your first day here I gave you oatmeal. You wouldn't eat it. Then I boiled you an egg and you ate it and I boiled you another and another. You ate twelve eggs that day and then got sick and I put you to bed and wondered, how is it I thought I could be a mother?

Beat.

Do you remember Rice Krispies? How much you liked them and I said yes, snap crackle and pop, I loved that too when I was a kid. Then you decided they were too loud, they hurt your ears. So I bought ear plugs and taped them to the box of Rice Krispies. And each day at breakfast you would very solemnly pour out the Rice Krispies, put in the ear plugs, pour the milk and eat them up.

Beat.

And when you were in *Alice In Wonderland*, you were such a nice eaglet.

KATIA: And the two of clubs.

MAGGIE: Yes. And at some point Alice says "Let me try to remember the things I used to know." I wrote it down on a scrap of paper in the dark of the theatre, still have the paper, the handwriting all skewed...It seemed like the most beautiful sentence I'd ever heard. "Let me try to remember the things I used to know."...The sound of it, cadence, and the...whimsy or something, how familiar I guess, the wish, and the impossibility of actually remembering what you used to know, and... and you, those early years, not knowing, not knowing what happened to you, to your mother, thinking about your mother so much, what happened to her, and did I do everything I could to know, to be sure...

Pause.

When we brought you here, they said the transition needed to be slow. I made your room very spare. One day I walked into your empty room and...began to cry...and then I thought, don't do this, don't get attached to the idea of her, of what should be. And I looked up and you were standing there. You looked so guarded, so lost, and I thought, okay. Let me try to serve this child. And then all of that turned out to be meaningless, or anyway, it fades in the light of…

KATIA: Of what?

MAGGIE: Of the love.

KATIA: Oh now you're getting corny.

MAGGIE: Just a fact. I fell in love with you.

KATIA: Too bad it didn't last.

MAGGIE: Yeah. Oh well.

KATIA: I think you're going to fall apart when I go.

MAGGIE: You do?

KATIA: Yes.

MAGGIE: Is that why you're not finishing your essays?

KATIA: No.

MAGGIE: I'm not going to fall apart. Anymore than I already am.

KATIA: I worry about you.

MAGGIE: Don't.

KATIA: Do you miss dancing?

MAGGIE: (*Light.*) I dance.

KATIA: Really.

MAGGIE: No.

KATIA: Why?

MAGGIE: Too hard. I like to go in, know where I'm going, the tasks, the pay checks, the interactions in the office, even the tensions and conflicts, I feel part of the world, part of this big machine.

KATIA: Mom.

MAGGIE: It's more an awareness of this hole, this absence…I miss creating a dance, creating something out of nothing, something that would never have existed if I hadn't made it…But the daily thing is, well, it's more a weight. A feeling of defeat.

KATIA: Well, you have to stop that. You're not over the hill you know.

MAGGIE: I know.

KATIA: No, I mean it. You should set a better example.

MAGGIE: Oh, well.

KATIA: I should be way more messed up than I am.

MAGGIE: You really should.

KATIA: You should go out more. You just stay at home in the dark.

MAGGIE: Not in the dark. I turn on a lamp.

KATIA: But really.

MAGGIE: I have plans. I'm going to write a baking column for *Popular Mechanics*.

KATIA: You should have a boyfriend.

MAGGIE: I will, next year. As soon as I announce I'm available they'll be lining up outside my door. They'll have to take a ticket.

> *Maggie looks over at the clock.*

Honey? I don't mean to be goal oriented…How about not trying to solve all the problems today.

KATIA: Mom.

MAGGIE: You can attend to them tomorrow, I promise, if you want to go to Russia, or really anything, and I'll try to be a better example, just do this because it's the thing in front of you.

KATIA: I've written it. I've written it a thousand times. I don't believe in the form. I don't believe in a coherent, cohesive statement, I don't believe in making an argument.

MAGGIE: Yes you do. Step up to the plate.

KATIA: Oh, please don't start with the baseball references.

MAGGIE: Would you just read me what you've written? I know it's there, you can find it.

KATIA: It's not finished.

MAGGIE: Then finish it. It doesn't help the blueberry farmer to be lying on the couch. So write the thing and do the thing and carry on. Because you get to. You have a choice. That's a very big deal. Take it.

> *Katia goes to her laptop, flicks it on. Maggie sits beside her as Katia reads aloud.*

KATIA: (*Reading.*) A memory house is a construct originating in the Middle Ages. The idea is if you visualize a house and you imagine putting facts and ideas in specific nooks and crannies in the house, you can always go there to get them. The visualization helps you remember. I find it hard to visualize a house. I find it hard to decide to remember.

> *Katia presses a button on the keyboard and continues to read.*

I discover a house. It has a rotting porch. But what can be done about it? It's my house.

A man who is my father and a woman who is my mother want to furnish the house. I do not give them a key. They stand, weeping, on the rotting porch.

I am a young girl standing beside a cart. A boy runs up and down the hill. I have a thought. I look at the hay in the cart and I think, I'll always remember this thought, I'll always remember thinking it, and when I learn to write I'll write it down. But when I learn to write I don't remember the thought, only the moment that I thought it.

> *Katia loses nerve and sits back. Maggie leans forward and continues reading.*

MAGGIE: I am in a hotel room. There are strange people there, a man who is to be called my father and a woman who is to be called my mother. They open a suitcase of clothes. I am to wear these clothes. I am to be taken away.

There is a large room, rows of beds, children lying in the beds, a dirty window, a grey sky. A girl is taken off a bed, put in a room, it's cold, no light, she kicks against door, she calls out, no one comes, she sleeps, she wakes, she sleeps.

Maggie looks over at Katia in silence, then returns to the keyboard.

A woman in a doorway, it's dark, I can't see her face, my face up against her legs, rough wool, smells of smoke and barn, dirt floor, kitchen, I lean against her legs, she picks me up, a chicken pecks at the floor, the woman sings a song.

I don't know where in the house to put things. I don't know why I'm here. I think my house is sinking.

Maggie looks over at Katia.

It's good.

KATIA: Mom.

MAGGIE: Trust it. It's good. Print it out.

Maggie goes over to where the box and its contents have been thrown. She gathers up the stuff and carefully put it back into the box. Katia sits on the couch thinking. She glances over at Maggie who folds the dress and places it in the box. Maggie notices the cork, takes it and brings it to Katia who acknowledges it and puts it into her pocket.

Katia picks up the laptop, goes and plugs it into the printer, types a command and waits as the printer begins to print out. Katia pulls on her coat as the stove starts beeping.

KATIA: I won.

MAGGIE: No way.

Maggie turns off the stove alarm and takes the pie out of the oven. Katia gets the pages from the printer, puts them in an envelope as her cell phone begins to ring. She answers it.

KATIA: (*Into phone.*) Hey…Sorry, I had to finish this stupid essay and fight with my mom. Yeah…(*To Maggie.*) Jake says hi.

MAGGIE: Hi, Jake.

KATIA: (*Into phone.*) You going over there now? Really? Yeah. I'm leaving now. Okay…You talked to her?…You're kidding. Okay. Now.

>   *Katia closes the cell phone, gathers up the envelopes, goes over to the pie.*

KATIA: It looks real.

MAGGIE: It's a miracle. (*Beat.*) Hon?

KATIA: Yeah?

MAGGIE: You don't mind if I apply to college too, do you?

KATIA: (*Light; it's fine.*) No.

MAGGIE: I need to better myself.

KATIA: What about your essay?

MAGGIE: I'm sending them the pie. Sometimes a nonverbal statement is the most eloquent.

>   *Katia starts out.*

MAGGIE: You coming back after?

KATIA: Some of us are meeting up there.

MAGGIE: Oh. Nice. Big party at the post office?

KATIA: Yeah.

MAGGIE: Okay. Call me to let me know where you are.

KATIA: See you.

MAGGIE: Bye.

KATIA: Thanks.

MAGGIE: See you.

Katia leaves. Maggie stands there, watching the door.
Lights fade.

END OF PLAY

NOTES ON GHOSTWRITTEN
by Naomi Iizuka

O n one level, *Ghostwritten* is a story about the aftermath of the Vietnam War. It's about a father who never returns from Vietnam and the impact that loss has on the lives of his children. It's a play about the Vietnamese people left behind and how their lives are inextricably intertwined with the Americans they encounter during the war. At its core, *Ghostwritten* is also a retelling of the *Rumpelstiltskin* story. There was something about the idea of a stranger from one's past showing up one day to collect on a debt that resonated with the story I wanted to tell.

Rumpelstiltskin is a strange and puzzling fairytale. It contains within its deceptively simple story several intriguing mysteries. Why does Rumpelstiltskin demand a baby as the price for spinning straw into gold? Why does the Miller's Daughter agree to his terms? Why does her salvation revolve around guessing his name? And what does it mean at the end of the story when Rumpelstiltskin splits himself in two? Like most fairytales, *Rumpelstiltskin* is a riddle built around powerful human desires and anxieties. Like many fairytales, it is a story about an absent parent and a lost child. It is also a story about a stranger who grants a wish and then exacts a terrible price. Most of all, it is a story about unforeseen consequences. We think we've put miles between ourselves and something in our past, and suddenly it appears in the rearview mirror bearing down on us. What do we do? How do we break free? Do we ever break free? Those are some the question that set the play in motion.

Ghostwritten originated as a commission from the Goodman Theatre and moved forward thanks to the generous support of the Joyce Foundation. I wrote the play with the guidance and wisdom of many people. They include Arthur Acuna, Neena Arndt, Jocelyn Clarke, Shannon Cochran, Dieterich Gray, Philip Himberg, Andre Holland, Mia Katigbak, Kim Martin-Cotten, Bruce McKenzie, Tanya Palmer,

Ryan Pavelchik, Lisa Portes, Lisa Tejero, Tiffany Villarin, Dan Waller, Thomas Weitz, everyone at Sundance Theatre Lab, the Hedgebrook Women Playwrights Festival, and all the people kind enough to take time out of their days and evenings to share their stories with me.

— Naomi Iizuka

BIOGRAPHY

Naomi Iizuka's other plays include *36 Views, Anon(ymous)*, *At the Vanishing Point, Concerning Strange Devices From The Distant West, Polaroid Stories, Language of Angels, Tattoo Girl, Aloha, Say the Pretty Girls, 17 Reasons Why*, and *Skin*. Her plays have been produced by the Goodman Theatre, the Guthrie Theater, Actors Theatre of Louisville, the Children's Theatre Company, Kennedy Center for Performing Arts, Huntington Theatre Company, Berkeley Repertory Theatre, GeVa Theatre, Portland Center Stage, the Public Theater, Campo Santo + Intersection for the Arts, Dallas Theater Center, Brooklyn Academy of Music's "Next Wave Festival," SoHo Rep, and the Edinburgh Festival, and workshopped at Sundance Theatre Lab, Hedgebrook Women Playwrights Festival, Midwest PlayLabs, the Public Theater's New Works Now, PS 122, Manhattan Theatre Club, and JAW/West at Portland Center Stage. Her plays have been published by TCG, Smith and Kraus, Heinemann, Playscripts, Theatre Forum, and American Theatre. Naomi is a member of New Dramatists and the recipient of a Howard Foundation Fellowship, a PEN/Laura Pels Award, an Alpert Award, a Joyce Foundation Award, a Whiting Writers' Award, a Stavis Award from the National Theatre Conference, a Rockefeller Foundation MAP grant, an NEA/TCG Artist in Residence grant, a McKnight Fellowship, a PEN Center USA West Award for Drama, Princeton University's Hodder Fellowship, and a Jerome Fellowship. She heads the graduate MFA Playwriting program at the University of California, San Diego.

ACKNOWLEDGMENTS

Ghostwritten premiered at the Goodman Theatre (Robert Falls, Artistic Director; Roche Schulfer, Executive Director) in Chicago on April 4, 2009. The director was Lisa Portes. The set design was by Linda Buchanan, costume design by Rachel Healy, lighting design by Keith Parham, and sound design by Andre J. Pluess.

GHOSTWRITTEN
by Naomi Iizuka

CHARACTERS (in order of speaking)

THE WOMAN FROM VIETNAM, a stranger with magical powers.

LINH, the Woman's partner.

SUSAN, a chef specializing in Asian fusion cuisine somewhere in the American Midwest.

BEA, Susan's daughter adopted from Vietnam.

CHAD, Bea's boyfriend, a doctor working in a large hospital in the American Midwest, and also **Not Chad**, a woodsman.

MARTIN, Susan's younger brother, the black sheep of the family.

TIME

Twenty years ago and today.

PLACE

A little village in Vietnam, a big city somewhere in the American Midwest, and the woods outside the city.

"I have nothing left that I could give," answered the miller's daughter. "Then promise me," said the little man, "if you should become queen, that you will give me your firstborn child." And so she promised him what he wanted, and for that he spun the straw into gold.

— *Rumpelstiltskin* by the Brothers Grimm

SCENE 1

> *A little village in Vietnam. Twenty years ago. An early morning mist.*
> *A Vietnamese man named Linh sits by the side of the road. He begins*
> *to sing a song. The lyrics are in a foreign language. The melody is*
> *beautiful and strange. The Woman from Vietnam appears. She begins*
> *speaking. She conjures a book from the ether. It is a beautiful, ancient*
> *book. She continues to speak. She is telling a story in Vietnamese.*
> *Linh translates.*

WOMAN: *Ngay xua ngay xua co mot nguoi dan ba.*
Mot nguoi phu nu My.
Va nang rat co don.
Va cach nha rat xa.
Nang da di du lich nua vong trai dat
den mot nga lang mho be o Viet Nam
mot noi goi la Dien Bien Phu.
Nang da di tim kiem mot cai gi do.
Cai dieu ma nang da bi mat.
Hoac la dieu gi ma nang chua bao gio co.

LINH: "Once upon a time there was a woman.

> *An American woman named Susan appears.*

An American woman.
And she was alone.
And she was very far from home.
She had traveled halfway across the world
To a tiny village in Vietnam
A place called Dien Bien Phu.
She was looking for something.
Something she had lost.
Or something she had never had."

WOMAN: *Trong mi deo lung cua nang la tap* Lonely Planet Guide:
Southeast Asia on a Shoestring.

Nang deo mot chiec dong ho dep va dat noi co tay.

LINH: "In her knapsack was a *Lonely Planet Guide: Southeast Asia on a Shoestring.*

On her wrist she wore a watch."

> *The Woman slams the book shut. It vanishes.*

WOMAN: (*To Susan.*) Where did you get that watch?

SUSAN: *Xin loi?*

LINH: "Excuse me?"

WOMAN: I said, where did you get that watch?

SUSAN: *Toi khong hieu.*

LINH: "I don't understand."

WOMAN: (*Grabbing Susan's watch.*) Your watch! Your watch! Where did you get your watch?

SUSAN: You're speaking English.

WOMAN: Yes. Yes, I am.

SUSAN: I'm sorry. I was thinking about other things, I guess. I've been traveling by myself. I haven't talked to another person in I don't even know how long. You have no idea how good it is to hear a little English.

WOMAN: Where did you get your watch?

SUSAN: Oh right. My watch. My dad, he gave it to me.

WOMAN: Your father?

SUSAN: It's kind of a long story.

WOMAN: Where do you come from?

SUSAN: Illinois. Do you know where Illinois is?

WOMAN: No, not really no.

SUSAN: If this is America, this is Illinois. Right in the middle.

WOMAN: What's it like in Illinois?

SUSAN: Flat, it's very flat. And all across the state, there's fields and fields of corn. And in the winter, the fields are covered in snow. It's like the whole wide world is covered in white, a blanket of white. And it's so quiet. And some days, the sun makes everything sparkle like the world is made of diamonds. And you look up at the sky, and it's so vast and so blue. You think: how can the sky be so, so blue.

WOMAN: You miss your home very much, I think.

SUSAN: I do. I don't know why. I shouldn't. There's nothing much to go home to, but yes I do. You know, your English is very good. Both of you.

WOMAN: (*Speaking on behalf of herself and Linh.*) Thank you.

SUSAN: How did you learn to speak so fluently?

LINH: Magic.

> *The Woman smacks Linh.*

LINH: Ow.

SUSAN: Magic, huh?

WOMAN: Don't listen to him. He's so silly. And such a big mouth. What a big mouth he has. Maybe he needs to keep it shut for a while.

> *Linh tries to pry open his mouth, but he can't.*
> *Susan doesn't notice.*

WOMAN: You probably don't believe in magic, do you?

SUSAN: You know, no, I guess I don't.

WOMAN: Why is that?

SUSAN: I don't know. To me, magic is fairytales. Magic is happily ever after. And I guess, well I guess I don't think the world is like that. I don't think it works that way.

WOMAN: How does it work?

SUSAN: I believe what you see around you, that's it, that's all there is. Terrible things happen, things that break your heart, and you just have to make the best of it. You know what? Don't listen to me. I don't know what I'm talking about. I don't know anything about anything. I don't know anything at all.

WOMAN: Do you live in a field of corn?

SUSAN: No, I live in a big city. No fields. No corn. Just big giant skyscrapers one after the next. You look up and all you see are big stone towers reaching far up into the sky.

WOMAN: Do you live in a tower?

SUSAN: I do.

WOMAN: Is it very wonderful?

SUSAN: It's small. Very, very small. And I live so high up that even if I opened up my window and shouted at the top of my lungs, there wouldn't be a single soul who'd hear me.

WOMAN: You live with your husband?

SUSAN: No. No, I don't have a husband.

WOMAN: You live with your mother?

SUSAN: No. No, I, I live alone.

WOMAN: In Vietnam, nobody lives alone. Everybody lives together, mother, father, brother, sister, everybody all together.

SUSAN: That sounds so nice. You have no idea how nice that sounds. Sometimes I wish, I just wish…never mind. I don't know what's wrong with me.

WOMAN: I think you're sad. I see it in your eyes. Don't be sad, lady from America. Do you know what time it is?

> *Susan looks at her watch.*

SUSAN: It's almost noon.

WOMAN: Are you hungry?

SUSAN: I am. I'm starving.

WOMAN: Good. Time to eat. I cook for you. (*To Linh.*) Go go go. Hurry up!

> *Linh quickly retrieves cooking utensils: a pan, chopsticks, a piece of flint, some wood, a bag of ingredients.*

SUSAN: What are you making?

WOMAN: You'll see. First, you start with fire.

> *The Woman strikes the flint. Flames.*

WOMAN: Then you take a pan and add two drops of oil.

> *The Woman pours oil from a small bottle into the pan. The sound of sizzling. She adds other ingredients. The Woman cooks.*

WOMAN: Juice from one lime.
Vinegar fish sauce sugar and garlic.
Two stalks of lemongrass.
One fist of coriander.
Ginger and chili pepper.
Mince. Chop. Slice.
Listen.
Can you hear that? The pan is speaking to you.

SUSAN: What does it say?

WOMAN: All kinds of things. Secret things.

SUSAN: What kinds of secret things?

WOMAN: Give me your watch and I'll tell you.

> *Susan hesitates a moment, and then takes off her watch and gives it to the Woman. The Woman gives it to Linh. He puts it on his wrist.*

WOMAN: We call this nuoc cham. Every dish we make begins with this. Here. Taste.

> *The Woman dips a finger into the pan and extends it to Susan. She tastes. Something inside her begins to crack open.*

SUSAN: Oh my God. What is that? It's…it's…Salty. And Bitter. And Hot. And Sweet. It's so sweet. It's like everything all at once. It's like nothing I've ever tasted before. It's so good. It's so good. It's amazing. It's like the most amazing thing in the world. Am I crying? I am, aren't I? I don't know why I'm crying. I don't know where this is coming from.

WOMAN: Give me a tear. One teardrop. That's all I need.

> Linh catches one of Susan's tear drops and lets it drop into the pan. The teardrop sizzles. The Woman dips a finger into the pan once more and extends it to Susan. She tastes. Something inside her breaks. The words come out like a geyser.

SUSAN: I'm 21 years old, I've never been in love, I don't know what that is, My family are like strangers, I don't know who they are, I don't know who I am, I don't have a skill or a talent or a passion, I don't have a burning desire, I don't have a dollar to my name, I don't know why I'm here, I don't know what I was thinking, this was a mistake—

WOMAN: Why did you come to this place?

SUSAN: It doesn't matter.

WOMAN: But you came here for a reason. You were looking for something or someone—

SUSAN: It doesn't matter, it doesn't matter anymore. How did you do what you did just now? That's what I want to know. I want you to show me. I want that more than anything.

WOMAN: What else do you have?

SUSAN: I just gave you my watch.

WOMAN: It's not enough

SUSAN: (Rifling through her knapsack.) I'll give you my money. It's not a lot, but it's yours. I have a camera. It's not a great camera, but I'll give that to you, too. Look, why don't I just give you my whole knapsack, everything in it. It's all yours. (Offering the Woman her knapsack.) Here.

WOMAN: I don't want your things. Your things mean nothing to me.

SUSAN: But that's all I have. I don't have anything else.

WOMAN: You could give me one of your fingers. Perhaps your right thumb.

SUSAN: I'm not going to do that.

WOMAN: You could give me your ear. I have a knife.

> *Linh pulls out a very large, very sharp knife. The Woman snatches it from him.*

I could slice it off right now.

SUSAN: I'm not going to give you my ear.

WOMAN: Maybe you don't really want what I have to give.

SUSAN: No, I do. I really do.

WOMAN: I don't think so. (*To Linh.*) Go go go. Hurry up!

> *Linh starts packing up cooking utensils and ingredients.*

SUSAN: Wait. Please. What else is there? There has to be something else. Please.

WOMAN: Well...maybe. Maybe there is. You know what, never mind.

SUSAN: Name it. Please. Anything.

WOMAN: No no no.

SUSAN: Please.

> *Linh tries to signal Susan not to continue down this path. He tries to do this without the Woman seeing him. The Woman sees him. She shoots him an evil look. He stops signaling.*

Please just tell me.

WOMAN: You could promise me your first-born child.

SUSAN: What?

WOMAN: You heard me.

SUSAN: You're kidding, right?

WOMAN: No. I'm not.

SUSAN: Why do you want my first-born child?

WOMAN: I have my reasons.

SUSAN: OK. Sure. Done.

WOMAN: That was quick.

SUSAN: I'm never going to have a child. It's never going to happen.

WOMAN: How do you know?

SUSAN: It's not in the cards. I wasn't born to be a mother.

WOMAN: How can you be so sure?

SUSAN: I just am. I have never been more sure of anything in my life.

WOMAN: Then we have a deal?

SUSAN: Yes. We have a deal.

WOMAN: Promise.

SUSAN: I promise.

The Woman grabs Susan and slashes Susan's palm with the knife, and squeezes Susan's blood into the pan. Something explodes in the pan. The sound of sizzling and hissing.

WOMAN: Now I will show you how to make food like you have never tasted before. I will show you how to make food that will bewitch and enchant anyone who tastes it. One taste and the world will suddenly glow with promise. Like their eyes can now see and their heart has cracked open. All it takes is one taste. Here. Taste.

The Woman dips a finger into the pan and extends it to Susan. She tastes. The world spins. It keeps spinning. An airplane takes off.

SCENE 2

The night sky. Light on Bea, a young Asian-American woman.

BEA: I have a memory. It's my earliest memory. I'm in an airport. I'm like maybe two or three and I'm with my mom. I remember she smells of breath mints and shampoo. And I remember thinking, this is what America smells like, minty and soapy and clean. And it's nice, it's so nice. We're sitting at the gate waiting to board the plane to go to the States, and I remember out of the corner of my eye, I see this man.

Light on Linh holding Susan's knapsack. He sees Bea. He tries to talk to her. He tries to open his mouth, but he can't.

And it's like he's trying to say something to me, but he can't. It's like his lips are sealed shut or something. And he's holding this bag and I'm looking at the bag and I slowly realize it's moving. It's quivering ever so slightly, so slightly you can barely tell, but it's moving, it's moving, like there's something inside of it that's alive. And I get up and I start walking towards him and all I want to do, all I want to do is look inside.

Linh exits. Light on Chad. A high rise apartment in a big city in the Midwest. Night. The present day. Chad is getting ready to go to work. Chad is a doctor in a hospital in the city. Bea is the girlfriend he lives with.

CHAD: So what happened?

BEA: My mom scooped me up, we boarded the plane, and I never saw the guy again.

CHAD: Ooooh spooky.

BEA: It was spooky.

CHAD: I believe you.

BEA: No, you don't.

CHAD: Bea, what do you want me to say?

BEA: You don't think that's weird and creepy to run into this guy with his lips sealed shut and this strange creature in his bag.

CHAD: Look, it was probably just some small animal like a rabbit or a ferret.

BEA: Why would this Oriental man be transporting a rabbit or a ferret?

CHAD: I don't know. Maybe it was a pet. Or maybe it was dinner. I don't know what he was up to. And you shouldn't say Oriental.

BEA: Fine. Asian. Whatever. I can't believe you're lecturing me about the word Oriental.

CHAD: It's a problematic word and I'm not lecturing you.

BEA: Fine.

CHAD: Bea.

BEA: You're not even Asian. You're like from *Wisconsin*.

CHAD: There are Asian people in Wisconsin.

BEA: Yes, but you're not one of them.

CHAD: Bea, I don't see where you're going with this.

BEA: I'm just saying, I can say Oriental if I want to say Oriental because I am Oriental, or whatever I am. I don't know what I am.

CHAD: You're a nice Midwestern girl.

BEA: I am *not* a "nice Midwestern girl." I am a strange and exotic flower.

CHAD: Come on, Bea, you've lived here practically your whole entire life.

BEA: So?

CHAD: So...do you even remember anything else?

BEA: What? You mean like from before I came to the States? No. Not really. I mean, some things. Kind of. I don't know, not really.

CHAD: You should ask your mom sometime.

BEA: I do! I have! All she'll say is that she was hitchhiking around Vietnam, and that she was kinda lost, and then she wandered into this orphanage and that's where she found me.

> *Bea feels something in her pocket. She pulls out a ziplock bag with some kind of indeterminate food inside. It's smashed and battered. She works it absentmindedly like a stress ball.*

CHAD: You should go back sometime.

BEA: To Vietnam? Yeah. Maybe. Someday. (*Beat.*) Chad, do you love me?

CHAD: Yeah. Sure.

BEA: No, I mean *really*.

CHAD: What? I love you, Bea. What's the problem?

BEA: Will you love me if I get like really fat?

CHAD: No.

BEA: Chad.

CHAD: Of course I will.

BEA: Will you love me when I'm old and I lose all my teeth? Or what if I'm like in a bad mood for a really long time?

CHAD: Like how long?

BEA: Like ten years.

CHAD: That's a long time, but yeah, yeah, I would.

BEA: What if I get sick? Will you love me if I get sick or something? Or what if my brain turns to mush and I don't even know who you are anymore?

CHAD: Yes, Bea. I will love you forever. What is that?

BEA: What? Oh. My mom made it. I've been carrying it around with me for like a week. It got kinda mushed.

CHAD: I don't care. Give that to me.

> *Chad grabs the ziplock bag and eats. He devours the food with gusto.*

Man oh man, this is fantastic. Your mom is like the best cook in the whole entire world.

BEA: I guess.

CHAD: You guess? Are you kidding me? This stuff is amazing. It's unbelievable. What is it?

BEA: Deep-fried mung bean dumplings. I think.

CHAD: Mung bean? What's a mung bean? Never mind. Don't tell me. I don't even want to know. All I need to know is that it's good. Oh my goodness, it's good. You sure you don't want any?

BEA: No, I'm not hungry.

CHAD: You are so lucky to have a mom who's like a chef. She's like a chef, she's like a famous chef, and you never eat what she makes. That's just crazy.

BEA: I do. Sometimes. I used to. She'd make this soup when I was a kid, this stuff called *pho*. If I was like sad, like if somebody made fun of me at school or something, she'd make it for me, and it always made me feel better. Like once I ran away from home when I was thirteen, my mom and I had this huge fight, and I was so mad at her, I was furious and I was like at the bus stop waiting to take off when suddenly I could smell it, I could smell it like simmering on the stove top—which makes no sense cause like the bus stop was all the way on the other side of town, but I could and somehow, whatever it was that made me so mad, it just like went away, and all I wanted to do was go back home and be with my mom. And so that's what I did. Whatever. It's stupid.

CHAD: No, it's not.

BEA: Yes, it is. It's totally stupid. Everything, it's all so stupid. I can't believe how stupid it is.

CHAD: Bea? What's going on?

BEA: Nothing.

CHAD: You're acting really weird.

BEA: I am not.

CHAD: Yeah, you are.

BEA: I'm not.

CHAD: You are.

BEA: I'm not.

CHAD: We're bickering like old married people.

BEA: We're not married.

CHAD: We could be. Married, I mean.

BEA: What? What did you just say?

CHAD: We could be married. We could be married tomorrow.

BEA: Tomorrow?

CHAD: Why not?

    Chad drops down on one knee.

CHAD: Bea, will you marry me?

BEA: Oh my God. Stop. Are you serious?

CHAD: I am *so* serious.

BEA: Oh my God, Chad.

CHAD: Bea, I love you. Let's get married.

BEA: Really?

CHAD: I'm on my knees, Bea.

BEA: I know. I see.

CHAD: Well?

BEA: Yes! Yes.

CHAD: OK so here's what we're going to do: we're gonna hop in the car as soon as I get back from work, and then we drive to Las Vegas, we tie the knot, and we live happily ever after. Sound like a plan?

BEA: Yes! Oh Chad, I love you. I love you so much.

CHAD: I love you too. Aaagh, I gotta go. I'm going to be late.

BEA: I know.

CHAD: Give me a kiss.

> *Chad and Bea kiss. It's a really nice kiss.*

BEA: Chad, I don't want you to go.

CHAD: I'll be back in no time.

BEA: I know, I know. It's just that I have something to tell you—

CHAD: You can tell me when I get back. I'll see you tomorrow as soon as I finish my shift. You know what?

BEA: What?

CHAD: We're getting married.

BEA: I know! I'm so happy!

CHAD: Me, too. All right, I love you I love you I love you good-bye.

BEA: I love you I love you I love you, too. Good-bye.

> *Chad goes. Bea touches her belly. The phone rings. It rings and rings. Bea answers it. Light on the Woman from Vietnam in the darkness.*

BEA: Hello? Is there anyone there? Hello?

> *Light on Linh holding the knapsack. He opens his mouth. His lips have been sealed for the last twenty years and now the spell is broken. He gulps in the air. The air tastes sweet. He sticks out his tongue. A single snowflake falls. It melts on his tongue. It begins to snow. A blizzard of white.*

SCENE 3

> *A Greyhound bus. Martin is sitting, unwrapping a burger and fries. Linh sits next to him. He holds Susan's knapsack. Linh steals looks at him.*

MARTIN: Nothing better than a quarter pounder with cheese. No special sauce, no bacon, no avocado, none of that. Just the meat, the bread, and the cheese. It's like a zen burger. It's like the *ur* burger. It's pure and beautiful beyond words.

> *Martin takes a bite of his burger. He savors his burger. He's lost for a moment in food ecstasy. Linh continues to steal looks at him.*

MARTIN: What are you looking at?

LINH: Nothing.

MARTIN: Martin. The name's Martin.

LINH: Linh.

MARTIN: What was that?

LINH: Linh.

MARTIN: Lynn, huh. No offense, Lynn, but that's a girl's name isn't it?

LINH: Not in my country.

MARTIN: Oh yeah? What country would that be?

LINH: Vietnam.

MARTIN: Nam, huh. That's a lot of history, lot of water under the bridge.

LINH: Yes.

MARTIN: I was not in Nam myself. I was too young. I did, however, see a lot of movies about Vietnam and so I feel like I have a little taste of what that whole thing was about. You think I'm an asshole, don't you? That's OK. I got a thick skin. I think a lot people think what I think. They just don't say it out loud.

LINH: Maybe that's a good thing.

MARTIN: (*Eating french fries.*) You know, no. I don't think so. I kinda think when you don't say things, it leads to a blockage, like an intestinal blockage where your intestines and your colon, they get all jammed up and impacted, and full of all this undigested crap that just kind of festers and rots in there. So me, personally, I'd rather just get it out there. Just spew it out. It's healthier, I think.

Linh eyes the french fries like someone who hasn't eaten in years.

MARTIN: You want a fry?

LINH: Oh no. I couldn't.

MARTIN: Aw come on. One fry. It's not going to kill you.

Linh eats the french fry. It is the most delicious thing he has ever eaten.

LINH: That is the most delicious thing I have ever eaten.

MARTIN: What did I tell you? (*Offering his fries.*) Go for it.

LINH: No no, I couldn't.

MARTIN: Here you go. They're all yours.

LINH: Really?

MARTIN: Go to town.

Linh devours the fries. A french fry lodges in his throat. He starts to choke.

LINH: Help. Help me.

Martin springs into action. He administers the Heimlich maneuver.

LINH: You saved my life. If you weren't here, I would've choked and died. I'm alive. Thanks to you, Martin, I'm alive.

MARTIN: Anytime, man.

LINH: Please, what can I do to repay you?

MARTIN: Don't worry about it.

LINH: Anything you wish. Name it. It's yours.

MARTIN: Anything, huh? What? Like you'd buy me a car or something?

LINH: I would obtain for you a car. If that is your wish.

MARTIN: What about a house? Would you *obtain for me* a house

LINH: If that is your wish.

MARTIN: Really? What about a job? Think you could arrange that. A job where they pay me a lot of money to do something. I don't know what. Something. Anything.

LINH: Your wish is my command.

MARTIN: OK, man, that's enough.

LINH: You wish anything. Anything in the world. Make a wish. And it will come true.

MARTIN: I said that's enough.

>*The sound of the miles going by. A Greyhound bus hurtles through the snowy night. Martin takes out a flask and begins to drink.*

MARTIN: One wish, huh? What are you? My fairy godmother? Is this like some kinda fairytale or something? Fuck that. You want a fairytale? I'll give you a fairytale: once upon a time there was this little boy. And he was out on the lake in the middle of winter and the ice cracked, and he fell through and almost drowned, and his big sister, she grabbed his arm and pulled him out, and wrapped him up in her jacket and carried him home. She saved his life. And then they grew up and the sister, she became this big fancy chef. She never cooked a damn thing when we were growing up, didn't even know how to boil water. And now here she is and she's like this big fancy chef and she owns this big fancy restaurant, and I'm thinking: how the hell did that happen? Things change, boy. They can change on a dime. One minute you're walking along minding your own business. The next minute you're falling through the ice. Or choking on a french fry. Or maybe you meet somebody and maybe, just maybe they save your life. The craziest things can happen. Man, I could tell you some stories.

Martin falls asleep. The bus wheezes to a stop. Linh gets up. He takes his knapsack. The knapsack quivers. Linh exits the bus and vanishes into the darkness. The bus keeps going Martin sleeps. He sleeps.

SCENE 4

The sound of a phone ringing in the night. Bea turns on a light. She answers the phone.

BEA: Hello?

Light on the Woman from Vietnam in the darkness.

BEA: Who's there? Please say something. Who are you? Do I know you? Hello?

WOMAN: *Me yeu con. Me yeu con.*

BEA: I don't understand. I don't know what that means. Please tell me what it means. What does it mean?

The Woman hangs up and vanishes. Light on Susan.

SUSAN: What does what mean?

SCENE 5

Morning. Light on Susan in the kitchen of her restaurant. A giant wok sits on the stove. Beside the wok are mountains of ingredients, familiar and exotic. Susan chops vegetables.

SUSAN: What does what mean?

BEA: What? Oh, nothing. I'm just, I'm just thinking out loud.

SUSAN: Thinking about what?

BEA: Nothing.

SUSAN: Come on, Beatrice. You can tell me.

BEA: I'm not Beatrice. I'm Bea.

SUSAN: I wish you'd try using your full name now that you're all grown up.

BEA: Mom, everybody knows me as Bea.

SUSAN: Yes, but that's not your name. Your full name, your *real* name is—

BEA: Please don't say it, please don't say it, please don't say it—

SUSAN: Beatrice.

BEA: Mom—

SUSAN: Why don't you like your name? It's a wonderful name.

BEA: It's just why would you ever name a little kid Beatrice?

SUSAN: Because it's a great name. I like it a whole lot better than Bea. I wish I had never given you a name people could make nicknames out of. I hate nicknames. You should call a person by their real name.

BEA: Mom?

SUSAN: What is it, darling?

BEA: Tell me again how you found me.

SUSAN: Oh my goodness, how many times have I told you this story? I found you in a little orphanage in a little village just north of Dien Bien Phu. You were the cutest baby I'd ever seen. Very chubby, very serious. I took one look at you and I knew right away that you were going to be my little girl. You changed my life. It was like I saw you and everything changed. It was like the world looked different all of a sudden. I couldn't imagine a time when you weren't in my life.

BEA: Why don't you ever talk about your own family?

SUSAN: You are my family.

BEA: You know what I mean.

SUSAN: Oh, Bea. I left home such a long time ago and I just never looked back.

BEA: Why not?

SUSAN: I don't know. Just because. That's just how it was. (*Offering Bea a taste of the food she's cooking.*) Here, have a taste.

BEA: No thanks. Did you always want to be a mom?

SUSAN: Yes. Of course. Always.

BEA: Me, too.

SUSAN: Well I hope you're not going to be a mom for a long, long time. Marriage and babies can wait.

BEA: Mom—

SUSAN: There's plenty of time for all of that. You know how I feel about this, Bea. Are you sure you don't want a taste? Come on, just a taste.

BEA: I'm not hungry. I thought you liked Chad.

SUSAN: I like Chad just fine. That's not the point. The point is you have to think about your career. It's very hard to build a career and be a wife and a mom. You need to focus on yourself for a while. What are you going to do with your life? Have you thought about that much lately?

BEA: I think about it all the time

SUSAN: Frankly, Bea, it feels like you're in a holding pattern waiting for your life to begin.

BEA: Mom, don't start—

SUSAN: You're a very smart young woman. You went to a wonderful college. I wish you hadn't majored in Drama—

BEA: Oh my God—

SUSAN: But we won't talk about that. The point is that you have a good head on your shoulders and you need to start getting focused. You need to be realistic. You need to have a plan. I think acting is a very difficult profession. I'm not sure why someone would choose such a difficult profession knowing how difficult it is.

BEA: Mom, you're like a *chef*. You think that's easy?

SUSAN: I have a gift, Bea. I have skills, yes. But I have something else, something very special. It's almost a kind of magic. It's hard to explain.

BEA: And you think I don't have that?

SUSAN: I'm sure you're a very good actress, whatever that means. That's not the point—

BEA: You always act like cooking is this big mystical thing.

SUSAN: It is.

BEA: You're like this hippie chick who figured out how to use a wok.

SUSAN: It's a little bit more complicated than that, I assure you.

BEA: YOU MAKE EGG ROLLS FOR A LIVING!

SUSAN: I wonder, Bea, if you've given any thought to law school.

BEA: Yes I have and I'm never going.

SUSAN: Please don't speak in absolutes.

BEA: I am never ever going to law school.

SUSAN: You are so willful. Why are you so willful?

BEA: Because I take after you.

SUSAN: What is that supposed to mean?

    Bea exits.

SUSAN: Don't you walk away from me when I'm talking to you. Bea! Bea! All right fine, you want to walk away from me?! Go! I don't care!

Go! I don't care if I ever see you again! And just for your information: I DON'T MAKE EGG ROLLS! I HAVE NEVER MADE AN EGG ROLL IN MY LIFE!

Susan retrieves a very large, very sharp knife. She starts chopping with a vengeance. She adds ingredients to the giant wok. The sound of sizzling and frying. She stirs with giant chopsticks. Smoke and sparks. Susan is working her culinary magic. She chops some more. The knife moves blindingly fast. All of a sudden, she cuts her hand in the same place where the Woman from Vietnam cut her hand many years ago. Susan bleeds. The Woman appears. Linh trails her holding the empty knapsack.

WOMAN: Hello, lady from America. Remember me?

Susan sees the Woman and Linh. She goes after Bea.

SUSAN: Bea! Come back!

WOMAN: Bea. I like that name.

SUSAN: Bea! Bea!

WOMAN: I think Bea's gone. I think she went away. (*Sticking her finger in the wok and tasting.*) Mmm. Delicious. Nice place, your restaurant. Very authentic.

SUSAN: What do you want?

WOMAN: I think you know.

SUSAN: OK listen to me: this restaurant, my restaurant, it's been doing very well. I've been blessed in so many ways. I have money now.

WOMAN: A lot of money.

SUSAN: Yes, a lot of money.

WOMAN: From feeding people food I taught you how to make.

SUSAN: And I understand how you might feel that way. I do. And so I'm prepared to write you a check, a very generous check. You can go back to your village and open your own restaurant. I bet you could open a whole chain of restaurants if that's what you wanted.

WOMAN: I don't want your money.

Susan retrieves her cell phone and dials Bea's number.

WOMAN: We had a deal. You made a promise. Now it's time to pay.

SUSAN: Look, I worked very hard to get to where I am. If you think how I got here is because of anything other than my own blood sweat and tears, you are sorely mistaken. (*To Bea's voicemail.*) Bea, it's mom. You need to call me right away. It's important. Please.

WOMAN: I'm never going to have a child. It's never going to happen.

Susan hangs up the phone.

WOMAN: Isn't that what you said?

SUSAN: Bea is not my child. She's not my real child. She's adopted. She doesn't count.

WOMAN: I see.

SUSAN: No, wait. That didn't come out right. That's not what I mean.

WOMAN: It doesn't matter what you mean. You made a deal. You think you can have something for nothing? You think you can take whatever you want and not have to pay? You think you can get away with it? Is that what you think? It doesn't matter. I'm not interested in you. I've come for Bea. And for what's growing inside of her.

SUSAN: What? What are you talking about?

WOMAN: Right now, it's just a tiny little creature pulsing in the darkness, no eyes, no mouth, no ears, the heartbeat so faint you can hardly hear it. But in a few short months, that creature will grow and transform into the most adorable little baby girl with chubby little cheeks and the tiniest little toes. And when it does, I'll be there.

Susan rushes out in search of Bea. Linh begins to sing. The Woman grows calm as though caught in a spell. Linh cautiously approaches her. He reaches out to her with the knapsack, and suddenly she lunges and thrashes, a whirling dervish of nails and teeth and hair, a blur of movement. And then she and Linh are gone.

SCENE 6

*A busy hospital in the city. Fluorescent lights and white linoleum.
Susan sees Chad standing in the hall. He's the doctor on call.*

SUSAN: Chad! Where is Bea? I need to find her. I need to find her right away.

CHAD: I don't know where she is. Have you tried calling her?

SUSAN: Yes I've tried calling her.

CHAD: What happened to your hand?

SUSAN: Nothing, it's nothing. It's just a little cut.

CHAD: Susan, is everything OK?

SUSAN: No, everything's not OK. Do you have something you want to tell me, Chad?

CHAD: Uh, no. I don't think so.

SUSAN: Are you sure you have nothing you want to tell me?

CHAD: Yeah. Positive. Susan, what's going on?

SUSAN: You tell me.

CHAD: I don't know. If I knew I wouldn't be asking.

SUSAN: You don't know.

CHAD: Know what? What's going on?

SUSAN: She didn't tell you. How could she not tell you?

CHAD: Tell me what?

SUSAN: Chad, listen to me, I need to find Bea. I need to find her as soon as possible. It's very, very important.

CHAD: Susan, what's going on?

SUSAN: Just tell her to call me. I have to go. I have to go cook.

Susan exits.

CHAD: Susan? Susan, wait—

As Susan exits, Linh enters. He's scratched, bitten, and bleeding. He's winded. He looks like he's been in a struggle with a large wild animal. Chad tries to get past him. He blocks Chad's path.

CHAD: Look I'm sorry, I'm sort of in the middle of something. I'm kind of in the middle of something. If you'll excuse me. I said if you'll excuse me…Oh. OK, I get it. You don't speak English. You don't understand a single word I'm saying. I AM IN THE MIDDLE OF SOMETHING.

LINH: Can you please keep your voice down.

CHAD: Oh. You speak English.

LINH: Yes. Yes, I do.

CHAD: I just assumed, you know, because…well, because…you know what, I don't know what I was thinking.

LINH: Listen carefully. I have something I need to tell you. My… pet is sick, you see.

CHAD: What pet?

LINH: In here.

CHAD: OK. Well, you know what, I'm not a vet. In this country, we have people doctors and animal doctors. I'm a people doctor.

LINH: What difference does it make?

CHAD: Well, actually, it makes a very big difference.

LINH: Please. You have to do something. You have to make her better.

CHAD: Look, I really wish I could help you, but I don't know anything about—

LINH: You make her better or else.

CHAD: Or else what?

LINH: Or else bad things happen.

CHAD: What kind of bad things?

LINH: Bad things.

CHAD: Oh, for heaven sakes, here, let me see.

> *Linh deliberates. He then carefully opens the knapsack. Chad cautiously looks inside.*

CHAD: Wow. Wow. That's amazing. I've never seen an animal like that before. I've never seen anything like that before. What kind of animal is that?

LINH: I don't know the name in English.

CHAD: And you say she's sick?

LINH: Very sick.

CHAD: Sick how?

LINH: She is very angry. She is so angry it makes her sick. It's eating her up inside. It's tearing her apart.

CHAD: Look, I don't know what to tell you. Maybe she's got a hair ball. Maybe she's got fleas.

LINH: No no no! You don't understand. This is about Bea.

CHAD: Bea? How do you know Bea?

LINH: We met. A long time ago.

CHAD: Oh my God. You're that guy. You're the guy with the animal in the bag, the rabbit, the ferret. Only it's not a rabbit or a ferret.

LINH: Please. We don't have much time.

CHAD: What are you talking about?

LINH: Just listen to me. Listen.

> *Linh whispers in Chad's ear. A commotion begins inside the bag. The sound of growling, hissing, the gnashing of teeth.*

LINH: Go now. Go. Hurry.

Chad exits. Linh begins singing again to the creature. The creature grows more agitated. Linh opens the knapsack tries to stroke the creature. She bites him. He howls in pain.

SCENE 7

Afternoon. Susan's kitchen. Susan cooks. Martin enters and sets his army rucksack down. He looks through Susan's kitchen, opening cupboards, examining their contents, sniffing ingredients. Susan doesn't see him. She is completely focused on cooking.

SUSAN: One large onion roughly chopped.
Ginger root and coriander.
Cinnamon and fish sauce.
Cardamom, basil, fennel, and lime.
Chili pepper, star anise, sugar, and salt.
Meat and bones and brain and heart.
And you take the heart, you take it in one hand, and gently, very gently massage it with the fingers of the other.

Susan massages the internal organ of an unidentified animal.

You want to bring the blood up to the surface. You can tell you're doing it right if you see a blush, because what that is, you see, that's the blood vessels releasing their last bit of blood, and that's what you want. You want the heart to fill up with all the life juices. And then you want to take the heart, just at the moment it's as full as it can be, and you want to chop it up.

Susan violently chops up the heart.

You really want to get in there. You'll need a good, sharp knife. You may be surprised. The heart is surprisingly tough. It's a muscle after all.

MARTIN: (*Grabbing the knife from Susan.*) Whoa whoa whoa, easy there, sis. You're gonna chop off a finger if you don't watch out.

SUSAN: Martin? God, you scared me. What are you doing here?

MARTIN: Paying a visit to my big sister. Hey there, sis, long time no see. (*Sniffing the soup pot.*) That smells great. What is it?

SUSAN: It's a traditional Vietnamese soup the natives call *pho*. It's a very, very special soup. It's not done yet. It has to simmer. The flavors have to come together. I'm forgetting something. What am I forgetting? Oxtail. Oxtail. Damnit! I forgot the oxtail.

> *Martin turns the garbage disposal on. The sound of blades grinding. Susan turns it off.*

SUSAN: Can you please not play with that please.

MARTIN: You ever think about sticking your hand in there? Like when you're washing a fork, do you ever think what would happen if you just stuck your hand in there and flipped the switch? Would it hurt? Or would you just be like in shock? Would it just chew you up so fast, you wouldn't feel a thing?

SUSAN: No, I don't.

MARTIN: I do. It's really good to see you, Sue. It's been a long time. How's Bea?

SUSAN: She's fine. Bea's fine.

MARTIN: Last time I saw her, she was just a little sprout. She must be all grown-up by now. Don't you wish Dad could've been around to see her. I bet he would've been proud.

SUSAN: Martin, why are you here? What do you want?

MARTIN: Oh gosh, lots of things. World peace…love…

SUSAN: Money.

MARTIN: Money, sure. You bet.

SUSAN: How much?

MARTIN: Sue, Sue, Sue. What do you think I am? You think I'm just gonna waltz in here and hit you up for cash? Look, I know I've had some fiscal difficulties in the past, and I know you've bailed me out, which I appreciate, I do, but Sue, it's not just about money. It's about respect. It's about dignity. I can earn my own way. How does that saying go? Give a man money and he can buy a steak. Give him a rifle and he can shoot the cow.

SUSAN: What are you trying to say, Martin? Just spit it out.

MARTIN: I want to come work for you.

SUSAN: Oh Martin no—

MARTIN: Now hear me out, I know my way around a kitchen, I can cook, and I work hard. I work my butt off when I'm motivated. I just have to be motivated.

SUSAN: Martin, you're not well. You haven't been well in a very long time.

MARTIN: I've had my ups and downs in the past, I know that, but as long as I stay on my meds, the lady at the VA hospital says everything'll be just fine.

SUSAN: I want to help you, Martin, I do—

MARTIN: Then give me a job.

SUSAN: Oh God—

MARTIN: I'll peel things, I'll pluck things, I'll chop 'em up into lots of little pieces. I'll wash the crud off anything you give me. I'll mop the floors till they sparkle.

SUSAN: Martin—

MARTIN: Sue, please. I don't have anybody else. You're my family, Sue. You're all I got.

SUSAN: I can't talk about this right now. I need to go get some oxtail. It's not the same without the oxtail. Now listen to me, Martin. I need you to do something for me. Once the soup starts to boil, you need to turn down the flame. Turn it down to a low simmer. Whatever you do, no matter what, you can't let the soup boil over.

MARTIN: I won't, Sue. I won't let it boil over. I promise.

SUSAN: This is important, Martin.

MARTIN: You can count on me, Sue.

SUSAN: As soon as it boils, turn it down to a low simmer.

MARTIN: A low simmer. I got it. I'll watch that pot like a hawk, Sue, like a hawk.

SUSAN: OK. All right. I'll be back.

Susan exits.

MARTIN: (*Shouting after her.*) DON'T YOU WORRY ABOUT A THING! I'LL TAKE CARE OF EVERYTHING! I WON'T LET YOU DOWN! NOT ME! NO SIRREE!

Martin looks around the kitchen. His gaze turns to the garbage disposal. He is drawn to it. He can't help himself. He switches it on. The roar of grinding blades.

SCENE 8

Outside an apartment building in the city. It's snowing. Bea is wearing a parka. She's shivering. It's really cold. She's really cold. She has a little suitcase. She sniffs the air. She smells something familiar. Her cell phone rings. It's Susan calling. She doesn't answer it. Chad appears.

BEA: Chad! Where've you been?

CHAD: I got held up. Look Bea, I need to talk to you—

BEA: I need to talk to you, too—

CHAD: I need to tell you something—

BEA: OK but there's something I need to tell you first—

CHAD: It can wait—

BEA: No, it can't—

CHAD: Yes, it can—

BEA: Chad, I'm pregnant.

CHAD: Yes, I know.

BEA: What?

CHAD: I mean, I had a hunch.

BEA: You did?

CHAD: Just a gut feeling. One of those feelings, you know, in my gut.

> *Bea's phone rings.*

CHAD: Who's that?

BEA: It's just my mom. We had a big fight. I don't want to talk to her right now. Let's go.

CHAD: Listen, Bea, I've been thinking. I don't think we should go to Las Vegas.

BEA: What? What do you mean we shouldn't go to Las Vegas?

CHAD: I think we should go somewhere else.

BEA: Like where?

CHAD: I'm thinking somewhere far, far away. Maybe a little cabin in the woods.

BEA: You mean like for our honeymoon?

CHAD: No, I mean like forever.

BEA: Forever? Chad? What are you talking about?

CHAD: I'm talking about living happily ever after.

BEA: In a cabin in the woods.

CHAD: That's right.

BEA: But what about your job?

CHAD: I'm a doctor, Bea. I can be a doctor anywhere. Besides, maybe I'll get another job. Maybe I'll be…a woodsman. I've always wanted to be a woodsman

BEA: What's a woodsman?

CHAD: You know. A woodsman. A man of the woods.

BEA: Did something happen at work?

CHAD: No. We gotta go. Let's go.

BEA: Chad—

CHAD: What?

BEA: It's just that we were going to go to Las Vegas and get married. That was the plan.

CHAD: Well now we're going to a cabin in the woods and living happily ever after.

BEA: I just think that's kinda weird.

CHAD: It's not weird.

BEA: Yeah, it's weird, Chad, it's totally weird.

CHAD: Why do you want to go to Las Vegas so much? What's so great about Las Vegas?

BEA: It's not about Las Vegas.

CHAD: Then what's the problem?

BEA: It's just—you just seem different.

CHAD: Different how?

BEA: I don't know. Just different.

CHAD: Listen, Bea, you gotta trust me on this. Our lives are about to change forever. We need to start looking at the big picture. The city is a dangerous place. It's no place to raise a child. The woods, Bea, that's where we need to be. It's gonna be great. We're gonna go and we're going to find a little cabin, and we're going to live off the land just like people did in the olden days. We're going to grow our own vegetables and pick berries. And we'll drink water from the well— we'll have a well. And you, me and the baby, we're gonna live happily ever after. Trust me.

> *Chad and Bea kiss.*

BEA: I didn't bring the right clothes.

CHAD: That's OK. We'll weave some new clothes.

BEA: Weave?

CHAD: Yeah. You know. Like on a loom or something.

BEA: I don't know how to weave.

CHAD: You'll figure it out. I'll chop wood and you'll weave clothes and we'll be just fine.

BEA: Chad?

CHAD: We gotta go. We gotta go now.

BEA: Chad—

CHAD: Listen to me, Bea. You have to trust me. No matter what, trust me.

> *A blizzard of white snow. Chad and Bea vanish.*

SCENE 9

> *Susan's kitchen. It's a mess. The soup pot is boiling over. The garbage disposal is going. The sink is overflowing. Water gushes from the garbage disposal. The contents of Martin's rucksack are scattered all over the floor, Martin is running to and fro. He's overwhelmed. Linh enters with his knapsack. He bruised and battered. His hand is now bloodied.*

MARTIN: Oh my God, thank God you're here. Something's wrong with the sink. I don't know how it happened. You gotta fix it. You gotta fix it right now.

> *Linh goes to the sink and fixes the leak. Martin recognizes him.*

MARTIN: Lynn? Is that you? What are you doing here?

LINH: Fixing a leak. Listen, Martin, have you by any chance given any thought to your wish?

MARTIN: Right, right. My wish. No.

LINH: Well perhaps you should.

MARTIN: You know, Lynn, I think I'll maybe save my wish for a rainy day.

LINH: But Martin—

MARTIN: Come on, man, enough. I got enough things to think about without you beating that dead horse into the ground.

LINH: But Martin—

MARTIN: Just drop it, OK? Drop it. Enough is enough. I got my hands full as it is.

LINH: What's that smell?

MARTIN: Oh no oh no oh no.

> *Martin goes to the soup pot. He turns off the flame. He looks in the pot.*

MARTIN: I forgot to turn down the flame. I forgot. How could I forget?

LINH: It's OK, Martin.

MARTIN: I burned the soup. Who burns soup? Who does that?

LINH: It's just soup.

MARTIN: No, Lynn, no. It's not just soup. You don't understand. Never mind. I gotta clean this up. I gotta clean this all up.

> *Martin begins cleaning up. There's a lot to clean up. Linh joins him. Linh sees the contents of Martin's rucksack scattered on the floor. He*

> *sees a fishing pole among Martin's things and picks it up.*

LINH: Do you fish?

MARTIN: What?

LINH: Do you fish? Never mind.

MARTIN: Why? You like fishing?

LINH: Yes. You?

MARTIN: Are you kidding me? I love fishing.

LINH: Me, too. Fishing is my most favorite thing. No one tells you what to do. No one push you around. No one says: Go here, go there, do this, do that or else. You just sit. And fish. And nobody bothers you.

MARTIN: Amen, brother. Peace. Tranquility. All the crap just fades away, all the pressure, all the stuff you wish you could fix and you can't, you just can't, soon as your cast your line, it just all goes away. (*Beat.*) You ever been ice fishing?

> *Linh shakes his head.*

MARTIN: Oh man, it's great. It's like the greatest thing in the world. You go out on the lake in the middle of winter, and you saw a hole in the ice, and then you drop a line down into the water and you wait. And you drink. And the temperature keeps dropping and you just keep drinking. Man, what I would give to be out on the lake fishing right this second. You wanna go? Fishing, I mean?

LINH: Me?

MARTIN: Yeah.

LINH: You are inviting me?

MARTIN: Ah it's a bad idea. I can't go fishing. I promised. See, I made a promise.

LINH: Yes. I understand.

MARTIN: I can't just take off. I have obligations.

LINH: I know. Me, too.

MARTIN: I mean there's gonna be hell to pay if I take off. I'm never gonna hear the end of it.

LINH: I know. I know exactly what you mean.

MARTIN: But, man, what I would give to go fishing. I would love that. I would love that more than anything. But I can't. I can't do it.

LINH: What if something happens?

MARTIN: Exactly. Wait. What could happen?

LINH: Something. Something bad.

MARTIN: No, Lynn, no, we can't think that way. We gotta stay positive. We gotta get outta here. We gotta do the thing we love, we gotta seize the day because life, life is short. All right, that's it, we're going. You and me, we're going fishing. I know the perfect place. My dad used to take me when I was little. It's great.

LINH: You would take me to your family's ancestral fishing hole?

MARTIN: Yes, Lynn, yes I would.

LINH: I am very honored, Martin. You are my good and esteemed friend.

MARTIN: That's nice, Lynn. OK, let's go.

> *Martin stuffs his scattered belongings into his rucksack. Linh looks at his knapsack and deliberates. Martin finishes packing.*

MARTIN: You ready? You got everything?

LINH: Yes.

MARTIN: What about your bag?

LINH: You know, I think I will leave my bag here.

MARTIN: Well all right then. Let's roll.

> *Martin exits. Linh looks at the knapsack. He touches the knapsack and speaks softly to the creature inside.*

LINH: *Me yeu con. Me yeu con.*

> *Linh exits. The knapsack sits on the counter of Susan's kitchen. And then slowly, it begins to quiver and undulate. The sound of growling*

and hissing, the gnashing of teeth. The sound gets louder. A hand thrusts itself out of the knapsack.

It's the Woman's hand. The Woman's hand frantically feels around the kitchen counter groping for something. The Woman's hand finds the knife that Susan was using. The Woman's hand grabs the knife and begins slicing and stabbing through the knapsack.

SCENE 10

The world transforms. The woods outside the city. Trees as far as the eye can see. The Woman is alone in a clearing sharpening her knife.

WOMAN: Once upon a time there was a woman.

Bea enters in her coat. She carries her little suitcase. The Woman puts away her knife.

WOMAN: And she was alone.
And she was far from home.

Bea sees the Woman.

BEA: Hello?

WOMAN: Hello.

BEA: I think I'm lost.

WOMAN: Really?

BEA: I think so, yeah.

WOMAN: Don't worry. I can help you. Follow me.

The Woman takes Bea's hand and they exit.

END OF ACT ONE

SCENE 11

Late afternoon. A desolate road somewhere in the American Midwest. Susan is studying a map. She can't find where she needs to go. She's getting more and more frantic. Lightning flashes across the sky. The Woman from Vietnam appears.

WOMAN: Once upon a time there was a woman.
And she was alone.
Only this time, she was not that far from home.
She was actually very, very close.
And yet, oddly enough, she was lost.

SUSAN: I will kill you. I swear to God. I will kill you with my bare hands—

WOMAN: Yes, but then you would never get your daughter back. She'd be lost to you forever. A child on a milk carton. A father who never came back from war.

The rumble of distant thunder.

SUSAN: What did you just say?

WOMAN: People disappear. It happens all the time. They vanish as if by magic. They just pick up and walk away, they walk away from their old lives because something inside them cracks open, and they cannot go on as they had been, they cannot be that person anymore. Or sometimes they have no say in the matter. Someone snatches them away, and they are too weak to resist. Or too young to understand what's happening. And the loss that is felt is so great, it's so great, it's like a monster inside of you tearing you apart— but I digress. You are clearly lost. But don't worry. This is your lucky day. I know where Bea lives, you see. And I can tell you right now it's not on your map.

Lightning.

SUSAN: What have you done to her?

WOMAN: I've taken very good care of her is what I've done. Bea and I have become very close. She's so sweet. She's like a little lamb.

SUSAN: Now you listen to me: if you harm so much as a hair on her head—

WOMAN: What? What will you do? It's over. It's done. I've won.

SUSAN: I'll sell my restaurant. I'll give whatever money I make to you, every cent I have I'll give to you. You'll have more money than you could ever imagine.

WOMAN: Will you never learn?

SUSAN: Look, I want you to consider renegotiating our deal. I want to see if we can maybe take a second look at some of the original terms of the contract. I think you and I, I think we can find many things we both agree on. I think we're really not that far apart. I think if we just sit down at the table and hash some things out, we can both walk away happy.

WOMAN: It's very difficult to bargain when you have nothing left to offer.

Thunder. The Woman starts to walk away.

SUSAN: No, wait. Wait. Take me. Take me instead. A life for a life.

WOMAN: How selfless, how maternal. But I don't want you.

SUSAN: But you did. Once upon a time, you did.

The Woman stops in her tracks.

SUSAN: You chose me. Of all the people in the world, you chose me. As if you knew me already. As if we had some connection, some thread that tied us together. But how could that be? You and I, we didn't know each other. We were strangers. I didn't even know your name. That's so strange. After all these years, I don't know your name. How can that be?

WOMAN: There are many things you don't know about me. Besides you never asked. I was just part of the scenery, part of the native color.

SUSAN: I'm asking you now.

WOMAN: Guess.

SUSAN: I have no idea. How could I know? How could I possibly know your name?

WOMAN: I tell you what: if you can guess my name, I will release you from your debt to me. We'll call it even. And I will go away and you can live happily ever after.

SUSAN: Do you mean that?

WOMAN: Why not? You'll never guess—

SUSAN: But if I do—

WOMAN: You never will—

SUSAN: But if I do, do we have a deal?

WOMAN: Yes. Fine. We have a deal.

SUSAN: Now tell me where she is.

WOMAN: Please.

SUSAN: *Please* tell me where she is.

WOMAN: Up ahead you'll see a lake. Beyond the lake you'll see a tiny, tiny dirt road. Take that road and walk deep into the woods. When you feel the first raindrop fall, turn left. Keep walking until you see the lightning flash, and a clearing will appear through the trees. In that clearing you'll see a cabin. You better go or you'll be late.

> *The Woman vanishes. Lightning. Susan crumples up her map and throws it away. She exits quickly. The sound of thunder.*

SCENE 12

> *The middle of a frozen lake. Martin and Linh are fishing. They've been fishing for a while. The fish aren't biting. Martin is drinking from a flask. Linh is shivering.*

> *It's very cold.*

LINH: Psst. Martin.

MARTIN: What?

LINH: I think I heard thunder.

MARTIN: Yeah? So?

LINH: Maybe we should call it a day. Build a fire. Drink some cocoa.

MARTIN: We're not leaving here till we catch some fish.

LINH: But I'm so cold, Martin. My lips are turning blue. I have lost all feeling in my toes.

MARTIN: Will you pipe down for Chrissakes. You're gonna scare away the fish.

LINH: (*Beat.*) Martin?

MARTIN: Jesus Christ. What now?

LINH: Are you sure this is the right lake?

MARTIN: Of course, I'm sure.

LINH: How do you know?

MARTIN: I just do. I feel it in my bones.

LINH: But this lake looks like all the other lakes.

MARTIN: I just told you I felt it in my bones, Lynn. Jesus Christ. Don't you think I'd know my ancestral fishing hole when I see it? What do you think I am?

LINH: I think you are maybe confused, Martin.

MARTIN: I am not confused, Lynn. My mind is sharp as a tack. If I say this is my ancestral fishing hole, then this is my goddamn ancestral fishing hole.

LINH: But we have been traveling for months now. Every lake we go to, it all looks the same. And no matter where we are, we never catch any fish. And I am so cold right now. I have never been this cold in my life.

MARTIN: It's not the destination, Lynn. It's the journey. It's all the good times along the way.

LINH: But the times I am having are not so good.

MARTIN: What are you talking about, Lynn? We're men and we're fishing. It doesn't get any better than this. No, this is the place. I'm positive. My dad used to take me here all the time when I was a kid. We'd sit here all day and fish, we'd catch so many fish, and he'd tell me these stories, all these crazy stories. Man, those were good times, those were the best times in the whole entire world.

> *The sound of ice cracking. And also another sound: a kind of primordial groaning.*

LINH: Did you hear that just now?

MARTIN: It's just the ice settling.

> *Linh studies the ice for cracks. He peers down the ice hole. Martin continues to fish and drink.*

LINH: How deep is this lake?

MARTIN: Deep.

LINH: How deep?

MARTIN: I don't know, Lynn. Deep.

LINH: It is so dark down there. Anything could be down there. All kinds of creatures. Angry creatures. Dangerous creatures.

> *Linh starts singing into the hole.*

MARTIN: Jesus Christ, what are you doing? Don't sing. You're gonna scare away the fish.

LINH: You know, Martin, I think maybe the fish are sleeping. I think maybe we should just let them sleep.

MARTIN: What are you talking about? Fish don't sleep.

LINH: Some do. Some fish burrow in the mud and wait. You think they're gone, but they're not. They're lying in wait, lurking in the darkness, waiting to strike.

MARTIN: (*Reeling in his line.*) Ah fuck it. This is ridiculous. Here, give me your watch.

LINH: What?

MARTIN: You heard me. Give me your goddamn watch.

LINH: Why do you want my watch?

MARTIN: I just do, OK? Give it to me.

LINH: I cannot. It belongs to somebody else.

MARTIN: Who?

LINH: It is a long story.

MARTIN: Never mind, I don't care. Just give me the watch.

LINH: I cannot, Martin.

MARTIN: Give me the goddamn watch.

LINH: No—

MARTIN: Give it to me—

LINH: No—

MARTIN: Gimme that.

 Martin snatches the watch and hooks it onto his fishing pole.

LINH: Wait. Wait. What are you doing? Wait.

 Martin drops the line with the watch as bait.

MARTIN: Fish like shiny things. Besides, it's just a cheap old Timex. What's the big deal? I betcha they start biting any second now. You watch.

 There's a tug on the line. And then another. Martin feels it.

MARTIN: What did I tell you? Hold on. I think I got something. I think I got something.

 There's another tug. And then another one after that. Martin starts reeling in the fish. Whatever it is, it's big. A cosmic tug of war between fish and man ensues.

HOLY CRAP! IT'S A BIG ONE! IT'S A MONSTER! JESUS CHRIST! I GOT IT I GOT IT I GOT IT!

The line snaps. Stillness.

Goddamnit. It got away.

LINH: Oh well. Next time.

MARTIN: What if there is no next time?

The Woman from Vietnam appears. Linh sees her. Martin does not.

LINH: OK. Time to go.

MARTIN: What if this was my last shot and I fucked it up? What if I just fucked it up like I always fuck things up?

LINH: It's OK, Martin.

MARTIN: No, it's not OK, Lynn. Don't you get it? This is my ancestral fishing hole. I should be able to catch a fish in my own goddamn ancestral fishing hole. What is wrong with me?

LINH: We should go now. It would be good to go now.

MARTIN: We're not going anywhere.

LINH: Martin, please—

Martin begins packing up his fishing gear. As he does so, the Woman approaches. Martin does not see her. Linh does.

MARTIN: No, Lynn, no. I'm not giving up, no way no how. I'm gonna hike out to the middle of the lake, find us another patch of ice, and then I'm gonna saw us another hole, and then I'm gonna catch us some fish. There are fish in this lake, this lake is teeming with fish, and I swear to God I'm gonna find them. I'm gonna catch something if it's the last thing I do. I'm gonna catch something if it kills me. *Martin exits loaded down with fishing gear. He does not see the Woman. The Woman is holding the watch. It's dripping wet. She puts it to her ear.*

WOMAN: Takes a licking and keeps on ticking.

> *The Woman holds out the watch to Linh.*

WOMAN: It's almost time.

> *Linh takes the watch. He feels something rising from his gut up into his throat. Somewhere else, Bea is very pregnant. She touches her stomach. Something is moving under the skin. Linh reaches into his mouth and pulls out a silvery fish. The Woman vanishes. The sound of ice cracking. Thunder. And then rain.*

SCENE 13

> *A cabin in the woods. Outside it's raining. Bea is very pregnant. She's wears a princess costume. She touches her stomach.*

SUSAN: Oh, Bea. You look like a fairytale princess.

BEA: It's just a costume for this play I'm in. I have to go to rehearsal in a minute.

SUSAN: It's so good to see you, Bea. I'm so proud of you. You're acting. It's what you always dreamed of doing.

BEA: It's nothing, it's no big deal. It's just this community theatre thing. It's just a bunch of locals. None of them really act, you know, professionally or anything. They all just sort of play themselves. It's stupid. It's totally stupid.

SUSAN: No, Bea, it's the first step. You'll see. Before you know it, there'll be all these other opportunities. You're so talented, Bea. You're a really good actress—

BEA: Mom, stop, just stop.

SUSAN: I've been so worried, Bea. You have no idea. It was like you dropped off the face of the earth. I missed you so much.

BEA: It's just been kinda crazy the past few months, finding a place, getting settled.

SUSAN: No, of course, I understand. I understand completely. Where is Chad?

BEA: Out. He's out.

SUSAN: Will he be back soon?

BEA: I don't know exactly when he'll be back.

SUSAN: Bea, you really shouldn't be alone right now. Chad needs to be here with you—

BEA: Just drop it, OK?

SUSAN: Listen, Bea, I think I owe you an apology. I think the last time we spoke, I think I maybe said things I didn't mean. I feel like you might still be angry with me.

BEA: I'm not angry. I just, I just have a lot on my mind is all.

SUSAN: And I want to help. Let me help you guys out. I'm sure you've had a lot of expenses, what with getting ready for the baby and the new cabin. I can write a check. I was also thinking I might start a college fund for the baby.

BEA: I don't need that kind of help.

SUSAN: But, Bea—

BEA: That's not the kind of help I need.

SUSAN: Please, Bea—

The sound of ice cracking.

BEA: You used to live around here, didn't you?

SUSAN: What?

BEA: When you were a little girl, you used to live around here.

SUSAN: Who told you that?

BEA: This lady I met when I first got here.

SUSAN: What lady?

BEA: Just this nice lady I met when I first got here. She said she knew you. From a long time ago.

SUSAN: What was her name?

BEA: Her name?

SUSAN: Yes, Bea, her name. What was her name?

BEA: It's…it's…That's funny. I can't remember.

SUSAN: Well what did it sound like?

BEA: Like, like…God, that's so weird. I'm completely drawing a blank.

SUSAN: Think, Bea. Try to remember.

BEA: It's on the tip of my tongue. I don't know. It'll come to me.

SUSAN: Bea—

BEA: So is it true you grew up around here?

SUSAN: Not too far from here.

BEA: With your mom and your dad?

SUSAN: Yes.

BEA: And Uncle Martin?

SUSAN: Yes.

BEA: And your dad, he died like in the war, like in Vietnam.

SUSAN: Yes.

BEA: But your mom, she's still alive.

SUSAN: She remarried and moved to Florida. She's a very toxic and unhappy person. I haven't spoken to her in years. You know all this already, Bea.

BEA: And Uncle Martin?

SUSAN: He has a lot of problems. He's an alcoholic and a troubled soul. He's not somebody I want in your life or in mine.

BEA: But I want my child to know where she comes from.

SUSAN: What does that mean? What does that even mean?

BEA: It means knowing where you come from. It means not growing up with this feeling inside of you, that you're missing something, some piece of the puzzle you're never going to find. Why can't you understand that? Why is that so hard for you to understand?

SUSAN: I understand.

BEA: No, you don't. How can you?

SUSAN: Bea, I do. I understand. Bea, please.

BEA: Tell me again how you found me.

SUSAN: Bea, you know this story. I've told you a thousand times.

BEA: I want you to tell me again.

SUSAN: I found you in an orphanage in a little village—

BEA: Just north of Dien Bien Phu. Yes, I know, I know that. You've told me that part already. What orphanage?

SUSAN: What do you mean? You mean the name? I don't know the name. It was just a shack, Bea. It was a terrible place. Dirty and dark and awful, it was awful.

BEA: Why did you go in there?

SUSAN: I don't know why, Bea. I was walking down the road and I saw it and I just went in.

BEA: That doesn't make any sense.

SUSAN: Bea—

BEA: That doesn't make any sense. Why would you just go into some dirty shack by the side of the road in some foreign country you don't even know? It doesn't make sense. Why would you do that?

SUSAN: I don't know. Because.

BEA: Because why?

SUSAN: Because.

BEA: Because why, mom? Why?

SUSAN: Because I heard something.

BEA: What? What did you hear?

SUSAN: This, this song.

BEA: What kind of song?

SUSAN: I don't know. I don't know. Someone was singing this song.

BEA: What was it like?

SUSAN: Like nothing I had ever heard before. It was beautiful and strange. I can't explain. It's hard to explain.

BEA: And so you went in?

SUSAN: Yes.

BEA: And you saw me?

SUSAN: Yes. You were sleeping. It was early morning. The sun was rising and the room was filled with all this golden light. And there you were. You were fast asleep on this straw mat laid out on the ground, this beautiful little girl, this precious child. And I took one look at you, and it was like I knew you. It was like I had known you my whole life.

BEA: Who was singing?

SUSAN: What?

BEA: You said you heard someone singing.

SUSAN: I'm not sure. I forget.

BEA: And then what happened?

SUSAN: I went over to you, and I picked you up, and I held you. I just held you. Bea—

> Susan gives Bea a hug. Susan hasn't hugged Bea in a very long time.

SUSAN: I love you, Bea. I love you so much.

The rain stops. The sound of Linh singing. Bea hears it. Susan does not. Bea pulls away.

BEA: I have to go.

Bea puts on her coat over her princess costume.

SUSAN: Bea, please—

BEA: I have to go.

Bea exits into the forest. The sound of Linh singing continues. And then the sound of a creature hissing, growling and gnashing its teeth.

SUSAN: Bea! Bea, wait!

Susan exits into the woods. On the lake, Linh has accumulated a small mountain of fish. He's trying to sing, but something is rising from his gut and into his throat. He stops singing in mid-phrase. He pulls another fish out of his mouth, a big, silvery fish. The Woman approaches him. She sharpens her knife. As she does, she recites all the names that are not her name.

WOMAN: Is it Ai? Is it Ang? Is it Be? Is it Bien?
Is it Cam, is it Canh, is it Chau, it Chi?
Is it: Dao, Diep, Dieu, Don?
Giang, Ha, Hai, Han?
Hang Phu, Hien, Hoa?
Lan, Lang, Lanh, Mai?
My, Nam Ha, Ngoc?
Ngu, Nguye, Nhu, Nhung?
Phuong, Quy, Sang, Suong?
Tam, Thien, Thuy, Trinh?

Guess. I dare you to. Go on. Guess.

The Woman plucks the fish from Linh. She slices through its belly with her knife. And then she vanishes.

SCENE 14

Lights up. The woods. An actor who looks like Chad but is Not Chad is sharpening his axe. He is dressed in a woodsman costume. Bea enters in princess costume. She's turned around. She's lost.

BEA: Hello? Can you help me? I think I may be lost. I'm looking for this lady. I think she lives around here—

Not Chad stops sharpening his axe. He looks up. Bea gets a good look at him.

BEA: Chad?

NOT CHAD: "There you are, my lady."

BEA: What?

NOT CHAD: "I have ventured deep into the woods, and I have seen many things."

BEA: What are you talking about, Chad?

NOT CHAD: Chad? Who's Chad?

BEA: What do you mean who's Chad? You're Chad. What is wrong with you? It's like you drag me to a cabin in the middle of the woods in the middle of winter and you tell me we're going to live happily ever after, and then we get here, and it's like you're gone. It's like the Chad I knew, the Chad I *thought* I knew, he's nowhere to be found, he just disappears, just vanishes into thin air, and now here you are and you're dressed funny, and you're acting like a crazy person.

NOT CHAD: I think you're confusing me with somebody else. I'm not Chad.

BEA: This is crazy, this is insane. If you're not Chad, who are you?

NOT CHAD: I'm the woodsman.

BEA: What are you talking about?

NOT CHAD: Like in the play? You're in a play, right? Or do you always dress like that?

BEA: No, of course not. It's a costume, for a play, yes, I'm in a play—what woodsman?

NOT CHAD: There's a woodsman. He shows up halfway through the story and saves the day.

BEA: The woodsman?

NOT CHAD: Yes, the woodsman—have you even read the script?

BEA: I have…I just…what scene is this?

NOT CHAD: The one where the woodsman tells the princess the secret name nobody else knows and saves the day. It's maybe the most important scene in the play. Why is it that everybody always forgets the woodsman? I don't get it because the woodsman, he's pretty much the hero of the story. He's the guy who takes care of everything, it's all on him, and the pressure he is under is unreal. If he messes up, if he drops the ball, all kinds of bad things will happen.

BEA: What kind of bad things?

NOT CHAD: Bad things. Look, do you want to do this scene or not?

BEA: I'm sorry…it's just…you just remind me of somebody I used to know is all.

NOT CHAD: And who might that be? My evil twin, my doppelganger, my shadow self?

BEA: I'm not sure.

NOT CHAD: You're acting really weird.

BEA: I am not.

NOT CHAD: Yeah, you are.

BEA: I'm not.

NOT CHAD: You are.

BEA: I'm not.

NOT CHAD: We're bickering like old married people.

BEA: What? What did you just say just now?

NOT CHAD: We're bickering like old married people. Only we're not married, thank God, because I'm the woodsman and you're the princess, and that's not the kind of relationship we have. He's a free spirit, a man of the woods, and she's a princess, a big, pregnant princess. Boy, are you pregnant. You are so pregnant. And I gotta be honest with you, I find it very disturbing. All those cells mutating, all that DNA bubbling and percolating, all that life, all that roiling life in your belly. It's spooky.

BEA: Well you know what? You don't have to think about it.

NOT CHAD: Well you know what? I do. Every time we do this scene together I'm going to have to look at your big huge belly.

BEA: Oh my God, who are you?

NOT CHAD: The woodsman! I'm the woodsman! How many times do I have to say it? I swear to God, your brain is turning to mush.

BEA: What?

NOT CHAD: It's the hormones, I know. They're raging out of control right now. You don't even know what you're saying. You're not in your right mind. Why are you even in this play? Shouldn't you be like in a birthing hut somewhere?

BEA: I'm an actress.

NOT CHAD: OK.

BEA: And I'm like new to the area. I thought this might be a nice way to meet new people and practice my craft.

NOT CHAD: So who is this Chad character?

BEA: Nobody.

NOT CHAD: Well clearly that's not true.

BEA: He's just somebody I used to know.

NOT CHAD: Where is he now?

BEA: I don't know.

NOT CHAD: Oh. I get it. He's the dad, right? The absent father.

BEA: That's none of your business.

NOT CHAD: What? Did he get scared? Did he just take off?

BEA: You know, this is really none of your business.

NOT CHAD: Well, clearly it is since it involves my evil twin. It's scary being a dad, it's really scary. The birth, the blood, the poop, this little creature who screams night and day. It's like a horror movie, only it's your life.

BEA: How do you think I feel?

NOT CHAD: You're not the only one going through this, you know.

BEA: Well, you know what? I kinda am. Look, I have to go.

NOT CHAD: Go where? We have a scene to do.

BEA: There's somebody I need to talk to.

NOT CHAD: Yes, that would be me. The person you're in this scene with.

> *Bea starts to go.*

NOT CHAD: OK, fine. You don't want to play this scene with me? I'll do it all by myself: "Pray tell me, kind woodsman, what did you see?" "I saw a creature, my lady, like no creature I have ever seen before. I thought it was a rabbit or possibly a ferret, but it wasn't a rabbit or a ferret, it was like nothing I've ever seen before, it was—"

BEA: What did you just say?

NOT CHAD: Uh…pray tell me, kind woodsman?

BEA: No after that.

NOT CHAD: A…a…a creature like no other creature?

BEA: After that.

NOT CHAD: …I thought it was a rabbit or possibly a ferret.

BEA: Yes. Yes. But it wasn't a rabbit or a ferret, was it?

NOT CHAD: No. No, it wasn't.

BEA: What was it? Tell me. I need to know.

The baby stirs inside of Bea.

NOT CHAD: Whoa. Are you OK?

BEA: I'm fine.

NOT CHAD: So, uh, how does it feel?

BEA: Scary.

NOT CHAD: That makes sense. I'd be scared. Just looking at you makes me scared. Have you picked out a name? It's OK, you don't have to tell me. I don't mind.

BEA: It's not that, it's just…my life is kind of a mess right now. I'm having this baby pretty much any day now, and I don't have a name, and I haven't done anything to prepare, whatever it is people do to prepare, like you can really prepare, I mean come on, how the hell are you supposed to prepare for something like this, and there's all these things that keep coming up, and I don't know where they're coming from, and I don't understand what they mean, and it's like my life doesn't make sense anymore, and the people in my life who I thought I knew, I don't, and everything is crazy and mixed up, and I don't know what comes next, and I'm scared I'm really scared—

Not Chad kisses Bea.

NOT CHAD: The woodsman kisses the princess.

BEA: Is that in the script?

NOT CHAD: No. It was an impulse. I just went with it.

The sound of an animal hissing, growling and gnashing its teeth.

BEA: What was that?

NOT CHAD: Just stay here, OK? I'll take care of it. I'm the woodsman. That's my job.

> *Not Chad exits with his axe. The baby stirs inside of Bea.*

> *The sound of hissing, growling, and teeth gnashing grows louder. Bea exits. Susan enters.*

SUSAN: Bea? Where are you? Bea!

> *The sounds of hissing and growling. Susan exits.*

SCENE 15

> *The middle of a frozen lake. Linh is sitting by the fishing hole next to a mountain of fish. Martin enters lugging his fishing gear. He's been walking in a giant circle and is now back where he started. Martin sees Linh.*

MARTIN: Linh, is that you?

LINH: Hello, Martin.

MARTIN: I think I must've gotten all turned around. I thought I was going that way. But I think I ended up going that way. And then I think I ended up doubling back that way. Where'd you get all that fish? Don't tell me, please don't tell me. You caught all those fish?

> *Linh nods.*

MARTIN: How did you catch all that fish?

LINH: It's kind of a long story. Maybe we go now. Maybe I cook you a fish.

MARTIN: No, Lynn, no. I'm not going anywhere. I'm going to cook my own goddamn fish that I catch myself. Jesus Christ, for once in my life, I'm gonna have a plan and it's gonna work.

> *The sound of the ice cracking under their feet.*

MARTIN: Oh God. It's cracking. The ice is cracking.

LINH: It's OK, Martin.

MARTIN: No, it's not OK, Lynn, it's really not OK. People always say things are OK when they're not OK. This is not OK. This is really not OK.

LINH: Sssh. Just follow me. Watch your step.

Linh leads the way across the ice. Linh and Martin walk very carefully. The sound of creaking ice.

MARTIN: Oh no.

The ice breaks with a giant crack. The Woman's hand thrusts itself out of the lake and pulls Martin down into the freezing water. Blackout. A tiny light flickers and then blinks on in the distance.

SCENE 16

A deserted diner somewhere on the edge of the woods. The middle of the night. Fluorescent light. The only light for miles. Bells on a door ring as Bea enters.

BEA: Hello? Are you open? Is anyone here? Hello?

The Woman appears drying her hands.

WOMAN: You're just in time.

BEA: It's you. I was looking for you.

WOMAN: And here I am. Magic. Sit.

Bea sits at the counter.

BEA: I never knew this place existed. I never saw it before. It's like it just materialized out of thin air.

WOMAN: Why, it's always been right here, right in front of your nose. Silly girl. You'd lose your head if it weren't attached to your neck. So forgetful. Lucky for you, I'm here to take care of you, make sure you eat, make sure you take care of that precious little life growing inside of you. Look I have a treat for you. I made you a very special delicacy from my homeland.

> *The Woman retrieves a plate on which sits the big, silvery fish that she was gutting. It's cooked.*

WOMAN: Eat up. Eat eat eat.

BEA: Oh that's so nice of you, but you know, I'm not very hungry.

WOMAN: Not hungry?

BEA: Not so much.

WOMAN: But you have to eat.

BEA: I really don't feel like it.

WOMAN: You eat it or else—or else you get weak. You're eating for two now after all.

BEA: You are so sweet. You've taken such good care of me these last few months. I don't know what I would've done without you. How will I ever be able to repay you?

WOMAN: Oh we'll figure something out.

> *Bea delicately cuts off a little piece of fish. She plays with the fish. She pushes the fish around the plate. The Woman grows more agitated.*

BEA: You know, my mom came to see me today.

WOMAN: Oh yes?

BEA: How is it you two know each other? I don't think you ever said.

WOMAN: It's a long story.

BEA: You know the strangest thing: she asked me your name and I couldn't for the life of me remember. Isn't that strange? I guess I've just been thinking a lot about names these days. It's so hard. I mean, how do you choose a name? Of all the names in the universe, how do you pick the right one? I mean, there are some really weird names out there. I mean like names you wouldn't guess in a hundred million years. How do you make sure you pick the right one?

Bells on a door ring. Not Chad enters with his axe. He sits next to Bea at the counter.

NOT CHAD: Hey. Hi. (*To the Woman.*) Can I get a menu?

The Woman retrieves a menu.

NOT CHAD: Can I get a glass of water?

The Woman exits.

NOT CHAD: You were supposed to stay put.

BEA: What was I supposed to do? Just hang out in the woods waiting for you?

NOT CHAD: Yes.

BEA: Well I wasn't going to do that.

NOT CHAD: OK we gotta go. We gotta get outta here.

BEA: What are you talking about?

NOT CHAD: I don't have time to explain.

BEA: Look, I'm in the middle of something kind of important here.

NOT CHAD: Just do what I say. Just trust me. You gotta trust me.

BEA: I did trust you, Chad, and look where it got me—

NOT CHAD: I AM NOT CHAD.

The WOMAN enters with a glass of water and sets it down.

NOT CHAD: No ice. Thanks.

The Woman exits with the glass of water.

NOT CHAD: OK let's go.

BEA: No, wait wait. You need to tell me what happens.

NOT CHAD: What are you talking about?

BEA: In the story, what happens? What happens next?

NOT CHAD: We don't have time for that.

BEA: Just give me a recap really quick. I need to remember how it goes.

NOT CHAD: OK all right. So once upon a time there was a princess and she needed to spin this straw into gold only she didn't know how when suddenly from out of nowhere this stranger appears and says I'll show you how to spin straw into gold but in return you gotta give me your firstborn child and the princess says sure and so the stranger spins the straw into gold and the princess lives happily ever after until one day she gets pregnant and the stranger shows up out of the blue and says time to pay up and she begs and she pleads till finally the stranger says guess my name and you can keep your baby and so the princess tries to guess but she can't so she sends this woodsman into the woods to follow the stranger and so the woodsman follows the stranger deep into the woods where he sees him dancing naked around a fire and singing this song which turns out to be—

> *The Woman reenters with the glass of water and sets it down.*
> *She doesn't go anywhere.*

NOT CHAD: You know, I haven't had a chance to look at the menu yet. I'm gonna need a few more minutes.

> *The Woman doesn't move.*

BEA: He just needs a few more minutes.

> *The Woman exits.*

NOT CHAD: Oh my god oh my god oh my god. We have to get outta here now.

BEA: But I have to figure out what it means. What does it mean?

NOT CHAD: What does what mean?

BEA: The story.

NOT CHAD: Right. The story. Can we just get outta here and then we can talk about it all you want, we can talk about it till the cows come home.

BEA: But she's part of it and it means something. It's a riddle. It's a kind of riddle. Something happened, something happened a long time ago. There was a woman and a stranger, and something happened between them, and there was a baby, a little girl, a little baby girl—OK, all right, so you've gone into the woods.

NOT CHAD: Yes.

BEA: And you come upon a clearing and you see this creature—

NOT CHAD: Dancing naked and singing around a fire—

BEA: And you figure out the creature's name—

NOT CHAD: I do and I run back to the castle as fast as I can, and I find you and I say: "Have no fear, my lady, for I know his name and I will tell it to you forthwith."

BEA: And I say—

NOT CHAD: And you say: "What is it, kind woodsman? Do not delay. Pray tell me quick." And I say, I say…what do I say?

BEA: Think.

NOT CHAD: "His name, my lady, his name…his name…his name is…ugh, I'm drawing a blank.

BEA: Think!

NOT CHAD: I am!

BEA: You have to remember!

NOT CHAD: I'm trying!

BEA: Try harder!

NOT CHAD: Stop shouting at me! You're stressing me out!

BEA: Look, this is the part where I need you. I need you to do your part. You're the woodsman.

NOT CHAD: I know. I'm doing the best I can.

BEA: Well it's not good enough.

NOT CHAD: Why are you so critical of me?

BEA: You're supposed to help me. That's the role as written.

NOT CHAD: That's what I'm trying to do.

BEA: Yeah? Well, you're failing miserably.

NOT CHAD: Well I'm sorry I'm such a failure.

BEA: Look, this is it, this is your big moment and you're blowing it because you don't have a clue! You're completely useless! It's like you're like this bit player who's got like one line to say and you can't even get that right! God, why do I have to play this scene with you?!

NOT CHAD: You know what, you don't. I quit.

> *Not Chad exits.*

BEA: Fine. Go! I don't care! Go! I don't care if I ever see you again! I'll just do the scene by myself!

> *Bea has a contraction. She exits. The Woman watches her go. And then vanishes.*

SCENE 17

> *The woods. The sound of creatures in the darkness. Susan is making her way through the trees.*

SUSAN: Bea? Bea, is that you? Bea?

> *Martin appears. He's wearing an old army uniform.*

SUSAN: Martin? What are you doing here? You know what? Never mind. I don't even want to know. Have you seen Bea? I'm looking for Bea.

MARTIN: I haven't seen her, Sue. I'm sorry.

SUSAN: You should be sorry. I asked you to do one thing, one thing. I should know better by now. I don't even know what I was thinking trusting you with anything. I don't know what I was thinking. I can't count on you for anything. (*Beat.*) What are you wearing? Is that Dad's old uniform? What are you doing with Dad's old uniform?

MARTIN: I found it.

SUSAN: What are you talking about? Where?

MARTIN: In the lake.

SUSAN: Oh Martin—

MARTIN: Sue, listen. Please. For once, just listen. I almost drowned just now and that's the truth. I was walking out on the ice and it cracked, and I fell through, and I fell and I fell, I just kept falling, and it was so dark and cold, it was so cold, and my lungs were aching and my ears were ringing, and the sound in my head was so loud, it was so loud, and I was scared, I was so scared. And then I saw him, Sue, I saw him. He was standing there watching me. And he looked just like he did in all the photographs. And he had something in his hands and I asked him what it was, and he held it up, and it was his old uniform. And I asked him if I could have it. And he came over to me and he set it down in my arms, and it was so heavy I could barely hold it. And I asked him if he was OK. I asked him if he was ever gonna come back. But he didn't say a word. He just walked away, and I tried to call out to him. I tried to tell him to wait for me, but I couldn't get the words out of my mouth. And then he was gone.

SUSAN: Martin—

MARTIN: I know you don't believe me, Sue. You never believe me.

SUSAN: Because you make up these ridiculous stories.

MARTIN: I'm not making this up—

SUSAN: And you believe them. You can't tell the difference between real life and make-believe. This isn't some fairytale, Martin. Our lives are not some fairytale. There are no happy endings. What you see around you, that's all there is. You need to wake up. You need to take a good hard look at yourself. You're a mess. Your life is a mess. Nothing you do turns out right. It's like there's something inside you that's broken. And no matter how hard you try, you can't fix it, you can't. (*Beat.*) What are you doing here, Martin?

MARTIN: I came home, Sue. It looks like you did, too.

SUSAN: This isn't my home.

MARTIN: ·Yeah it is. You were born here. You grew up here.

SUSAN: And I left as soon as I could. I hate it here.

MARTIN: See now, I don't get that. You got the forest and the lake and all the cornfields stretching as far as you can see. And in the winter, it's like the whole world is covered in snow and it's so quiet. And some days, it's like the sun makes everything sparkle, like the world is made of diamonds and it's so beautiful. And you look up at the sky, and it's so blue. You think: how can the sky be so, so blue. (*Beat.*) What? What is it?

SUSAN: You sounded just like him just now is all. That's like something dad would say. Well, you wouldn't remember. How could you? You were too young.

MARTIN: I remember. I remember all kinds of things. I remember me and dad, how we used to go fishing. I remember how we'd go out on the lake. I remember we caught so many fish, so many we couldn't even count them all.

SUSAN: You never went fishing with dad, Martin.

MARTIN: Yeah, I did. I remember it. I remember it like it was yesterday.

SUSAN: No, Martin, no. You remember the stories I told you of when I used to go fishing with dad. You've got to stop this. You've got to stop this right now. You almost drowned pretending you were going fishing with dad.

MARTIN: That's how you see it.

SUSAN: No, Martin, that's not "how I see it." That's the truth. The truth is dad died in a jungle on the other side of the world when you were barely old enough to walk. The truth is he didn't teach you to fish because he never had a chance to teach you, because by the time you were old enough to learn, he was gone.

MARTIN: Why do you do that, Sue? You always act like you know everything, like you have all the answers, but you don't.

SUSAN: Martin, I know you've been through a lot.

MARTIN: You don't know the half of what I've been through.

SUSAN: It's hard. I know that. It's hard thinking about dad, how he died so far away from home, no one to bury him, no one to visit his grave.

MARTIN: I don't think he died, Sue.

SUSAN: Oh, Martin—

MARTIN: Don't tell me you never thought the same thing. When we were kids, I used to have this feeling like he was still alive. Like I'd look up one day and he'd be there, just standing there watching me. Don't tell me you never had that feeling.

SUSAN: No, I never did.

MARTIN: See now, I don't believe that. 21 years old, saved up all your money you ever made and where did you go? Most people, they save up to go to Paris, Rome, but you, you go to Vietnam. Of all the places in the world, why Vietnam?

SUSAN: I don't know. I don't know why.

MARTIN: Yeah you do. You were hoping to find him. You were hoping maybe you'd catch a glimpse of him in some little village somewhere. Or maybe you'd see some little kid coming out of a shack, some little Asian kid who kinda looked like you.

> *Light on Bea in her cabin. She touches her belly. Bea sings the song that Linh has sung throughout the play.*

SUSAN: What have I done? Oh Martin, what have I done?

MARTIN: It's OK, Sue.

SUSAN: No, Martin, it's not, it's not OK.

MARTIN: Don't cry, Sue. Please don't cry.

SUSAN: Oh, Martin, I don't know what to do. There's nothing I can do.

MARTIN: I wish I could make it better.

SUSAN: I know. I know you do.

MARTIN: Sue, listen to me. I'd give everything I have to make it better, everything I have I'd give it to you. If I had one wish left in the world, I'd give it to you.

SUSAN: Why would you do that for me, Martin? After everything, why would you?

MARTIN: You're my family, Sue. You're all I got.

> *Linh appears.*

MARTIN: Linh? (*Beat.*) Oh my God. It's real, isn't it? Any wish and you'll make it come true.

> *Linh nods.*

MARTIN: Make a wish, Sue.

SUSAN: I don't understand.

MARTIN: Just make a wish.

SUSAN: Martin—

MARTIN: Please trust me, Sue. Trust me.

SUSAN: Her name. I want to know her name. Please. Tell me her name.

LINH: It is not a name you read or write. It is not a name you say.

SUSAN: What does that mean? If it's not a name you read or write, and it's not a name you say, what kind of name is it?

> *Susan hears the song Bea is singing.*

SUSAN: Oh my God. Oh my God, of course. But I can't remember, I can't remember how it goes. How does it go?

> *The Woman appears. Bea sees her. Bea stops singing.*

WOMAN: You called for me. You called my name.

BEA: I want to know how the story ends. How does it end?

SCENE 18

A cabin in the woods. The Woman tells Bea a story.

WOMAN: Once upon a time, there was a girl who lived in a land far away. And in her land there was a terrible war, and fire rained down from the sky and the earth trembled and shook. And one day when the world was quiet, the girl went into the woods by the village where she lived, and in a clearing she saw a creature, and he was wounded and he was scared. And she took him back to her village, and when night fell, they lay side by side on a straw mat, and fell asleep. And when the girl awoke the next morning, she saw that the creature was like none she had ever seen before. His hair was the color of sunlight. And his eyes were the color of the ocean. And she saw he was crying. "Why are you crying," she asked. And the creature said, "Because my heart is breaking." And the girl asked, "Why is your heart breaking?" And he said, "because I am a demon and I have done terrible things." And the girl took pity on the creature. And she held him close and she said—

BEA: *Me yeu con. Me yeu con.*

WOMAN: Yes.

BEA: I love you. It means I love you.

WOMAN: Yes.

BEA: How do I know that? I don't know how I know that. It's like something I remember from a dream I had, like a story someone told me a long time ago.

WOMAN: They lived together for many years as man and wife until finally the creature passed away. And later, many years later, the girl who was no longer a girl came upon his watch. She knew it was his the instant she saw it. And she wanted it more than anything, for it was all that was left of him. That and their child, a beautiful baby girl, more precious than anything in the world, because she was the last piece of him she could hold in her arms. And then that *woman* comes, that thief, and takes the baby away, steals her like you steal a loaf of bread. Do you know how it felt to come back and see you were gone, do you have any idea?

BEA: I need to go. I need to go now.

WOMAN: Go? Where will you go?

BEA: I don't know. I don't know where. I just have to go. I can't stay, I can't stay here.

WOMAN: Of course you can. You can stay here with me.

BEA: No. No, I can't.

WOMAN: Don't you want to know how it ends?

> *The Woman reaches out to Bea.*

BEA: Don't. Please don't.

WOMAN: Can't you see? I have waited a lifetime for this moment. My child, my beautiful little girl.

BEA: I'm not your little girl.

WOMAN: What are you saying?

BEA: Don't touch me. Don't you touch me.

WOMAN: What are you saying? What are you saying to me?

> *Light on Susan. She begins to sing a song. It is the same song that Linh sang. The Woman hears it. She begins to back away from Bea.*

WOMAN: How could she? How could she have guessed?

> *The Woman transforms into a creature. Howling and growling, the gnashing of teeth. The woman tears herself apart. And then she vanishes. Susan and Bea remain.*

BEA: I remember now. I remember everything. I remember my mother was out in the rice fields. I remember I was alone in our hut and it was morning, and you came in and you picked me up and you took me away.

> *Susan approaches Bea.*

SUSAN: I love you so much, Bea. I loved you from the moment I saw you, more than I ever thought I could love another person. You are the most precious thing in my life.

Susan reaches out to Bea. Bea pulls away.

BEA: Why did you do it?

SUSAN: Bea—

BEA: Why did you do what you did?

SUSAN: Bea, please try to understand. You were all that was left. It was like seeing a ghost. Only you weren't a ghost. You were this beautiful little girl, so innocent, so alive.

BEA: What are you saying?

SUSAN: I took one look at you and I knew. I knew.

BEA: Knew what? Tell me.

SUSAN: That you were my father's child.

> *Bea vanishes. Blackout. The world spins. It keeps spinning. An airplane takes off.*

SCENE 19

> *The diner. A year later. Springtime. Martin is clean shaven, sober. On the stove top, a pot of soup simmers. He adds spices to taste. Susan is lost in thought.*

MARTIN: Sue?

SUSAN: I'm sorry.

MARTIN: I lost you for a second there. You were somewhere else. Where did you go?

SUSAN: I don't know. I was just...I don't know.

MARTIN: Here. Wait. Hold on. The soup's almost done. (*Holding a spoonful of soup.*) Taste.

> *Susan tastes the soup.*

MARTIN: Well?

SUSAN: It's good.

MARTIN: See. I told you I could cook. You didn't believe me, but it's true. I know how to cook. (*Beat.*) Can you believe it? A whole year and it's gone by like that. Wink of an eye. How does that happen?

SUSAN: I don't know.

MARTIN: It's going to be great, Sue, I'm telling you. This place is gonna be great. We're gonna cook and people are gonna eat our food, and it's gonna be great. We're like partners, Sue. We got a restaurant. We got a restaurant in our hometown. You and me, sis. Can you believe it? Man, life's strange. Like how we ended up back here after everything. I mean for me, well I could've ended up anywhere, but you, you had this big fancy restaurant, you had this whole other life and you just walked away.

SUSAN: I was ready for a change. A little home-style cooking, a little comfort food.

MARTIN: I get that. It's good to be home, huh.

SUSAN: Yeah. Yeah, it is.

MARTIN: (*Beat.*) So, uh, have you heard from Bea?

SUSAN: Not yet. I'm sure she'll write or call when she gets to where she's going.

MARTIN: Sure she will. It's just something she needs to do. She just needs to see for herself, Sue, she needs to go and figure it out for herself. She'll be back.

SUSAN: I hope so.

MARTIN: Hey listen, Sue, I was thinking…nah, never mind.

SUSAN: What, Martin? What is it?

MARTIN: I was just thinking I might take off, go fishing, but you know what, it's OK, I don't need to go. There's stuff to do. I mean there's all kinds of stuff to do.

SUSAN: No, Martin, it's OK. Go.

MARTIN: Yeah?

SUSAN: Yeah. Go. I mean it, go.

MARTIN: You are the best, Sue. You watch: I'm gonna catch us some dinner and then I'm gonna cook it up and it's gonna be delicious. I'll be back, OK? I'll be back in no time.

> *Martin kisses Susan, grabs his fishing pole and his tackle box, and exits. Susan stirs the soup. She tastes it. Bells on a door ring. Linh enters. Susan sees him.*

LINH: I wanted to say good-bye. Here. This is for you.

> *Linh holds out the watch. Susan takes it.*

SUSAN: It was in a little box wrapped in brown paper. I remember that. And it had all these stamps from—well, from Vietnam I guess. And I opened it and it was his watch. And later my mom came home from work and she said: well, I guess that's all that's left of your dad. Just a cheap old Timex. And I never thought about who sent it to us. I never gave it a second thought. Not till now. You were there that day, weren't you? And you didn't stop me. Why didn't you?

LINH: He was a good man, your father. He lived in our village for many years. I promised I would take care of his family after he was gone. That was my promise to him. Please tell your brother we will go fishing again. We will do that someday. Please tell him that.

> *The sound of an airplane taking off. The world spins. It keeps spinning. Susan recedes from view.*

SCENE 20

> *An airport in southeast Asia. The hum of arrivals and departures being announced. Bea holds a baby in a sling. She checks on the baby. Chad enters.*

CHAD: Our luggage should be here any minute now. Is she still sleeping? I can't believe she's still sleeping. She slept through the whole flight.

That's incredible. We're maybe the luckiest parents in the universe. (*Looking at the baby.*) Look at her. She's so beautiful, Bea. Who do you think she looks like? Not me, I don't think. And I don't think she looks like you. Maybe she looks like some long lost relative we don't know. Maybe someone we'll meet while we're over here. Or not, and that's OK, too. Remember, Bea, no matter what happens, you're discovering your roots and that's a good thing. Bea? Did you hear any of what I just said?

BEA: I'm sorry, Chad. I'm just, I'm a little out of it, I guess.

CHAD: Of course you are. We just flew halfway around the world. We're in like Saigon or no, not Saigon. Ho Chi Minh City. That's what it's called now. Ho Chi Minh City. Look, I know things have been a little rough these past few months. I know I was kind of absent and just not there for you, and I'm really sorry. I haven't really been myself. I think the whole parenthood thing, it's just been a lot of change, but it's like the counselor says, we just have a lot of stressors in our life right now, and that's what parenthood does, it just brings up a lot of stuff, you know, stuff about our own parents, how we were raised, what it means to be a good father, a good mother, family stuff, you know, all this subconscious family stuff you don't even think about, I mean I know I didn't think about, but I really think it's going to be OK.

> *An announcement can be heard over the PA system. The message is garbled, impossible to discern.*

CHAD: Wait a second, wait a second. Did you hear that? I'm going to go check on our bags. You stay here. Don't go anywhere.

> *Chad kisses Bea and exits. Linh appears. He begins to sing his song from the beginning of the play. As he does, the airport fades away. Bea looks up and sees him. He approaches her. He stops singing. He holds out the book from the beginning of the play. Bea takes it. She opens the book.*

SCENE 21

Bea reads from the book. As Bea reads, the Woman and Susan appear.

BEA: Once upon a time there was a woman.
And she was alone.
And she was very far from home.
She had traveled halfway across the world
looking for something.
Something she had lost.
Or something she had never had—

> *Bea looks at the Woman and Susan. A babel of English and
> Vietnamese spills outwards from the pages of the book, the sounds of
> small town America, the sounds of the jungle, the sounds of war, the
> sounds of babies being born. The roar
> of an airplane as it splits the sky in two.*

END OF PLAY

NOTES ON LAS MENIÑAS
by Lynn Nottage

A Yoruba proverb states "The white man who made the pencil also made the eraser."

Las Meniñas began as a mission to rescue an African princess from a French convent where she was locked away for nearly three hundred years. The adventure began in the Sterling Library on the campus of Yale University with a book examining the African presence in early Europe. I found myself rereading one particular paragraph that detailed an extraordinary episode in the French court of Louis XIV, the Sun King. It described the romance between Queen Marie-Thérèse (wife of Louis XIV) and her African servant, Nabo, a dwarf from Dahomey. He was a gift to her from Admiral Francois de Vendome, duc de Beaufort, from the King of Dahomey. The book went on to briefly talk about Louise-Marie, a Moorish nun who spent her life sequestered in the Benedictine convent of Moret-sur-Loing by royal decree. It was speculated that the Moorish nun was the fruit of the Queen's illicit romance with the African dwarf. The birth and death of the Moorish nun in 1732 became one of the great mysteries of the era, perplexing French historians.

I began to do my own research into the life of Louise-Marie, "the black nun of Moret." What I discovered excited, intrigued, amused, and frustrated me. It reinforced what I already knew to be true. Louise-Marie was twice a victim, once of circumstance and secondly of the callousness of history. She was omitted from the historic record, and conveniently erased by those perhaps frightened by the implications of the truth.

A remarkable painting by of Queen Marie-Thérèse and Nabo exists. The Queen is dressed in stately clothing and seated by Nabo, who kneels subserviently beside her. Upon closer examination the two appear to be exchanging flowers. There is something about the Queen's posture that demands a deeper reading. Her eyes appear to gaze downward and sideways at Nabo and he looks up at her with adoration. I believe the painting was their unspoken way of going on record, of not permitting their taboo relationship to be completely erased. With *Las Meniñas* I have decided to rescue Louise-Marie, Queen Marie-Thérèse, and Nabo from obscurity, to refocus the spotlight on the complicated role that race and gender played in the French royal court.

The playful and irreverent tone of the play reflects the great fun that I had researching it. I will go on record as saying that I believe the romance between Queen Marie-Thérèse and Nabo did occur. I recognize the absurdity of the events, and understand how they might be viewed with incredulity and skepticism. We assume that history is fixed, but it is constantly being be reshaped by new voices, like mine, joining the conversation. And, I must confess that I have an agenda, not unlike most historians; it is to explore and recapture history using my own unique lens. Historians often obfuscate, consciously or unconsciously, that which does not reinforce the prevailing notions of the day, allowing the perspectives of those in power to become fact, record, history. As a result, women and people of color are relegated to the margins of history. My pen has enjoyed challenging convention, turning upside down our widely held beliefs about the period and demanding that our presence be acknowledged. *Las Meniñas* is my attempt to shed light on events that took place in the court of Louis XIV, and rescue a forgotten piece of history.

— **Lynn Nottage**

BIOGRAPHY

Lynn Nottage's plays include *By The Way, Meet Vera Stark* (Lily Award); *Ruined* (Pulitzer Prize, OBIE, Lucille Lortel, New York Drama Critics' Circle, Drama Desk, and Outer Critics Circle Award); *Intimate Apparel* (New York Drama Critics' Circle Award, Steinberg Award); *Fabulation, or The Re-Education of Undine* (OBIE Award); *Crumbs from the Table of Joy; Las Meniñas; Mud, River, Stone; Por'knockers;* and *POOF!*

Nottage is the recipient of the 2010 Steinberg Distinguished Playwright Award, the Dramatists Guild Hull-Warriner Award, the inaugural Horton Foote Prize for Outstanding New American Play (*Ruined*), the Lee Reynolds Award, and the Jewish World Watch iWitness Award. Her other honors include a 2007 MacArthur Foundation Fellowship, the National Black Theatre Festival's August Wilson Playwriting Award, the 2005 Guggenheim Grant for Playwriting, the 2004 PEN/Laura Pels Award for Drama, as well as fellowships from the Lucille Lortel Foundation, Manhattan Theatre Club, New Dramatists, and New York Foundation for the Arts. She is a graduate of Brown University and the Yale School of Drama, where she is currently a visiting lecturer.

ACKNOWLEDGMENTS

Las Meniñas premiered at San Jose Repertory (Timothy Near, Artistic Director; Alexander Urbanowski, Managing Director) in San Jose, California on March 23, 2002. The director was Michael Donald Edwards. The set design was by Gordon Svilar, costume design by B. Modern, lighting design by Robert Jared, choreography by Carolyn Houser Caravajal and Marcus Cathey, and sound design by Jeff Mockus.

Las Meniñas was developed in Genesis 2000 at Crossroads Theatre Company. It received a developmental workshop at the 2000 Hedgebrook Women Playwrights Festival, co-produced by Hedgebrook and ACT Theatre.

LAS MENIÑAS
by Lynn Nottage

CHARACTERS

LOUISE MARIE-THERÈSE

QUEEN MARIE-THERÈSE

KING LOUIS XIV

NABO SENSUGALI

QUEEN MOTHER / MOTHER SUPERIOR

PAINTER / DOCTOR

LA VALLIÈRE / LADY SERVANT

COURTIERS

TIME

1695, looking back on 1664.

PLACE

France.

NOTE: The Courtiers serve as servants, attendants, candle bearers, and guards as well as the movers of the set.

ACT ONE, SCENE 1

Louise Marie-Therèse, a light-complexioned black woman, kneels on the floor of her cell in the convent Moret. She wears the austere clothing of a novice and a highly ornate gold cross around her neck. It is a sharp contrast to her unassuming attire.

The Mother Superior, a striking older woman, pours a pitcher of steaming water into an old bath tub.

MOTHER SUPERIOR: It is almost time, child. Are you prepared?

LOUISE: Already, Mother? May I have final words with my sisters?

MOTHER SUPERIOR: You don't have much time. Your bath is ready. I will call on you shortly.

The Mother Superior tests the bath water and exits. Louise listens for a moment, then slowly rises.

LOUISE: (*Nervously, to audience.*) Shhh! Close the door!

Louise looks around suspiciously.

Shhh! I'm not demented as the Mother Superior might have you believe, and no you won't go blind if you listen…Now quiet, sweet sisters, and I will tell you again.

Louise smiles gloriously.

This is the true story of the seduction of Marie-Therèse…the Queen of France.

The lights rise on Queen Marie-Therèse, a plump blond, dressed in the exquisite clothing popular in the French court during the 1660s. She sits in an ornate chair sipping a glass of wine.

Next to the Queen sits King Louis XIV, a lovely young man more elegantly clad and adorned than his wife. He covers his mouth with a handkerchief to keep down a belch. It erupts.

They pose for a portrait, which is being painted by an expressionless artist.

Members of the court adoringly watch their King and Queen.

LOUISE: It started with a box.

Lights rise on an ornate box, neither too big nor too small.

A gift from the Queen's cousin Monsieur De Beaufort, to take the Queen's mind off of her husband's improprieties, which had yielded several healthy children who wandered the court freely like plumped wild pheasants.

The Queen curls her upper lip and sips her wine.

Yes, it started with a box. The day after the King belched up a most prodigious worm, a foot in length, following his afternoon ride. The Queen took the worm as a powerful sign and readily accepted the gift.

The Queen speaks with a rough Spanish accent.

QUEEN: You see now! Mi primo give me a gift. Look at the size of the box...Louis, it could be treasure, gold, from the New World...He been there you know, my father sent he. How could I not accept it?

The King flirts with a pretty courtesan.

KING: I'm sorry, did you say something, Marie? Speak French, for God's sake I do not know what you are saying.

He belches.

QUEEN: I'M TALKING OF DE BOX DAT ARRIVED FOR ME DIS MORNING!

KING: Not louder Marie, in French. Please, my ears are dying!

LOUISE: The scandal, oh the scandal that was to follow this Queen, the princess of Spain.

Lights fade on Louise-Marie. The Queen traipses over to the box, and examines it for a moment. The painter throws his arms up in frustration.

QUEEN: A gift! What is the best gift that you ever received? Did it come in a box dis size or bigger?

The King shrugs, disinterested.

QUEEN: Do you remember whether that gift was given to you by someone you love, or someone you did not know?

She places her ear to the box and giggles.

Mercy, supposing it is so splendiferous that I cannot repay it. Oh dear! Now I'm afraid to open it.

The Queen smells the box, she knocks on the box.

KING: Oh for God's sake, please open it.

The Queen finally opens the box. A very short African man raises his head over the edge, gasping for air. Horrified, he peers at the powdered members of the court. He is a "little person," petit. The Queen claps her hands with unbridled pleasure.

QUEEN: Ay Dios mio. Es un African. A little one at that. Look Louis, es fantastic.

The King, disinterested, can't be bothered to look away from Madame de la Vallière.

QUEEN: Isn't he lovely? No?

KING: If you like. Now come sit, my dear, so we can finish—

QUEEN: —I like very much…

She claps her hands again.

Oh goodness, I wonder what he does. Should I say something to him?

KING: If you like.

The Queen isn't sure what to say. She looks to members of the court for guidance. Madame de La Vallière, the king's lovely, haughty mistress speaks.

LA VALLIÈRE: Perhaps the little moor will give us a song, Your Majesty.

QUEEN: Ah yes! Bueno…Sing for me!

Nabo, the African dwarf, does not respond. He stares incredulously at the Queen.

Well?…Sing, little man!

Nabo still does not respond.

QUEEN: SING! COMPRENDE?

NABO: (*Timidly.*) I can't!

QUEEN: Oh?

A moment.

Give us a dance then!

NABO: I don't.

The Queen, mortified, searches her mind for another prospect.

QUEEN: …Then what is it dat you perform?

NABO: What can one perform after being in a box for three days? I was promised six goats and some beads, and I closed my eyes and I had crossed the ocean. And now I'm scented, powdered and stuffed in a box. If I perform, it's functions of the body, and that Your Majesty is private. Each place I go, they expect me to perform. What? I do not know. And they pack me back in a box and send me on. I've traveled halfway across the world in this box. And I'm tired, tired, tired…of it!

KING: Oh?

The King sits erect, quite surprised by Nabo's frankness.

QUEEN: He's tired, Louis! Delightful!

The Queen again approaches the box with a balance of caution and curiosity.

Are you hun-gry?

NABO: Yes, yes.

The Queen's eyes grow large with enthusiasm.

QUEEN: Is it true?

NABO: (*Apprehensively.*) What?

QUEEN: What they say, of course…is it true dat human flesh tastes like wild boar?

NABO: I wouldn't know.

QUEEN: Sweet mother, you've probably never had wild boar.

> *Claps her hands.*

Den you will have.

NABO: I won't have to eat human flesh as well? What kind of barbarous place is this?

> *The Queen roars with delight. The court joins in her laughter.*

QUEEN: Did you hear dat, Louis? Barbarous! What a wonderful fool I have.

> *The King rolls his eyes.*

KING: Lovely gift my dear, but be careful…remember what happened to the last one.

> *He winks at La Vallière.*

KING: I'm bored. I'm tired of sitting, I feel like a ride or fête or something.

> *He yawns, stands, and gazes at Nabo in the box, then prepares to leave.*

QUEEN: Where are you going?

KING: Pardon me, I have pressing affairs of state to attend to.

> *The King takes La Vallière's hand. The entire court stirs.*

QUEEN: But, Louis—

KING: Shhh!

QUEEN: But—

KING: Smile.

> *The Queen smiles to reveal a mouthful of rotten teeth.*

There, now that's where your charm lies. You needn't strain yourself with anything else.

The King exits, followed by La Vallière and his entourage.
The Queen's ladies remain at a distance.

QUEEN: That es your King, not nearly as impressive as his portrait.

She nods to the patient painter.

My compliments!

The painter nods.

Louis, his work es of a nefarious nature, wrapped in lace and velvet... and extremely productive...But what of me? Left to have my portrait painted alone. (*To Nabo.*) You, sit with me.

NABO: I can't!

QUEEN: WHY?

NABO: I can't get out of this box.

QUEEN: Oh? I'll call someone to help...Naturally I can't really be...

The Queen signals to her ladies, they're useless. Nabo frantically waves his arms, desperate to be free.

QUEEN: Sweet Mother, I'll...

Finally, the Queen struggles to lift Nabo out of his box. After considerable effort she manages to free him. They tumble head over heels. The Queen's ladies quickly straighten her clothing. Nabo, dressed as a French nobleman, bows.

Please, no need for that. I'm bored by formalities. Save it for Louis. If you can't relax with a fool, who can you relax with?

NABO: You call me fool, but it isn't my name.

QUEEN: Well? I will give you a name then.

NABO: I have one!

QUEEN: You do?

NABO: Nabo Sensugali.

> *He bows again.*

QUEEN: I don't like it! I can't say it! Jorgito or Pedro, you like Pedro?

NABO: No!

QUEEN: You're indignant for a man that came in a box. I could put you back in dere and ship you home.

NABO: Indeed? I welcome such punishment, for this liberal tongue deserves no mercy. Send me home!

> *A moment. The Queen roars with delight.*

QUEEN: Pedro…You don't mean dat of course! You're teasing me! Besides, you do what I say…Pedro!

NABO: Nabo!

QUEEN: (*Whispered.*) Pedro…

NABO: Nabo!

QUEEN: (*Furiously.*) DON'T TAKE AN IMPERIOUS TONE WITH ME! (*Whispered.*) Pedro…Please? Por favor?

> *She smiles.*

You're no fun, are you? You know I can force you! But dat would poison our friendship and dat's not any way to begin.

> *She grins.*

Come here…Come and sit by me…

> *Nabo begins to kneel by her side.*

…in de king's chair.

NABO: If I must.

QUEEN: (*Growls.*) YOU MUST!

> *The Queen strikes an elegant pose for the painter. Nabo tired, reluctant, takes a seat next to the Queen.*
>
> *Lights rise on Louise.*

LOUISE: And there it began in the king's chair with a painter re-shaping her likeness, molding that haphazard smile into an enigmatic smirk. With the image of Nabo lightly drawn in, uncommitted …a mercurial impression barely perceivable.

The Queen smiles at Nabo. Lights fade on the Painter and Nabo.

LOUISE: And so, sisters, sat the Queen many years later, sipping wine, trying, as she did, to remember beyond her illness. And I, a child in the company of a queen, charity's ward.

The Queen, now worn and tired, turns to Louise Marie.
She coughs uncontrollably, then regains her strength.

The Queen lets a few drops of wine from her glass fall to the floor.

QUEEN: (*Whispered, barely audible.*) Dios de Salve, Nabo.

LOUISE: What was that you said?

QUEEN: Did I say something? Oh sweetness, forgive me I can't remember now…Oh yes, shall we have more wine?

Louise pours wine for the Queen. The Queen gets lost in a memory.

So many lavish rooms and faces and words I couldn't understand. It wasn't my home until I could invite someone else in. Comprende? And I laughed and laughed and—

LOUISE: And laughed?

QUEEN: Yes, how did you know?

The Queen begins to laugh loud and robustly, but is suddenly overcome by a wave of melancholy.

What was I saying? Oh yes. You really should see our gardens? I've been told they're the most beautiful in de world.

LOUISE: And the King, is he as handsome as they say?

QUEEN: Yes, to many.

LOUISE: Are there truly celebrations that have no end?

QUEEN: They always end, my child, even in Versailles.

LOUISE: Indeed. I'd very much like to see Versailles, Your Majesty. I want to hear everything there is to know about your world, but these walls are my home. And dreams are a beggar's fortune, that's what the Mother Superior says. So why tell me these things?

QUEEN: I enjoy your innocent conversation. Having little wit, the court offers small comfort.

LOUISE: But Your Majesty, your gift of friendship is a small cruelty. I'd rather not be your confessor if I must listen to your tales with such eager resignation. Perhaps it would be better to torture some other novice with your beautiful stories. Why have you chosen me?

QUEEN: My dear child, everything happens according to a divine plan. And each time I ask why, I move a little further away from God.

LOUISE: You uphold ignorance as a virtue?

QUEEN: Shall we not ask questions of one another. Yes, I think it best. Don't you?

> *The Queen strokes Louise's face.*

You're so pretty. I was never pretty.

> *The Queen begins to cough. Mother Superior enters and places her hand on Louise's shoulder.*

MOTHER SUPERIOR: Look Louise, you've upset the Queen. Naughty girl. Say you're sorry.

LOUISE: I'm sorry.

QUEEN: Louise, I want you to know—

MOTHER SUPERIOR: You are not well, and it's so cold in here. Perhaps on another visit, Your Majesty.

> *The Queen coughs.*

LOUISE: (*To audience.*) And she left…never to return. Did I take wine with the Queen? You ask. Am I mad? You ask. Well, judge not dear sisters and allow me to speak on this eve of my wedding to the Lord, for these words shall never again pass my lips, and these truths have an audience.

The Queen's cough transforms into laughter.

The lights rise on the Painter and Nabo.

QUEEN: (*To Nabo.*) I think more wine is absolutely necessary…
Don't you?

She turns back to Nabo, smiling.

The Mother Superior and Louise retreat into the darkness.

NABO: If Your Majesty pleases.

*A servant pours wine for Nabo. He sips it and pours a quick libation
on the ground.*

QUEEN: What was that?

NABO: A libation for an ancestor I wish not to forget.

QUEEN: Oh? Libation? How silly to waste good wine on an ancestor.

*They share an awkward silence. Nabo and the Queen steal glances
at each other. The Queen touches Nabo's hair. He recoils.*

QUEEN: Bueno! Much different…May I?

She reaches out her hand like a child.

NABO: No!

QUEEN: Well. With my other fools I do as I please. Aren't you supposed
to entertain me?

NABO: How does one entertain Your Majesty?

QUEEN: HOW DARE YOU ASK ME A QUESTION!…(*Whispers.*)
I don't know.

NABO: Perhaps that is the problem!

QUEEN: Oh no! I can't bear de embarrassment of a fool without
wit. It's like a truffle without sugar or a day without gambling. It's a
wonder how—

NABO: In my country we tell stories, we have a tradition of sharing
tales to—

QUEEN: A story? (*Disappointed.*) No, no, no! You tumble delightfully! You sing some silly little song that rhymes! Like, like, well, anyway... a story? But surely you must be acquainted with one of our new dances—

NABO: No, not really your majesty. I am—

QUEEN: (*Exasperated.*) Not even the chaconne? But everyone knows it. Where are you from?...Give me your hand.

> The Queen stands. Nabo stands, she clumsily leads him through the steps of the chaconne, he is unable to follow.

QUEEN: No, no...or...Something short and rhythmic like de orientals.

> The Queen demonstrates; performing a clumsy approximation of an Asian dance. She loses herself in the dance. Nabo watches amused and bewildered.

> The painter merely looks away with embarrassment. As the Queen's frenzied dance ends Nabo and the attendants applaud. The Queen, momentarily flustered, curtsies. She smiles, emphatically, revealing her mouthful of rotten teeth.

QUEEN: Sweet mother, I've never done dat before. Was I good?

NABO: You had energy.

> The painter coughs.

QUEEN: Indeed...Not like Louis. He danced a ballet last night. De role of Apollo, my favorite. All the court was dere, even los niños. I haven't seen a showing like dat since I arrived in Paris drawn by a hundred grey horses.

> The King appears with two dancers.

Apollo in his full glory.

> The King dances a short ballet and exits with the two dancers.

It was beautiful. I haven't de grace or de delicacy. Que Lastima ... Now, tell me your—

NABO: Nabo.

QUEEN: I prefer Pedro.

NABO: It isn't—

QUEEN: Voila! I'm pleased you've come my little friend. I tire of my wicked Doña Molina, she forgets what good friends we were in Spain. I like having someone to spend time with me until I close my eyes and sleep, and when I awaken you'll be dere to help me with all the things dat I do during the day. Wouldn't dat make the ladies jealous.

The Queen savors the notion.

NABO: What is it that you do, Your Majesty?

QUEEN: I do whatever I like.

NABO: Which is?

QUEEN: Oh I see...I'm Queen of France, I don't know...I rule.

The Queen smiles fatuously.

NABO: Forgive me for asking, but why am I here?

A moment.

QUEEN: Why? Don't you like your wine?...Mi primo, my cousin gave you to me. He knows how much I love little...back in Spain we had a number of...but none of dem were...De court was always filled with laughter and little people.

NABO: I see. But as you may have observed I am at the end of my wits. I'm afraid I can't make myself or anyone laugh.

QUEEN: Over time you can acquire a sense of humor, I've seen it happen.

NABO: Dear me, does it mean I'm to stay here?

QUEEN: You're mine...aren't you?

NABO: No. He said that if I—

QUEEN: Oh yes, I'm sure of dat.

NABO: But that implies that at some point I relinquished my own will, which I have not. And therefore I belong to no one, unless that someone is me.

QUEEN: I'm confused.

NABO: You are.

QUEEN: No, I've changed my mind, it's you dat is confused. (*Without a pause.*) Painter, he came in a box addressed to me, you saw. I let him out, didn't I? But now he says he belongs to no one. But clearly he was given to me, which makes him mine, even if he didn't belong to mi primo. And my goodness if every man had a free will, then imagine the chaos that would be imparted. Dat's finished, let's move on to other things...What was your—

NABO: Na-bo!

QUEEN: Nabo. Dat's right. De name is growing on me. It floats very quickly off de tongue. Not like dese French names dat take so long to get out, dey ferment in your mouth and leave a bad taste. (*Protracted.*) La Vallière! Ha!

> *The Queen walks over to the canvas and studies the painting.*

That's not me! You've given me a healthier, more masculine look dan I appreciate.

> *She sucks in her cheeks.*

Thin me out, more color in the cheeks, and extend my chin. How come Louis gets color and I don't.

PAINTER: Your Majesty, I paint what I see.

QUEEN: No, you paint what I see!

> *She steps up to the canvas.*

How can you be so insensitive to my needs? Must your brush also favor the King's whore, La Vallière? What about me?

PAINTER: Your Majesty—

QUEEN: Enough! If we were in Spain I'd have you executed, but de French are so caught up in decorum. (*To Nabo.*) Don't you find that?

NABO: Yes, decorum…

The Queen corners Nabo.

QUEEN: I am beautiful Pedro, yes?

NABO: You're asking me?

QUEEN: Yes. I want to know whether you find me beautiful.

NABO: As Queen you define what beauty is and by that standard I imagine that, yes you are.

QUEEN: Really?

She shoots a vicious look at the painter.

Thank you, Pedro. You'll have a fine room, I'll see to dat, with a view of the garden. Do you like the garden? Should we look now? I love the garden. Can you smell it? I like the idea of the garden smelling aromatic all year round, don't you think? I've been finding the court to be particularly rank this season, a change in the sensibility, comprende?

The Queen walks up to Nabo and touches his hand.

De things we give up for peace in the land. I carry my duty out admirably, the pious Queen. On my knees half the day, praying… Do you know what I'm praying Nabo?

NABO: No.

QUEEN: Dat he'll contract syphilis from one of his whores and die and I'll rule…Now we have a secret between us and dat makes us friends. You give me one and it's sealed.

A moment.

Go on.

NABO: …When I said you were beautiful, I lied. I find you plain.

The Queen sits.

QUEEN: I don't find you beautiful either. True!

NABO: Beauty is not the only virtue in the world.

QUEEN: I'm so short on dem, I thought I should possess at least one.

Nabo walks over to the Queen and places his hand on hers.

QUEEN: Bittersweet words, you're de only one dare tell me the truth. And who are you?

NABO: Someone not unlike yourself.

QUEEN: Are you equating yourself with a queen?

NABO: No, with a sad woman a long way from home.

QUEEN: You have no shame!

NABO: You, Your Majesty, own it.

QUEEN: What a miserable fool you've become.

The Queen throws herself into the chair, covering her face with her hands, and pouts. Nabo takes her hand down from her face. She brightens up suddenly.

QUEEN: Yes? Not even a little beautiful?

NABO: A little.

QUEEN: Indeed. Beauty is overrated. Beauty? We'll have no more talk of this, I think not. Now won't you make me smile a tiny bit even? I demand that you do!…Please…Tell me one of your stories den…

Nabo enacts his tale. Lights rise on Louise.

LOUISE: And he began.

NABO: This is the story of a family, not a heroic tale, but a simple story of four souls bound by their love; a mother, a father and two sons.

LOUISE: And he wove a resonant tale of a small ancestral plot from which all the world could be seen, a vast mat of quivering trees. He carried her through the crevices and contours of the terrain, from the burial rites to the harvest, to the arrival of an intruder who claimed the eldest son as his own.

QUEEN: Oh no!

LOUISE: (*Savoring the telling.*) He marched her across the savannah, through the forest to the ocean. In the port city he took her through the streets, where the smell of singed flesh, frankincense and stewed goat overwhelmed the Queen, who gasped just once at the telling.

    The Queen gasps. Louise closes her eyes.

He told of the terrible struggle that ensued, and the son's attempts to flee, to find his way home. Then of the unpleasant trip to the place where—

NABO: —the sun was covered over and the damp air formed mold on the young man's clothing, and the wind blew cold.

LOUISE: A land where tufts of smoke came from people's mouths as they spoke—

NABO: Where he was treated like an animal…a goat on a string, led about—

QUEEN: Shame!

LOUISE: The young man's family waited for one day, then one month, and then one year. He never returned.

NABO: But it didn't stop him from dreaming of home—

QUEEN: STOP! It's too sad. Pedro. Imagine if something like that were true.

NABO: It is.

QUEEN: Wretched…I'll pray for dat young man.

NABO: Would you help that young man get back?

QUEEN: Yes, of course.

NABO: I am he.

QUEEN: You? But if I sent you back, I wouldn't have you. And I've grown very fond of you, my friend. We share a secret, dat bonds us.

    The Queen places her hand on Nabo's shoulder.

QUEEN: Don't you like me?

NABO: If I must.

QUEEN: …You must! We can be friends. Yes?

> *The Queen bends in front of Nabo. She goes through the motions of taking a string from around Nabo's neck and placing it around her own.*

QUEEN: …You've just begun to entertain me.

> *Nabo registers the horror.*

LOUISE: This Queen who only the night before damned God for her creation.

SCENE 2

> *The ladies in waiting prepare the Queen for bed. Louise stands on the Queen's bed.*

LOUISE: And what will be said about of our Queen Marie-Thérèse? Who will dare speak of the unfortunate alliance that brought peace between Spain and France, but no peace to the bedroom? What whispers will become record? And whose word history? Will it be the clever Madame de Montespan who once told me that the Queen always retired first having spent a good part of the day roaming the court in search of the King. Her King was always tender, stroking his wife's side before falling off to sleep.

> *The ladies exit. Louise climbs off the bed.*
>
> *The Queen seductively spreads herself across the bed.*
>
> *The King enters in his lavish night clothing. He hurries quickly into bed and rolls over on his side feigning sleep. After a few moments, the Queen sits upright in the bed.*
>
> *Louise giggles.*

QUEEN: You're not a sleeping.

The King does not respond.

Where have you been?

The King still does not respond.

Do you know what night it is?

The King rolls away from the Queen.

You're not a sleeping.

KING: I'm exhausted, Marie. And if I'm not "a" sleeping now it is because I must endure your miserable dismantling of the French language.

QUEEN: I recognize dat smell!

KING: Of ennui.

QUEEN: La Vallière.

KING: Hisssss…I thought we forbade that in this bedroom.

QUEEN: It's La Vallière. I smell her, I smell her, I smell her, I do.

KING: You know how it is…you rub up against a woman these days and wear her scent for the next month or so. It could be anyone that I'm wearing at this moment.

QUEEN: INSOLENCE!

KING: My God woman, learn something new for a change! Like subtlety, now that's a word of beauty when spoken by a woman of breeding.

QUEEN: You promised me tonight.

KING: It's my prerogative to will my own intentions. And I choose not to keep my promise.

QUEEN: Damn you to a fiery hell, keep going back on your promises. Just wait and see.

KING: I'm afraid I prefer the wait. Have you been eating sweets in bed again?

QUEEN: No.

KING: 'Tis a shame, you did have a full set of teeth when you arrived.

The King peels a piece of candy off of his face.

QUEEN: May I kiss you?

KING: Must you?

QUEEN: It has been—

KING: I know—

QUEEN: We're not out in de court you needn't be coy with me.

KING: Good night Marie!

QUEEN: No, no, no!

The Queen jumps up and down on the bed. The King climbs out of bed.

KING: I'm tired. Tomorrow I have a full day of pageantry and what-not. One of those damn Barons, Dukes, or Marquis or something from up North is coming. It's only appropriate that I out show him…But I need my sleep if—

QUEEN: I want another baby…I es lonely, Louis. Please, por favor.

KING: You just got a new fool, didn't you?

QUEEN: He isn't a fool. He's my companion.

KING: Well, you should try and make friends with one of the ladies if you're lonely, wouldn't that be more befitting…They're all over the place for God's sake just choose one…Madame De Montespan is pleasant, wouldn't you enjoy spending time with her in the country. They're always asking after you.

QUEEN: Dey are?

KING: Yes.

QUEEN: Dey pretend as though dey don't understand what I say. Dey whisper.

KING: It's not whispering Marie, it's etiquette, savior-faire, a lady needn't be heard in every room of the palace.

QUEEN: It seems a lady doesn't have a place in dis palace. Did La Vallière beg you for her last child. Did she?

KING: La Vallière didn't eat sweets in bed. Good night Marie. Maybe tomorrow morning I'll find this conversation charming.

QUEEN: I'm going home den.

KING: To start a war?…Oh but would I love to go south this summer…

> *The King kisses the Queen, then pushes her aside.*

There! No war.

QUEEN: I hate you, Louis. I'm going to tell my auntie.

KING: Don't tell Mama.

QUEEN: Will!

KING: Then tell her! Goodnight!

> *The King rolls over and pulls the covers over his head. Louise sits on the bed.*

LOUISE: She told the Queen Mother.

> *The lights rise on the Queen Mother. The Queen goes to her side.*

QUEEN MOTHER: I didn't sleep with Louis's father until I was early forty, and I only did so because I had grown bored with my other… experiences.

QUEEN: Other experiences?

QUEEN MOTHER: Yes.

QUEEN: Sweet Mother! Did you love de King's father?

QUEEN MOTHER: …At times. He was dying for most of his life, which didn't make for a gratifying companion, but gave me fodder for plump conversation. In the end he had an erection twice, Louis and Phillipe. Maria, we queens have but one function, produce a King and then love whomever, whenever, why ever. You'll die young if the king is the great love of your life, because you will always be chasing the scent of his mistress, and there is nothing less pleasant on a man's breath. I tell you because you are my niece, my daughter, my cousin and a Spaniard!

QUEEN: I would never take a lover! Are saying that I should?

QUEEN MOTHER: It wouldn't be Christian for me to say it aloud.

The Queen Mother nods yes.

QUEEN: De King would never approve.

QUEEN MOTHER: It is no fun if he does.

QUEEN: Sweet Mother! Can you love two?

QUEEN MOTHER: Only if you're adventurous.

Laughs robustly.

Anyway. Let me sleep Maria. I'm old and growing sentimental with the remembrance of more fecund times.

QUEEN: I would never take a lover and forsake my chance at heaven.

Patting the Queen on her hand.

QUEEN MOTHER: My dear, we'll stroll tomorrow. Bring along your Boy. They carry him everywhere, I'm afraid his legs will atrophy if he doesn't walk. It happened you know to one of the Bavarian princes.

QUEEN: Really?

QUEEN MOTHER: Yes…During one of those ugly peasant insurgencies, the wretches stormed the castle. Everyone managed to escape, but that poor unfortunate prince. My dear he'd been carried so often he simply never learned how to walk. It was then that he discovered that the power of name was not necessarily enough to carry him to safety. He was killed by an Italian actor by the name of Fabrezio, who'd been insulted by…anyway, bring the child.

The Queen Mother slowly retreats into the darkness.

QUEEN: Good night Auntie.

The Queen Mother disappears. The Queen continues to wander through the night.

LOUISE: The Queen wandered the court, absently. Once even bumping into a drunken courtier who grabbed her bosom, kissed her chin and traveled on.

The Courtier man handles the Queen then rushes off. The Queen gasps. Louise laughs and wanders with her.

Shhh. Say nothing yet, and I'll conjure their faces. We're free, but a moment, in their memory. Sisters, these walls, our prison and savior, tonight are a palace. This tongue a door, and behind it a bed chamber.

The lights rise on Nabo asleep in a small bed, designed for a man of his modest proportions. Next to his bed is a small makeshift altar with cowrie shells, a small clay pot and several burning candles.

QUEEN: Nabo?

The Queen shakes Nabo awake.

NABO!

Nabo, still half asleep, gazes at the Queen. She sits on the edge of his bed.

QUEEN: I couldn't sleep.

NABO: Uh?

QUEEN: Wake up!

NABO: Yes, Your Majesty.

QUEEN: I always thought dat life was continuous here, dat the games never ended, you just join in when you're ready. But my goodness, everyone sleeps.

LOUISE: But according to Comtesse de Clagny, the Queen says—

QUEEN: I am surprised dat the court isn't awake when I am, you'd think they'd be more considerate then dat.

LOUISE: And in Madame de Arnaud's diary—

QUEEN: Tis a pity de court hasn't learned to stay awake all night. If so, they'd realize that the sun rises from the east even when Louis is asleep.

NABO: Do you wish me to dress?

QUEEN: Oh?

Thinks.

No need. I think your attire is charming. Carry on.

Nabo starts to get out of bed.

NABO: As you please.

QUEEN: So formal.

NABO: You are Queen.

QUEEN: Yes, of course.

NABO: Is there something that you need? Is there a reason why you are here, Your Majesty?

QUEEN: (*Snaps.*) Reason? Why shouldn't I be?

NABO: Well—

QUEEN: Yes?

NABO: I'm afraid how it may appear. Please, Your Majesty, I don't wish for trouble.

QUEEN: What trouble do you speak of?

NABO: Oh...I've heard stories about the sort of things that happen when certain lines are crossed. If you understand what I'm saying?

QUEEN: I don't! Which means this conversation should probably end!

NABO: I didn't mean to overstep, Your Majesty. But—

QUEEN: (*Sing-song.*) Lines, lines, where are dese damn lines dat everyone keeps talking about, so many drawn I can barely remember where to stand, sit, or shit! It's a ridiculous French notion. Nonsense! I can do as I please!

NABO: That's what frightens me.

QUEEN: You! Afraid of me?

NABO: Yes.

QUEEN: What a thrill, no one's ever been afraid of me.

The Queen moves closer to Nabo. He modestly pulls the covers up around his body.

You pull back, Why?

NABO: You're sitting on my bed…

The Queen bounces up and down on the bed.

It's not very big.

QUEEN: Oh come, you don't mind that I'm sitting with you?

NABO: You are Queen.

QUEEN: If I wasn't would you want me to? (*Pause.*) WELL?

NABO: At this moment, in the middle of the night at the edge of my bed with this cold breeze blowing in from the door which was left ajar sending a chill down my back, Your Majesty?

QUEEN: Well?

NABO: (*Nabo forcing out the words.*) YES!

QUEEN: I thought so. You know I sensed it, from the moment I saw you. I knew we'd be friends. Can I tell you a secret?

NABO: Another one?

QUEEN: Yes… (*Whispered.*) When I couldn't sleep, I thought, who will I go to for comfort? And you're the only one I could think of, my little African man.

NABO: Surely that's not true.

QUEEN: Yes. It is de truth.

The Queen moves closer to Nabo.

NABO: I didn't know that I was to perform both day and night.

QUEEN: Oh? NOT LIKE THAT! YOU'RE A DWARF! You're black like night.

She roars with delight.

How could you think?

She stops laughing abruptly.

QUEEN: Would you want me like that?

The Queen awaits a response. Nabo climbs out of bed.

Of course you would, I don't need to ask.

NABO: Perhaps the Queen should go back to bed. I will take you. We'll get you something sweet and then back to your room. You'll catch a cough dressed up in your night clothing.

QUEEN: But, I don't want to go! No! No. I'll stay here with you, si! We'll let Louis wonder where I am tomorrow.

The Queen climbs into Nabo's bed. Her feet dangle over the edge. Nabo curls up on the cold floor.

LOUISE: And his face touched the cold, and he knew there'd be little sleep for him in this land.

Nabo sits up.

NABO: Are you sleeping?

Nabo stands up and creeps toward the Queen. He slips the pillow from beneath her head and holds it above her face, as if going to smother her. He struggles with the notion of suffocating the Queen for a moment, then gently lifts her head and places the pillow back under it. He does a warrior dance as if evoking a distant spirit for strength.

He kneels before his makeshift altar.

NABO: Please mighty Legba, why am I here? If I do as she says will she let me go? If I'm very funny will they give me more food? If I kiss her will she free me?

LOUISE: In his small room facing the darkness, he stood wondering how he had gotten so far from home.

Louise blows out the candle.

SCENE 3

The King strolls with La Vallière by his side. He addresses several members of the court, who laugh generously.

KING: I simply grew tired of his constant braggadocio and asked him to prove his assertions. When he couldn't, the embarrassment was too much and he placed poison in his brandy. He lived, much to my delight, because I get such a chuckle when I see him.

The court roars with delight.

Without his shoes he couldn't be much taller than Marie's fool, with them he was a virtual giant. It took him years to properly learn how to balance on the heels. I did see him once walking alone in the garden, when a tremendous gust of wind whipped up and tipped him over. I watched for hours from my window as he struggled to stand, which he could not do. It was not until evening that he was finally rescued by the gardener. Alas, when he showed up for dinner with the English ambassador, he told those supping that he had been attacked by highwaymen and dirtied in battle.

The court roars with delight.

I'm still going to appoint him as an ambassador, I admire his gumption and willingness to challenge the natural order. But he does believe in God and Louis, which makes him more than fit.

One member of the court laughs. The King cuts his eyes.

Who are you?

The courtier does not respond.

GET OUT!

The courtier exits quickly. The Queen enters with Nabo trailing behind her.

KING: So, you've finally found me?

QUEEN: Who says dat I was looking for you?

The King glances over at La Vallière.

KING: Anyway, the other day I was speaking with him in this very room and—

QUEEN: I thought that I'd come for my final sitting with the painter. Am I wrong to think dat the portrait must be complete in time for the fête? Really, I had no idea I'd find you here. None what so ever!

KING: I was telling a story. Now I've lost my concentration. I'm growing impatient with you, Marie…The other day I was—

QUEEN: A story? Nabo told me de absolutely most funniest story this morning. I nearly spoiled myself with delight.

> *Nabo takes a few steps back.*

KING: You interrupted my story again to tell me one that Nabo told you…that Nabo, Nabo? Who is…?

QUEEN: Silly, he is my companion, of course.

KING: Where is this companion? Show yourself!

NABO: I am here Your Majesty.

KING: Oh? You? So Nabo, you have a story that is better than mine?

NABO: Oh no, Your Majesty.

KING: The Queen seems to think so…tell it!

NABO: I'm sorry, Your Majesty.

KING: TELL IT!

NABO: I…I was explaining to Her Majesty that when I first arrived in France, I'd never seen white powdered makeup or a wig. As fate would have it, I…I was engaged by a patron who was quite beautiful, oh yes! Finely dressed with his white powdered face and a high standing wig, which gave him the illusion of a glorious head of hair. I must confess the ladies found him very comely and often visited. He inspired some of the finest poetry in this country.

> *The King raises his eyebrows.*

I mean the world. So you can imagine my surprise one evening when I went into his sleeping chamber to say good night and found an old balding man tucked in my patron's bed. "Who are you?" I demanded. For what was this shriveled old man doing there? I tried to pull him out of my patron's bed. But he refused to budge, insisting that he was my patron. "Oh no," I said, "my patron is a beautiful man with a full head of hair, a man who is still in his golden years." He slapped my face, I slapped his. "Fool!" he said. "Indeed!" I said. So I found my patron's sword and drove this man triumphantly from the house. That evening as I was searching for signs of my patron's disappearance I came upon his wig placed lovingly in a cradle as if a child. Next, I found my patron's face in a jar of rouge and a compact of powder. Oh dear. I could still hear the old man yelling from the cold. I thought, should I let him in to give me a thorough beating or should I let him freeze to death and claim he went mad?

KING: What happened?

NABO: He went mad.

> The King laughs, the members of the court join in. Louise enters the light.

KING: An amusing story! Tell another.

> The Queen smiles.

LOUISE: At that moment the dinner bell chimed.

> The dinner bell.

KING: Oh! Dinner time. Bring the fool around later, Marie. He amuses me.

QUEEN: (Excited.) I'm glad he pleases you.

KING: Will you be joining me for dinner?

QUEEN: (Beaming.) Yes.

KING: I didn't think you'd miss that.

> The King and Queen exit, followed by the court and Louise. La Vallière scowls at Nabo as she leaves.

PAINTER: I heard that story before. Performed by the Italian commedia in Abruzzi. They did it better. I was painting some overripe Italian nobles who had a love for the theatre and engaged me to paint them as classic characters from the Greek and Roman tragedies. Agamemnon, Lysistrata. My favorite was Medea, clutching her babies in arm.

NABO: I heard the story in Lisbon as I was traveling with the Sultan from Alexandria. One of the Portuguese seamen kept telling it over and over again. The Queen is easily amused. I cough and she laughs, I fart and she laughs.

PAINTER: Yes. It doesn't surprise me. I've been here so long I'm beyond surprise. Years ago I'd be immobilized with astonishment, but, now all I feel is—

He can't find the right word.

NABO: Numb.

PAINTER: Precisely.

The Painter takes out a flask of wine.

NABO: Until this evening no one other than the Queen had spoken to me. For a while I thought I was a figment of her imagination. Imagine that horror.

PAINTER: I've lived worse while serving this court. For a while I thought I was invisible. I'd speak and no one would respond, it was almost a year before I was acknowledged. And those first words were "IDIOT, you made me look like a moor!" I'd grown so accustomed to being ignored that I was overcome by emotion and fainted.

NABO: What you must hear.

PAINTER: The hell. Some days I worry that I will be put to death for what I've heard. But I make them look magnificent, despite my better judgment. They all look the same, you know. Or haven't you noticed. They're all related, you know. The same grandfather and grandmother. It's disgusting! All of them! But! I am a painter, a fine painter. I do what I can.

NABO: Indeed.

PAINTER: You know, I have been studying you. You have a remarkable complexion. You should let me paint you.

NABO: Me?

PAINTER: You're as fine a subject as any of them.

He passes Nabo the flask.

Nabo, relax, have some wine with me. Come, come they won't be back for hours. (*Giggles.*) What would you say if I told you that she likes you? It's good for you.

Nabo takes a quick swig.

NABO: The Queen?

PAINTER: Yes, indeed. There'll be a portrait yet. I've already composed it in my head. So, tell, what do you think of our Queen of France? Huh? Do you like her?

NABO: Do you?

PAINTER: I don't like any of them. In fact, I hate them all. And in every portrait that I paint I write in tiny letters in the lines of their forehead or the sides of the eyes, "I hate you." Come and look.

NABO: I don't read.

PAINTER: Pity…It's no fun having this secret alone. (Giggles.) So, this may be indiscreet, but, but what is it like in the palace beyond these public rooms?

NABO: It's magnificent. No detail left to the imagination.

PAINTER: Have you been to her bed chamber?

NABO: No, of course

PAINTER: Forgive me, I only ask because I've often wondered what color scheme they've chosen. I imagine green and gold, with allegorical sketches. That's what I see!

Louise enters. The lights fade on Nabo.

LOUISE: I met the painter many years later, when he was older and fading in memory. He painted a portrait of the Mother Superior turning her craggy face into one of an angel of mercy…(*To Painter.*) Is it true, Monsieur, that you were in the court of Louis XIV?

PAINTER: Yes...you look so familiar to me.

LOUISE: Perhaps we've met before.

PAINTER: I think not!

The Painter laughs. He studies her face.

PAINTER: No, you know who it is you remind me of, an African, yes, a dwarf of very fine character from Dahomey. He served the Queen about seventeen years ago. Funny man. You resemble him.

LOUISE: Me? Resemble an African?

She laughs.

PAINTER: It had always been rumored but I would never have guessed. They grew close, you know.

LOUISE: Surely you joke with me, monsieur.

PAINTER: Forgive me, perhaps I've said too much.

LOUISE: (*To audience.*) He told me he had a portrait, but he never came back to show me...(*To Painter.*) What was the African's name?

PAINTER: Bobo...I believe.

Lights rise on Nabo.

LOUISE: (*To audience.*) He remembered a few stories, vague at best.

PAINTER: (*To Nabo.*) Let me paint you, Nabo. Without the adornments. Your face.

Nabo takes off his wig.

NABO: I hope I'm not here long enough for you to finish.

PAINTER: I've seen fools come and go from all over the empire. You'll be here.

LOUISE: A sketch, colors selected, hues blended. Frustration. And finally found in a damp cellar a portrait of a nameless African man.

SCENE 4

The King and La Vallière lounge on the sofa whispering intimately. The members of the court sit alert attempting to glean bits of conversation. Louise walks amongst the courtiers.

LOUISE: And then there was La Vallière. Pretty, fertile thing.

La Vallière laughs, Louise laughs, mockingly.

She was the king's diversion, skilled in the art of—

The Mother Superior suddenly appears, a daunting presence looming in the background.

MOTHER SUPERIOR: Masturbation! Do you like masturbation? You must! Why else tell such tales? It is untrue, no matter who told you otherwise. Silence your tongue, child! I won't hear of it! What are you doing? Is this how you prepare for your vows on this blessed evening? Sisters, I beg you to close your ears to this insanity.

The Mother Superior walks briskly into the darkness. Louise hesitates before defiantly resuming her story.

LOUISE: (*Hushed.*) Please, stay if you will, for what does she really know of desire? If my tale surprises you, then let it be the surprise of a warm hand upon your thigh. What is the danger of a story, if it offers up such divine contentment? But now the Queen awaits us in the courtyard, darkness encroaching.

The Queen enters wearing hunting attire, trailed by Nabo similarly dressed. The Queen taps her foot, awaiting acknowledgment.

QUEEN: (*Without a breath.*) I've been waiting outside in the carriage for nearly an hour. Do you know what that means? I could have caught my death, dere's such a terrible wind. It's dark. I hate to travel at night. We'll arrive at the Chateau and nothing will be prepared. I'll have to sleep on de floor like a peasant. Do you want me to sleep on de floor like a peasant?

Nabo peers at the King from around the Queen's skirt.

KING: Oh? Marie. What is it? Calm yourself. If you're having trouble, I'll summon Doctor Fagon.

The Queen throws her hat and gloves on the floor.

QUEEN: Are you coming?

KING: Were we scheduled to leave this evening? Perhaps my secretary failed to notify me. Anyway, I've decided that I won't go to the country this month.

The Queen stops short. Nabo takes the Queen's hand attempting to calm her.

QUEEN: But Louis—

KING: La Vallière has persuaded me to stay. It appears a troupe of Italian—

LA VALLIÈRE: Performers.

KING: Yes, are booked for next week. La Vallière says it's fabulous and shouldn't be missed.

QUEEN: La Vallière says? La Vallière says? I'll play no role in this farce. I've all my bags packed and loaded. I've assembled my household and closed off my apartment. There are nearly thirty people standing outside dese window awaiting you in the cold.

KING: Then I'll have my valet fetch them capes. I'm afraid I'm not going.

La Vallière claps her hands.

LA VALLIÈRE: You won't be disappointed. Better than Moliere, I'm told.

QUEEN: Putana.

La Vallière yelps, retreating for behind the King.

KING: Marie!

NABO: Temper, temper. Let it go and one will always be chasing it.

KING: Marie! (*Aside.*) You've embarrassed us.(*To court.*) My apologies to all.

He grabs the Queen's arm and leads her towards the door.

KING: (*Aside.*) I want you to board that carriage and leave tonight. Now get out!

QUEEN: Have you forgotten your duties? Daddy won't like it.

Pero, quién te has creído que eres tu? Eres un paleto Borbón. Nosotros los Hapsburgos hemos sido emperadores mil anos.

The Queen throws a tantrum, stomping across the room in an undignified manner.

KING: What sort of primitive dance is this?

QUEEN: Te Mandará con La Vallière a los infiernos.

The Queen storms out. Nabo follows.

LOUISE: The gentle Queen rampaged through the palace in a rage that's still legendary. Tearing portraits from the walls and shredding tapestries with her bare hands. A most unchristian display for such a devout Catholic. Possession was blamed, a trance induced by proximity to an infidel. It was Nabo who finally calmed her.

The Queen pushes open the doors to her bed chamber. Nabo scrambles behind, attempting to calm his Queen. The Queen shoves her servants out of the room and slams the doors shut. The Queen fumbles about the bedroom searching for something to destroy.

Finally, the Queen flings herself on her bed. Louise retreats into the darkness.

QUEEN: If Louis is not going to the country, then I'm not going either. I defy you, Louis! Look Nabo, I'm not shaking.

NABO: That's right, Your Majesty don't let him take your pride. Once he has that you're bankrupt.

She holds out her rock steady hands.

QUEEN: I wish I were not so cowardly.

NABO: And I wish I had longer legs. If I had longer legs I'd have been gone. We don't always get what we want as you well know.

QUEEN: Shame! I have suffered my fifth insult of the day. I will not tolerate another. I'm going to bed and don't wake me until spring when my garden's in bloom. I don't think I can bare one more indignity this season.

The Queen begins to weep.

NABO: Your Majesty frightens me, are you all right?

He dries her tears with a handkerchief. He hugs her. She closes her eyes and rocks, pressing her face against his.

QUEEN: What kind of queen am I that quivers in the arms of a fool?

NABO: What kind of fool am I that cradles in my arms a queen? Shall I let you go, Your Majesty?

QUEEN: Only if you like?

NABO: Pardon me if I say that I like very much holding Your Majesty.

QUEEN: And I like very much being held.

NABO: Shall we go on sitting this way?

QUEEN: No bells have tolled and no bolts of lightning have struck.

NABO: My God does not punish for such acts.

A moment. The sound of laughter is heard from the corridor. Nabo and the Queen quickly release their embrace. They stare awkwardly at each other, attempting to find appropriate words. The laughter ceases and they immediately re-embrace. The Queen lets out a long sigh, which transforms into a moan. She turns her face into Nabo and they kiss spiritedly and passionately. Nabo pushes the Queen away.

NABO: There is danger around this corner.

QUEEN: We pay the price for the things we desire. I've offered my teeth for my excesses.

NABO: Now look good. Your anger shouldn't drive you to places from which you'd otherwise run.

QUEEN: Nor should your desire to be free, rob me of my virtue.

They embrace.

NABO: In all my travels I've never held someone as close as I hold you now.

QUEEN: In all my life I've never been held by one as tenderly.

NABO: Not even the King?

QUEEN: Not even the king. Dear God, what should we do?

NABO: You are Queen.

QUEEN: Yes. No. Wet your finger.

> *Nabo wets his finger. The Queen leads his hand beneath her dress. Louise enters the light.*

LOUISE: With a kiss he now possessed the kingly prize. With a kiss he tasted empires past and future. With one tender kiss she drew him in and they faced the possibility of freedom.

END OF ACT ONE

ACT TWO, SCENE 1

Lights rise on Louise's decrepit cell. She sits on the edge of a tub, slowly unbuttoning her gown as she speaks. She wears a simple undergarment.

LOUISE: Well, well, sweet sisters, I detect some disbelief. How could I have conjured so elaborate a tale on this, the eve of my wedding.

Are you still contemptuous of my story? What further evidence do you need? Have you had tea with the Queen and shared intrigues with nobility?

The Mother Superior dressed in black from head to toe moves from the darkness into the light. She walks across the space slowly, punctuating her statements with the gentle rise and fall of her elbows, like a young bird preparing for flight.

MOTHER SUPERIOR: I held you in my arms not long after your birth. You came with the storm clouds that lasted a full week, colicky and hungry for a swollen nipple. It was the night that the great tree fell against the rectory and tore a hole in the roof, Father Josephus nearly drowned in rain water. He coughed up a river of water for days.

LOUISE: I'm not listening.

The Mother Superior smiles.

MOTHER SUPERIOR: It's my turn. It was I who carried you in and placed you in a bundle next to my bed. I, who put aside a multitude of questions for a homeless child.

LOUISE: And that three hundred livres bestowed to the order annually. Yes Mother, I came with an excellent dowry.

Louise laughs.

MOTHER SUPERIOR: My final reward is to have you join us. But, if you're to take your vows with us you must first purge your imagination of these exaggerations. How can you wed God, when you still harbor the tales of the devil. The Queen? The King?

She crosses herself.

Do you know what your assertions could do? Shall we pray?

She closes her eyes and rattles off the Lord's prayer.

AMEN!

LOUISE: (*Whispered.*) Amen!

The Mother Superior wipes her brow and sighs.

MOTHER SUPERIOR: Avert catastrophe! That's the message I'm receiving from the Lord! More a command actually than a message. AVERT CATASTROPHE GOOD SISTER! (*Whispered as though confessing a sin.*) Why at Moret we have such a simple life, we are women of virtue. Women of noble birth enter our ranks in numbers far greater than any convent in France can boast. If we were a royal court it would be the finest in this nation. There's no place for your perfidious tales of *bastards, fornicators,* and *drunkenness.* Tales of Moorish infidels weaving vulgar jokes, unchristian even before their execution. I am nauseated.

She moans as though wounded.

AVERT CATASTROPHE! Words! Words! Sickening and potent like some potion to rid the body of vapors. Queens! Kings! Cursed! Malediction! How did our ranks swell with such pernicious tales of debauchery and niggerdom.

She begins to weep.

I can't stop weeping. I shall drown in the sea of licentiousness. I'm praying now for your soul.

She prays in Latin. The Mother Superior picks up her pace while traversing the stage as if in search of some answer. She suddenly stops.

MOTHER SUPERIOR: You've left me no choice. I must beat this demon from within you. Drive this homunculus out before it can do anymore harm to our reputation. How can you wed God unless you have purified your soul?

The Mother Superior removes a black leather whip from beneath her robes. She lifts the whip to strike Louise. She mimes delivering the strokes.

LOUISE: Tell me, sweet sisters, what troubles her so deeply that to look upon me is to beat me?

Mother Superior fades into the darkness.

Louise strokes the ornate cross hanging about her throat as the stage swells with a chorus of female voices singing somber, sacred music. Louise dreamily crosses out of the light as the music shifts from sacred to secular. A loud gasp is heard. The lights rise on the Queen gasping. She is surrounded by her ladies in waiting, who tug the strings of the stiff corset about her waist, trying to conceal her swollen stomach.

QUEEN: PULL! Pull! I say pull!

LADY SERVANT: It is no good Your Majesty. Perhaps

Two young maids attempt to pull the Queen's corset tighter and tighter. The Queen screams with pain.

QUEEN: Don't say it! Tighter! Tighter I say!

LADY SERVANT: Your Majesty I'm afraid we will hurt you.

QUEEN: I must get into this dress. It's my costume for tonight's fete! Louis is Apollo and I'm to appear as his twin, Artemis. I'll spoil everything. The dressmaker spent over two months refining dese costumes. The beads were imported from the Orient. We are to make a grand entrance through the garden, it's been rehearsed since the beginning of the spring. Ay!

The Queen lets out a wretched cry. One of the servants begins to weep.

LADY SERVANT: I'm sorry, Your Majesty, but I can't do this any longer…I'm afraid my queen will die.

QUEEN: If your queen dies then she will be buried in dis dress as the Goddess Artemis. Deo Volente! Now pull by God! You worthless wenches!

The women pull the corset so tight the Queen cannot utter a word. Waving her arms wildly, she struggles to indicate to them to loosen it, but they misread her instructions and pull tighter.

The women slip the elaborate dress over the Queen's head, and then proceed to powder her face. Fully adorned the Queen looks like a fragile porcelain doll.

QUEEN: (*Gasping.*) How do I look?

LADY SERVANT: Magnificent, Your Majesty.

The women applaud. The Queen attempts to bow, but cannot.

QUEEN: You see!

The sound of chamber music from outside.

The music!

Recounting what she must do.

I step out, bow to the King, he bows to me, he takes my hand and... and...and we move to the barge...and...and...Quick! Help me to the door.

LADY SERVANT: Are you sure, Your Majesty?

The Queen shoots a look at the servant. She moves with great difficulty, sidling back and forth. Before they reach the door, the Queen grows weak and faints. The women, unable to support her weight, let the body slide to the floor.

LADY SERVANT: We've murdered the Queen!

The women furiously fan the Queen. She slowly comes to and they lift her to a chair.

LADY SERVANT: Are you all right?

The Queen takes in air.

QUEEN: No! Ah! Quick! Quick wench! Go through mi closet and see if there's another Goddess I can appear as. Juno maybe! Something large and flowing. Loosen me quick I can feel the mushrooms and barley wine coming up.

The Lady Servants disrobe the Queen, who lets out a tremendous sigh of relief. One Lady Servant ventures to speak.

LADY SERVANT: Has it not been four months since Your Majesty last bled?

> *The Queen shoots a quick disapproving glance at the young woman.*

> *Sickened by the sunrise and the ring of the dinner bell.*

QUEEN: What are you suggesting?

LADY SERVANT: That you're in the family way, so swollen suddenly. It would be glorious news! Something grand to announce at the height of the fete as the toast is being made. It would be a true celebration!

QUEEN: (*Horrified.*) Impossible! And you won't repeat that again. Foul vapors fill my belly and a simple emetic will purge dis bloat.

LADY SERVANT: If that's how you'll have it, Your Majesty, but there will come a time when you can no longer hide it.

QUEEN: Insolence! Would you talk to…to…to Louis dat way? I have it on authority that the deserts are richer and more prone to linger in the belly dis season. Now find me something else to wear.

> *The fête music grows louder. Nabo enters ringing bells and dressed as Bacchus/Legba for the fête. He wears an African mask and a huge phallus strapped to his front.*

> *The Queen stares at him, covering her mouth with disbelief. She races offstage, trailed by her servants.*

> *A simple drum beat sounds for his performance.*

NABO: Ananse spider had roamed the earth for many years, when suddenly he felt the presence of death pursuing him. Oh no, not yet, he thought. He hadn't had time to spread his seed, to keep his tradition of trickery alive. So from village to village he roamed, his erection swelling and growing. But every woman that he encountered was married or barren or withered or old. Finally in a tiny village at the foot of a great mountain he spotted the most beautiful woman he'd ever seen. Her hair twisted in spirals, reaching for the sky and her skin blackened and glowing with a shea butter sheen. As he hung in a baobab tree lazing in the midday sun, he decided she would be the woman to bear his child. As fortune would have it, she was the wife of the moon. How opportune, he thought, All I need to do is slip into her hut at night when the moon's hanging high in the sky. So Ananse spider crept into the moon's hut that night and seduced his wife. He used the Moon's slippers to hide his footprints so there'd be no record of his visit. When the moon returned in the morning to sleep with his wife, he found that she was already satisfied. This happened day after day until the moon finally sensed some deception. So the next night the moon decided to go only three quarters of the way into the sky, and the night after that only half way into the sky. But it was too late, for Ananse had been sated and the moon was forever to be suspicious, only rarely returning completely to the sky, in order to keep an eye on his wife at night.

Nabo bursts into laughter. A burst of seeds shoot out of the head of the phallus. All others are silent.

Lights rise on the King dressed as Apollo.

KING: Vulgar! Moon? Spider? Why did the spider speak? Does a spider have an erection? Nonsense! It's a barbaric tale and I found it hard to follow. It smacks of paganism! Where's the humor? A most inappropriate tale and now that it's been told I declare that it should never be spoken again. Bring on another fool to start these festivities. I've grown bored with this one.

A battery of trumpets sound. The King departs.

NABO: Yes Sire. Yes Sire.

The lights fade on all but Nabo.

NABO: Yes Spoiler, yes Spineless, yes.

The lights rise on the painter cleaning his palette and packing his belongings.

PAINTER: Ah! And you thought no one was still watching!

NABO: That was my Nana's tale. Where I come from a spider can speak, a rock can dance and a tree can weep.

PAINTER: I'd like to see that place some day. Yes, indeed. If I could walk in your tiny shoes and purge my feelings before the King. Oh the stories that he'd be forced to endure.

He makes retching sounds.

NABO: You wouldn't wear those shoes for very long if you knew the places where they've been. Rolling, tumbling, tortured daily with their ticklish needs. You'd trade my shoes for a pair of worn sandals.

PAINTER: Oh you're wrong, I wouldn't be caught dead in a pair of sandals.

He laughs, then stops himself.

PAINTER: (*Whispers.*) I imagine you've heard.

NABO: Nothing that need be whispered.

PAINTER: Come closer. (*Whispers.*) She's with child, you'll soon have another to entertain.

NABO: With child?

PAINTER: You must know.

NABO: I do not. I swear.

PAINTER: These ears are never wrong. It is the truth, spoken by a lady of repute. Only this morning the Queen relinquished her meal in the chapel.

NABO: Pregnant? Performing for the King during the festival, I've seen little of the Queen.

PAINTER: (*Whispers.*) I'll tell you something, she can't bear a child more ghastly than her first.

He makes an apelike face. A moment.

It's no secret, the Queen's the ugliest woman in all of this court. If she wasn't queen they'd turn her out to pasture. Moo! It's a wonder, you know, that the king…

He grabs a hold of Nabo's phallus.

NABO: Come. She's not without charm. In the late afternoon light she can be thought to possess a few pleasant features.

PAINTER: In the late late afternoon perhaps.

The Painter laughs, then grows suddenly melancholy. He packs his brushes.

PAINTER: I thought I'd lost the ability to laugh. If I may say, I'm going to miss you.

NABO: Am I to be sent away?

The Painter laughs.

PAINTER: No, I am. It appears this painter couldn't transform the man into a God. The Apollo of my imagination wasn't to the King's satisfaction.

NABO: But it is a remarkable painting, my friend.

PAINTER: You think so? But nevertheless, I am being released. And suddenly I feel at ease.

NABO: Now, I were in your shoes.

PAINTER: But Ananse spider wears the shoes of the moon…

The trumpets sound. The painter disappears as quickly as he appeared.

Nabo rings his bells, resuming his festive dance. He stops abruptly.

The lights rise on Louise.

LOUISE: A child? A child.

SCENE 2

The Queen Mother and the Queen stroll down the palace corridor. Courtiers bow as they pass.

QUEEN MOTHER: What news, dear child. What news! You glow! Pregnancy does have the tendency to bubble the blood in the cheeks. Don't look so frightened, the first is always the most difficult. You'll have no trouble with this one. Kaplunk!

QUEEN: How'd you find out?

QUEEN MOTHER: How? How? I thrive on such precious gossip. You spend all your mornings in your bed chamber and all your evenings in chapel. The signs are there.

QUEEN: Does everyone know then?

QUEEN MOTHER: Everyone! Who is everyone? Of course not! I pay dearly for news that intrigues me. I recommend that you find help that's more discreet. I'm thoroughly disappointed; I didn't even have the pleasure of a good old fashioned barter. Regrettably when you reach my age you must take short cuts in this sport of gossip. When I tried my hand at governing I found gossip to be the most incisive tool. I was well-seasoned then. Alas, they weren't quite ready for me.

> *The Queen Mother kisses both of the Queen's cheeks.*

You're so slow at learning the ways of the French Court, without intrigue we might as well be English, humorless, passionless, and without reason.

> *She stops and fans herself.*

Maria, I'm hurt.

QUEEN: Where Auntie?

> *The Queen Mother slaps her chest.*

QUEEN MOTHER: I thought I'd at least be the first to know. Ha! Does Louis know?

QUEEN: Not yet, Auntie.

QUEEN MOTHER: That's right, spring it upon him at just the perfect moment. Everything is political and there's nothing more potent than a queen's womb.

QUEEN: I didn't want to say anything until I could be sure. Dere's no need to get him excited for nothing.

QUEEN MOTHER: Hmmmmm?

QUEEN: (*Half-hearted.*) I will tell him dis evening.

QUEEN MOTHER: Is there some information that has no price?

She lifts her eyebrows.

QUEEN: I don't understand what you're asking.

QUEEN MOTHER: If you don't understand then perhaps I am mistaken.

QUEEN: Maybe this once, Auntie.

The Queen Mother takes the Queen's hand.

QUEEN MOTHER: All is well?

QUEEN: Yes.

QUEEN MOTHER: Sometimes we make mistakes, but none that are too big to fix, it is the power of our rank. There are explanations for everything in this age of science, but still little can be stated with certainty. Don't look so worried, I'm here.

QUEEN: I'm afraid for what grows in my belly. I've dreamt of a child unnatural. It's not yet the fourth month and I feel it moving in my stomach as though it wants to get free. Ay! Dios mio! What if I give birth to a basilisk or some other horrible creature like the women from the Far East who sleep with pagans.

QUEEN MOTHER: We all have our fears. We all have our problems, some are solved with prayer and others with vinegar, mustard seed, a rat's liver and ginger root.

The Queen gasps.

Yes.

The Queen Mother bows to a passing courtier.

Maria, some day I will tell you all.

She slaps the Queen's hand.

But today I prefer to stroll and enjoy the lovely men, ah yes, and women. The times have changed. Heed my advice, send your fool away, Maria.

She resumes walking.

QUEEN: Nabo? Why Auntie?

She does not follow.

QUEEN MOTHER: So much time spent with an infidel could give rise to talk. I've heard that a soul as black as his could permeate your womb.

QUEEN: No! I'm going to the chapel dis moment to pray. And each morning from now until the birth I will spend on my knees. It isn't the case.

QUEEN MOTHER: It wouldn't be the first case, you know. (*Whispers.*) The De Medicis.

The lights fade on the Queen Mother as they rise on Louise. The Queen falls to her knees.

LOUISE: She prayed for a healthy beautiful boy without the dull eyes of her first born son. She prayed that she'd awaken from her dream in the Spanish palace with her circle of tiny ladies and the little wicked Dona Molina at her bedside stroking her hair. She prayed that the gentle Nabo was of princely proportions. What a cruel predicament.

Louise and the Queen are on their knees swaying back and forth in prayer.

QUEEN: I will repent! I will repent!

The West African drum sounds. The Queen sways to the rhythm, fighting the impulse to move. Louise begins to dance.

QUEEN: I will cleanse! I will cleanse!

Louise's dance becomes more impassioned. The Mother Superior appears from the darkness.

MOTHER SUPERIOR: Where'd you learn such a preposterous dance? Stop!

Louise collapses to the ground.

LOUISE: (*To audience.*) So I'd planned my wedding to a Spanish prince, more comely than the gardener's son. We'd escape these stone walls on his dappled horse. So I waited day one, so I waited day two, so I waited day three, day seventy, day four hundred, day one thousand.

The Mother Superior cracks the whip and disappears.

I waited and waited, but he never did come.

Chamber music plays.

SCENE 3

The King, the Queen, La Vallière, Doctor Fagon, and members of the court play cards in an antechamber.

The Queen belches, a monstrous belch.

KING: It's not your turn, Marie!

La Vallière laughs flirtatiously as the King places a card.

LA VALLIÈRE: (*To King.*) I'm not going to play cards with you, you're too clever for me.

The Queen throws a card down. Louise enters.

LOUISE: As the Queen's belly grew, they worshipped all day at the card table.

LA VALLIÈRE: Lovely day, don't you think?

DOCTOR: Special for this time of year. I look forward to a ride in the country, do you?

QUEEN: Yes.

LOUISE: And they gossiped.

LA VALLIÈRE: She's not his daughter from what I was told. His wife was barren, an accident involving an ox. Yet he traveled up north in the child's company.

KING: At his age he deserves applause not chastisement. I've known many a man that was seduced by the luster of a child's cheek.

The Queen bitterly throws down a card.

It's not your turn, Maria.

He picks up the card and shoves it in the Queen's hand.

KING: I will remove you from the game if you cannot follow the rules. Do you have money to wager? Or is this another exercise that shall cost me?

The Queen Mother enters assisted by a supple young man. The craggy-faced woman does her best to remain upright, though gravity pulls her forward and she occasionally has to be straightened out. Louise exits.

QUEEN MOTHER: Grand afternoon to all. Please don't stand on my account.

She waits for all to rise before continuing. The men stand. The women bow their heads.

QUEEN MOTHER: Ah! There you are Marie. Have you shared the news?

The Queen looks down. The Queen Mother shoots a piercing glance at La Vallière.

QUEEN MOTHER: Perhaps Madame de la Vallière is curious to hear the Queen's news? No?

La Vallière smirks.

I believe that Maria has something to share.

The Queen Mother claps her hands for emphasis.

KING: Can't it wait, Mother. We're in the middle of a game.

QUEEN: Yes.

QUEEN MOTHER: No!

KING: I'm not in the mood for talk. Save your thoughts for supper time. Concentrate on your cards, Marie.

QUEEN MOTHER: And once the news has been told you will scold her for not sharing it sooner. It is good news.

KING: Which will make it all the more pleasurable over a good meal.

DOCTOR: There!

> *The Doctor lays down a card, quite pleased with himself. The King acknowledges the defeat with a nod of the head. He quickly scribbles out an IOU note.*

KING: I now owe you two hundred livres. Collect it from the Minister of Finance tomorrow morning.

DOCTOR: Sire, it was my pleasure.

KING: Don't display too much glee Fagon. It is un-sportsmanlike. But I forget you physicians do so enjoy the pains of others.

> *The King rises and pulls out the chair for the Queen first and then La Vallière. Doctor Fagon stands and nods.*

You see what happens, Mother, when you and Marie strain my concentration. You're used to defeat, but I—

QUEEN MOTHER: No speeches for God's sake we're not in a session.

KING: Don't start, Mother. Stay out of my affairs.

QUEEN MOTHER: Your affairs are mine, a mother's prerogative. Don't ever forget how and why you sit where you are! NOW TELL HIM MARIA!

QUEEN: (*Tongue-tied.*) I—

LA VALLIÈRE: Oh go on now, I'm dying to know what news could bring such light into the Queen Mother's eyes.

KING: Should I sit or stand Marie?

QUEEN: I—

KING: I'll sit therefore I won't be disappointed if I had bothered to stand and it wasn't worthwhile.

QUEEN: Maybe I should wait until supper. Nothing better than good news on a full stomach.

KING: So it is.

> *The King leads his entourage toward the door. They follow at an*
> *appropriate distance behind him. The Queen Mother pinches*
> *the Queen.*

QUEEN: (*Yelps.*) I'M PREGNANT!

> *The King stops short. The courtiers applaud. The King silently counts*
> *the number of months on his fingers. He is not sure that it is possible.*

KING: Pregnant?

> *Again, he silently counts the months on his fingers.*

KING: Fagon, can this be confirmed?

> *Fagon shrugs his shoulders.*

QUEEN MOTHER: Nonsense. A woman's body tells her what she
needs to know.

KING: Hysteria is not uncommon, particularly during these spring
months. It is not unknown for maladies and other disorders to be
contrived for mere entertainment. Remember that poor Duchesse,
lovely thing she, well, remember. Can this be confirmed, Fagon?

> *The doctor examines the Queen, gently rubbing her belly, looking*
> *into her mouth and stroking her hair. He smells her breath.*

DOCTOR: She's all the signs of early pregnancy, Sire. Her tongue is a
solid pink and protrudes slightly. Her breath sour. Her hair is coarse
and her hands warm and moist. I'd say she's pregnant.

> *The King once again counts on his fingers the number of months.*

QUEEN: Are you pleased?

KING: (*Hesitantly.*) Yes, wonderful news. Fagon. Fagon.

> *The King summons the Doctor to his side.*

KING: (*Whispered.*) Could it be some other sickness that causes
these symptoms?

DOCTOR: I'm delighted that all the outward signs are there. She is pregnant.

KING: Is there some way, other than the usual way that the Queen could be ripe. If you understand what I'm saying. I can't recall when I rested with the Queen last, but I'm sure this child is mine. She's a pious queen.

DOCTOR: Of course. Have you eaten food from her plate?

KING: Yes.

DOCTOR: Kissed her lips after seven?

KING: Yes.

DOCTOR: Dried her tears or touched her saliva.

KING: (*Thinks.*) Yes, yes! That's it!

> *The King steals a glance at the Queen clutching her belly. His face grows long and troubled.*

DOCTOR: These are all quite scientific considerations, Sire. Congratulations are in order.

KING: Yes of course.

> *The King returns to the company of the women.*

KING: We'll have the church bells rung and a feast for all who can fit.

> *He throws his arms in the air and gestures wildly. He stops to think, suddenly inspired.*

I'll commission a musical extravaganza, which will be played as the boy is being delivered. The first sounds that he hears will be the celestial bellow of the horns drawing him from his watery sanctuary.

> *Muted French horns play a pastoral melody.*

No!

> *The music stops.*

It should be silent so his cries can echo throughout the palace. All the doors of the Louvre flung open so the sound will carry out into the air.

I'm to have another son!

> *The court claps. The King acknowledges the applause with graceful bows of the head, suddenly delighted.*
>
> *He kisses the Queen's hand, then exits in a flurry with his entourage following behind at an appropriate distance. Louise traipses on stage carrying a glass of burgundy wine.*

LOUISE: Cheers! Louis! Another son to inherit the empire. Cheers! Marie! Another son to be tutored, pampered, and plumped up for leisure. His mind afflicted with inherited madness. Matri, Patri, Avus, Avia...And years after that first celebration. They'd send his mistress and some pastries.

> *La Vallière, with a basket in hand, sheepishly a approaches Louise. She over-extends her arm in a hollow gesture of politeness.*

LA VALLIÈRE: Louise Françoise de La Baume Le Blanc, The Duchesse de La Vallière.

LOUISE: Pleased. Louise Marie-Thérèse.

> *La Vallière eyes Louise inspecting her clothing.*

LA VALLIÈRE: Dear child, you're not so black as they say.·

LOUISE: Nor do you resemble the witch so described. Lovely dress.

LA VALLIÈRE: I'll give you the name of my dressmaker, wondrous creature.

> *La Vallière gasps in feigned disbelief.*

If the window were larger you'd get glorious light in the morning. It would actually be quite lovely. Oh dear, I couldn't bear the confinement of a convent with prayer as the central event of my day.

LOUISE: (*Aside.*) She retired to a Carmelite house not soon after our meeting, it seems the King took another lover.

LA VALLIÈRE: Should we take our meal in the garden? Spiced mutton and stuffed plums in anisette, what a treat.

LOUISE: It sounds delicious, but I'm not permitted outside these walls no matter how tempting the offerings.

LA VALLIÈRE: Even on a day like today? That's ridiculous. Someone should speak to the Mother Superior.

LOUISE: Someone already has, I'm afraid.

She laughs.

LA VALLIÈRE: Then this will do.

She inspects the cell with abrupt twists of her head. She spreads a blanket across the floor.

LA VALLIÈRE: The Queen asked me to come in her stead. A fever took hold three days ago and it rages through her body. Doctor Fagon says it will pass after a complete blood-letting.

LOUISE: Give her my well wishes.

LA VALLIÈRE: Yes, I will. I think the Queen is most generous to give charity to one such as yourself. I know how much she looks forward to visiting the convent. She always seems reinvigorated after conversations with you. I've come to try my hand. I too need to be uplifted. I understand that you have a magician's touch.

La Vallière awkwardly lowers herself to the blanket.

LA VALLIÈRE: Come child, it will be like a picnic in the meadow.

LOUISE: Picnic in the meadow? It sounds lovely, but I wouldn't know.

A moment.

Louise bows her head. La Vallière can't stop herself from staring. Louise catches her and La Vallière averts her glance.

LA VALLIÈRE: I've come so far. Don't you want to see what I've brought?

LOUISE: If you haven't brought me freedom, it is of little interest to me.

Louise knocks the basket out of La Vallière's hand. A loaf of bread and some wild flowers spill out.

LA VALLIÈRE: I'm sorry. If I could have brought—

Louise drops to her knees and kisses the hem of La Vallière's skirt.

LOUISE: You have persuasion with the King. I thought at least you'd bring something more inspired.

LA VALLIÈRE: My influence is no longer in fashion.

LOUISE: But you could still plead my case. Ask him why I have been punished. Ask him to come, so I can present my case directly.

She takes hold of La Vallière's dress.

LOUISE: By my age, most of the young women here have been promised to men and those that haven't are given a trade. I must know whether there is some plan for me. I must know whether I am to grow old here.

LA VALLIÈRE: Don't you know? Hasn't anyone ever told you?

LOUISE: Told me what?

La Vallière begins to laugh hysterically.

LA VALLIÈRE: This is going to cheer me up.

LOUISE: What are you saying?

LA VALLIÈRE: The Queen is your mother, Louise. You are never going to leave here!

LOUISE: My mother? Then it is true. Is the king my father?

LA VALLIÈRE: Oh no! Has the Queen never uttered a word? Have you never looked in a mirror?

LOUISE: Not since I was a child. Then surely, my blood must be worth something to somebody.

LA VALLIÈRE: Don't you know? Your blood?

LOUISE: Am I that different from you? I bleed. I laugh. I weep. I feel no difference when I touch my face.

LA VALLIÈRE: Where the royal blood ebbs, the African blood flows. Your face is that of disgrace.

LOUISE: African? Me?

LA VALLIÈRE: Have you never asked yourself why your skin is brown, though you see no sun? Why you live here, so neatly tucked away from the world? Clever girl—

LOUISE: What questions do your bastard children ask of you?

LA VALLIÈRE: They know when to bow their heads, and when to hold them high. They too will never inherit what is rightfully theirs, though their blood flows directly from the throne. Child, I understand—

She stands and straightens her clothing.

LOUISE: Do they worship simple pleasures and know their father's touch?

LA VALLIÈRE: It is getting late and I don't want to make the journey back in the dark.

LOUISE: Royal blood? What use is this blood if it makes a prisoner of me?

Louise grabs the bread knife and slashes it across her wrist.

LA VALLIÈRE: No! MOTHER SUPERIOR! MOTHER SUPERIOR! MOTHER SUPERIOR!

La Vallière gathers her basket and exits hastily. The Mother Superior enters and wraps Louise's wrist with a handkerchief.

MOTHER SUPERIOR: You bleed again, so devoted are you to our suffering. You've a few more liters to meet the saintly requirement. Purify my sweet virgin. Purify!

Weakened, struggling to stand.

LOUISE: Cheers! Papa! I'd never seen an African other than the stained glass windows of Balthazar bending over Christ with a gift, wearing his azure turban more magnificent than the others. As the light shone through the window at noon I imagined he was my father casting purple hues across my forehead. I'd pray to him, a king from a far off land who ruled countries more beautiful than France. A king who'd been in the very presence of Christ. In Madame de Montespan's version my father was not a king. In mine sometimes he is.

Lights up on Nabo, who sits by his altar with a bottle of wine, drunk. He pours a libation before the altar.

NABO: Wine wasted on an old friend that has abandoned me. Well Legba, wine used to make you rise up. Dance. I can't hear you, too far from home now. Look at me with a foolish heart that has grown too large for my body. Legba, do me this one last favor and point in the right direction home. I don't know anymore.

Nabo stands.

LOUISE: The good Curé said that the Virgin Mary is black from head to toe, and is most beautiful in the eyes of God. As a child I ran from the taunts of children. "Gypsy swine, Gypsy girl." But God sees nothing but the naked soul, said the Curé and he taught me how to read the gentle words of the bible. Sweet sisters, when did blackness become a sin?

He walks in circles, his pace grows quicker as he speaks.

NABO: I know that Dahomey is to the south and I know the great river runs east past my village and I know the palace faces… Well I know when the sun rises…well I know that when my Uncle bowed to Mecca he always turned…

Nabo turns in circles.

NABO: Well I know poor Nabo, you will never get home at this rate.

QUEEN: (*Offstage, echoing.*) NABO! NABO!

NABO: Well well Legba tomorrow will be the day that we have another discussion.

He pours another drink as an offering.

QUEEN: (*Offstage.*) Nabo! Pedro!

Nabo rolls his eyes.

Nabo!

LOUISE: The Queen summoned him to the countryside where she was convalescing. She'd acquired too much fluid in the ankles and needed to be carried everywhere like an Oriental princess. Eight months pregnant, ghastly!

The Queen sits by the country hearth warming her feet. She drinks brandy wine from a silver chalice. Her eyes grow large as she hears stirring outside her chamber. Louise leaves the light.

One door panel swings open. Nabo tumbles in. The Queen does not respond.

NABO: You're not surprised?

QUEEN: Of course not, I called you here. I missed your company—

NABO: And I, yours.

QUEEN: Really? What took you so long? Did anyone come with you? What did you bring me? Where is everyone? Did dey come?

Nabo shakes his head.

QUEEN: The Queen Mother?

Nabo shakes his head.

Ladies from the court?

Nabo shakes his head.

Musicians?

Nabo shakes his head.

QUEEN: Anyone?

NABO: The King thought it best that you have a companion and believes none gives you more pleasure than myself.

He bows graciously.

QUEEN: How thoughtful of the King. I'm surprised that he knows I'm still alive. Has Louis really asked after me?

NABO: (*Lying.*) He's pale with worry.

QUEEN: Liar! Have the decency to lie with some panache.

NABO: If you'd like.

QUEEN: Yes, very much!

NABO: The King sighs at supper, he cries out for his queen whenever

QUEEN: Stop! Cries? Louis never cries. Try again!

NABO: The King has been heard to whisper after his morning treks. Maria!

> *The Queen leans forward.*

Maria! He is sickened by the news of your illness.

QUEEN: Yes, go on.

NABO: And, and, and—

QUEEN: Regrets that—

NABO: That he cannot be at your side at such a delicate time. He sent me to convey this message.

QUEEN: So thoughtful. And my child?

NABO: As robust as when you left.

QUEEN: Does he miss his mama?

NABO: At three, he barely takes the nipple of the wet nurse.

> *The Queen lies back and sighs with relief.*

QUEEN: Bueno! I had thought that all had forgotten, left me to rot and wither in dis sedate countryside. Even the ladies are abandoning me one by one, afraid that such a prolonged absence from the court will destroy their rank. Nonsense! Bring me my powder! I suddenly feel better.

> *Nabo fetches the Queen's compact of powder.*

Let's do something!

> *He douses her face with the white powder giving her a ghoulish glow.*

NABO: Shall I begin with a story?

QUEEN: No, all of your stories have sad endings.

NABO: Oh, the Queen is in a mood today. I thought you'd given up

Nabo for some other entertainment. But I can see my competition has been sweets and wines and puddings.

QUEEN: Silence! I'm not fat, I'm fecund. Si?…Nabo, tell me the truth, did Louis send me here to die? I've heard from my little wicked Molina that as I rode north, the King went south with his mistress. She's pregnant again. And here I am with his child from a few tears I shed and shared with him. I know this to be so.

NABO: Of course, I dare not cry for fear of spreading my seed, my sadness could yield an empire.

The Queen weeps slightly, collects herself and carries on as if nothing happened.

QUEEN: Please, I sent for you for merriment.

NABO: Merrymaking is perhaps where our problem lies.

Nabo sinks down next to the Queen. Her face is contorted with horror.

LOUISE: And there they sat for almost a full day. Frozen. Paralyzed by the possibility. Can you imagine? He was going to father a child with the Queen of France, the Princess of Spain, the divine vessel; he, a man no larger than a child. A court jester. A fool.

Nabo laughs hysterically, to the irritation of the Queen.

QUEEN: Stop it!

A moment. Silence.

QUEEN: I'm so cold, I can barely summon a servant to stoke the fire. And there's no one to help me in and out of my chair to circulate the blood in my ankles. I'm practically a prisoner, confined to this chamber full of portraits. I'm carrying the royal heir, for God's sake. RIGHT? CLARO QUE SI.

NABO: Can you be so sure?

QUEEN: Hush. It is the King's child, of that the doctor is certain.

NABO: Are you?

QUEEN: Don't even say aloud what I know you are thinking. I don't want to see you now! GET OUT! Blackie!

NABO: Fattie!

QUEEN: Little Man.

NABO: Ugly cow!

QUEEN: FOOL! FOOL! FOOL!

NABO: Inbred, big jawed, thick-ankled, wench!

> *The Queen falls back in her chair and howls like a wounded animal.*

QUEEN: GET OUT!

> *A moment.*

NABO: You've forgotten the kind words you had for Nabo not so long ago.

QUEEN: Forgotten yes, my memory is like cheesecloth.

NABO: Do you want me to remind you?

> *The Queen shakes her head.*

NABO: You are my sweet little Nabo.

QUEEN: NO!

NABO: You touch me as the King does not.

QUEEN: NO!

NABO: Ay dios mio! TE AMO, TE AMO!

QUEEN: (*Ecstatic.*) NO!

> *Nabo moves close to the Queen and plants a kiss on her neck.*

NABO: You

QUEEN: You are wicked, Nabo. Tempt and taunt me. I should be above such devilish seduction. STOP!

NABO: Would it be so horrible if the child bore Nabo's face?

QUEEN: It would be impossible for me to be with your child. You can't be virile at your size. Why your seed is incompatible with royal needs. NO!

The Queen is suddenly horrified by the question and turns her back on Nabo.

Be thankful that you're not its Papa, it would mean your end! It would mean my end! And I'm fond of your insolent presence.

NABO: You're right. Let us pray it isn't true. What am I thinking?

QUEEN: I am the vessel of empires to come. I can't afford to bring anything other than a royal child into dis world. It's what I'm bred for, Nabo. My sole purpose. If I cannot provide that, then what will become of Maria? You were shipped in a box and I, a carriage. When you first peered up over the edge of that little box I recognized you. Look at me, Nabo. They think I'm stupid. They think I've no feelings, no cares. They think I can be treated like spoiled meat.

The Queen presses her fist into her stomach.

QUEEN: I could pound my belly and let the King know that I HAVE SOME POWER TOO. I have some say in the shaping of this nation. I deserve to be treated decently instead of shipped off to Fontainebleau and quickly forgotten. I came with a most excellent dowry. I brought peace to this land and I will take it away. Oh, what havoc this child could bring!

The Queen raises her fist to pound her belly. Nabo stops her and presses his face against her stomach.

NABO: No! Don't!

QUEEN: You are mi angel, Nabo. Sometimes I feel that we are in love. Is that strange? Could we be in love?

NABO: In desperation.

Nabo kisses the Queen. As the lights fade around them, Louise enters smiling.

SCENE 4

Louise stands alone in a circle of light, she slowly unbuttons her novice clothing.

LOUISE: On this, my wedding night, with not a relative alive to bear witness to my testimonial. And this story is almost complete save for my birth and when it occurs, so will the death of Louise Marie-Therèse. Be patient, sisters, and allow me this sweet selfish remembrance.

She peels off her novice clothing, revealing a crude slip beneath. She steps into the tub, slowly lowering herself into the water.

LOUISE: The night before my birth everyone had a dream. They all sat up in their beds sweating out fears. It was a birth most anxiously undesired. What manner of beast would burst from between the Queen's legs if dreams be purveyors of the future?

Nabo screams. Lights rise on him in a little bed, his chest heaving up and down.

NABO: Oh dear Legba, I dreamt of my end which came with a child bearing my face. I dreamt this child was bound in cloth and couldn't breathe. The child was gasping and I couldn't free her.

The Queen yelps. Lights rise on the Queen sitting in her bed chamber. The Queen Mother wipes her forehead with a cloth.

QUEEN: It was a most terrible dream.

QUEEN MOTHER: Your screams shook the palace.

QUEEN: Is there any way to stop this birth?

QUEEN MOTHER: You are no more than a day from delivery.

QUEEN: How many sins can one commit before admission to Heaven is impossible?

QUEEN MOTHER: It is a question for the clergy, I've never cared to know the answer myself.

QUEEN: I've had a premonition that dis child will be born grotesquely disfigured, without a face, a monster.

QUEEN MOTHER: These signs change their meaning at will, what you see now may mean something different tomorrow. Only an oracle, pagan or a butcher can read these signs with clarity.

A labor pain hits, and the Queen doubles over in pain.

QUEEN MOTHER: It is time!

The doctor rushes to the Queen's side with a number of servants. The Queen is stretched across a bed. The doctor and the ladies crowd around the Queen.

DOCTOR: Push!

The Queen cries out.

Push!

LOUISE: Push!

With one final scream the Queen's cries are drowned out by the sound of a baby crying.

Louise, soaking wet, suddenly rises in the tub.

DOCTOR: She's here.

The doctor takes a close look at the child and immediately wraps her in a blanket.

The ladies burst into spontaneous applause, as they struggle furiously to get a glance at the child. Their whispers swell into a chorus of "Let me sees." They fall suddenly silent.

LA VALLIÈRE: Let me see. Let me see.

La Vallière bursts into laughter. The doctor attempts to stifle the laughter.

QUEEN: Let me see her! What? Why are you laughing? Let me see her!

She begins to laugh herself and then stops.

QUEEN: What? Why are you laughing?

The Queen reaches for the baby. The Queen Mother peeks at the child, shrieks and faints.

My baby! Can I hold my baby! My baby! My baby!

Laughter drowns out her cries. Church bells ring. The lights fade on Louise and the Queen as they rise on the King and Doctor Fagon. The King takes a pinch of snuff, sneezes and wipes his nose in his blouse.

KING: Tell them to stop ringing those damn bells. I didn't hear what you said.

The church bells continue to chime.

DOCTOR: (*Reluctantly.*) Brown, brown…Your Majesty. The child is brown.

KING: Brown? Are you sure? What does that mean? Is it a good sign? Is it a scientific term?

DOCTOR: No, no I'm referring to the color of its skin.

KING: BROWN?

DOCTOR: We fear that the Queen's fool having looked upon Her Majesty so often transformed the infant's complexion through a trauma during the pregnancy. This shouldn't last long, perhaps a month or two and then her true color will return.

KING: I see. A look! It must have been a very penetrating look. It's not the first I've heard of such an affliction, it did pass with the De Medicis not long ago. The royal womb tends to be more fragile, a divine vessel is more susceptible to outside irritations. It is why I'm told so many perish at birth.

DOCTOR: Oh yes! Quite right! How do you wish me to handle this?

KING: She'll need a name nevertheless! We will call her Louise Marie-Thérèse. Did you take that down?

The doctor pretends to take down the information on his hand. He bows obsequiously.

The Mother Superior crosses the stage holding a child in her arms. She gently rocks the infant, intermittently blowing kisses. Lights rise on Louise.

MOTHER SUPERIOR: You know, you'll have to take another name when you take your veil.

LOUISE: Yes, I know.

MOTHER SUPERIOR: I am your mother and the Lord is your father. I am your mother and the Lord is your husband.

The Mother Superior continues to rock the child as she moves across the stage and disappears.

KING: When can I see the child?

DOCTOR: The Queen rests. I haven't yet told her. The child

KING: Can I see whom she resembles?

The doctor clears his throat.

DOCTOR: Perhaps the King would care to wait. Until—

KING: Nonsense. Prepare the child for a viewing.

The doctor goes to the door.

DOCTOR: BRING OUT THE CHILD!

A nursemaid rushes in with the baby and shows her to the King. The King, aghast, loses his balance, nearly tumbling to the ground. A courtier brings him a glass of wine, which he drinks down quickly.

DOCTOR: May I recommend that she be placed elsewhere until her affliction heals? Someplace where her complexion won't be affected by so many curious eyes. I know an excellent little Benedictine convent.

The bells stop ringing. Mother Superior grabs Louise from behind.

MOTHER SUPERIOR: My dear Father Josephus nearly drowned in rain water. At Moret we have such a simple life, we are women of virtue. Women of noble birth enter our ranks in numbers far greater than any convent in France. If we were a royal court it would be the finest in this nation.

KING: Will this affliction clear?

DOCTOR: Not to my knowledge, but

> *A moment.*

KING: She is a girl after all, she wouldn't be…I'll have my valet, Bontems, deliver her this evening. We'll make arrangements to have her baptized in the convent. She must be baptized, I insist. The Queen is as pious as they come, that must be known by all. It is a pity that from now on she's to spend so much time in prayer, so young.

DOCTOR: Sire, I could announce the child's death if—

KING: (*Louder.*) It was stillborn you say? It always saddens me to prepare for a birth and a death on the same day.

DOCTOR: (*Whispered.*) They are excellent nuns and will care for the child well.

KING: I must have them prepare my mourning clothing. (*Whispered.*) The good sisters must be informed that the child is to know nothing of its birth. She is to be sequestered from the rest of the world until her death, or until her discoloration mends itself. I'm sure the Benedictine's will be sympathetic if I let my generosity be known.

DOCTOR: And if the Queen insists on knowing the truth?

KING: Excuse me, I must dress for the funeral. And go and comfort my wife.

> *The King exits. The courtiers burst into laughter.*

LOUISE: It was whispered, my nose was broad and flat. It was whispered that my hair was kinky and tight. It was whispered that I was born with two horns and hoofs for hands. They whispered as they prepared for a royal funeral. Hysteria seized the Queen and it took three women to hold her down.

> *Lights rise on the Queen being strapped to the bed by three women. She pulls at her hair, shrieking and crying.*

LADY SERVANT: She's dead, Your Majesty.

QUEEN: I heard her cry!

LADY SERVANT: She was born still!

QUEEN: I heard her cry!

LADY SERVANT: Calm, and drink this. In all of the excitement you are confused.

QUEEN: No! I want to know where my baby is! I want the King! I want him to tell me where my baby is. She isn't dead, I heard her cry. I heard her crying. I heard her crying! You tell the King that if anything has happened to my baby I will start a war that will take generations to pass. Now get out of here you LIARS!

The Queen hisses at the women, who scramble quickly out of the room. She twists and turns attempting to loosen the restraints.

Nabo emerges from beneath the bed carrying a withered flower.

NABO: The flower stood through most of the night, it was only your yelling that gave it a fright.

QUEEN: Come, come. Untie me!

Nabo unties the Queen's arms.

QUEEN: They've taken my baby, Nabo. They said she was grossly deformed and I should not look upon her. They said she was born still. It was for my own good, Fagon said. For my own good, nursemaid said, but nothing good has come of this day.

NABO: She was mine too, not the King's to give away. I heard the cries of a child this very morning echo through the palace.

QUEEN: She was brown from what I could see and they laughed and laughed like in my dream. She was beautiful from what I could tell. Tiny. Let's find the child and run away.

NABO: Where? Where can a queen run with an African dwarf? If I could get away I'd have been gone long ago.

QUEEN: We'll go to the land of your stories. To Africa?

Nabo laughs.

NABO: You wouldn't survive there.

QUEEN: Why not? You've survived here.

NABO: Some of me, but not all.

QUEEN: To the New World.

NABO: Old values have taken root.

QUEEN: Then I'll kill myself.

> *The Queen screams violently.*

I am Queen of France.

NABO: And what does that mean? You are so innocent, Maria.

> *He kisses her forehead.*

NABO: When you could love the whole world. You choose to love me. A truly noble heart.

QUEEN: No, you chose me. I'll bear the shame if only they will let me have my child.

NABO: She has no place in this court. No Maria.

QUEEN: We can go elsewhere.

NABO: Where? With what?

QUEEN: I have jewels.

NABO: I once asked you to let me go and you refused.

QUEEN: You are free, I know this now. Please, take me away from this place.

NABO: I wouldn't be free if I did. Where I go I'm not a fool, I don't think you yet understand that. I'm not servant or slave. And if you came I'd be all of those things.

QUEEN: Please, I can't have two losses in one day.

NABO: I've had many, you'll survive the pain…but as things stand, I'm lucky if I survive this day. We can spend all night making plans, but don't you know, Your Majesty, my fate was sealed when I foolishly sold my life for six goats and some beads.

La Vallière enters and taps Louise.

LA VALLIÈRE: (*Laughing.*) No one told you?

LOUISE: But my father was—

LA VALLIÈRE: An African dwarf.

LOUISE: (*To Queen.*) Why didn't you ever tell me?

QUEEN: (*To Nabo.*) We can run away.

> *The Queen's servants and Doctor Fagon appear and lead the Queen offstage Louise follows them. Nabo picks up the wilted flower, then is seized by two guards.*
>
> *Lights rise on the King pacing. He stops and sits behind a desk. Nabo is brought before the King, who makes a show of going through a pile papers. Nabo bows.*

NABO: A joke for the middle of the day, Sire? Something to take the edge off the affairs of state?

KING: No. It is a pity, I really do like you, more than I like her in fact. I'm sorry…

> *The King glances at the document searching for Nabo's name. He speaks casually.*

KING: *Nabo Sensugali*, I have before me a warrant for your execution. I've passed my judgment, I hope you don't mind too much, but I promise I won't make an event out of it and you'll have a Christian burial. You are Christian?

NABO: Actually I—

KING: Yes, then I imagine you are.

NABO: Perhaps the punishment does not fit the crime. Sire, may I know what I have been charged with?

KING: Treason.

NABO: Treason, I see. Of what nature?

KING: A penetrating look that threatened the welfare of the royal heir.

NABO: The gallows? It's so large a punishment for one so small. If you factor in my height, I'm one half the size of an average man and therefore I've committed only half the crime. Sire, you could always exile me to a far off land, like Africa.

KING: The thought has crossed my mind, but I believe execution is more demonstrative in this instance. It's the Queen's honor that's at stake.

> *He sips his wine.*

Talk has already reached epidemic proportions. I can't have the Queen's reputation tarnished any further.

NABO: Yes, you can't have that.

KING: We both know it's talk. You and the Queen, what a foolish notion. Why, you're half the size of an average man. I'm three inches taller than that.

> *He coughs.*

KING: This child does not exist as far as I'm concerned. I wish it had died at birth and then its odd discoloration could be explained away. But it survived, I'll not pretend otherwise. I…I care for my wife, despite what many think. She is my innocent angel, whose love has been unconditional. Familiarity is often more comforting than true love, which makes the heart violent and is accompanied by fits of rage, great passion, and ultimately hurt. I know with Marie I will never suffer that great hurt.

NABO: Is it necessary to take a man's life twice? As is my case. You've taken mine once when I entered this court, which means I'm already dead and therefore your judgment has been enacted. Can a dead man be killed, and if so by what means? Redundancy is not a kingly trait.

KING: Then you're familiar with kingly attributes.

NABO: Oh yes, Your Majesty.

KING: Hmmm?

NABO: May I ask another question?

KING: Go on!

NABO: May the Queen see her child? Her sanity hangs by a thin thread.

KING: I—

NABO: My life for hers and the child's.

KING: That's not possible. Officially this conversation is not even happening, I'm out for a ride.

NABO: If we never had this conversation, is it possible that I never existed? The Queen never did give birth, which means she has no child, which means no crime has been committed.

KING: That is true. The truth. No crime committed.

He signs the paper before him.

NABO: So you signed me out of existence and tomorrow I will never have been here.

KING: Yes.

NABO: I gave a woman a few moments of love. I should be thanked for that. I was shipped to and from empires bizarre and unwelcoming in a box no full size man could survive. Bought, sold, bartered and brokered until I do not know who I am. Laughed at, kicked, and disgraced, I've learned more than most men about this human race. And if my tongue were acid you'd now be dead. I've made kings weep with joy and queens whine with delight. Months of pleasure I've given your court, and I am to pay for the one moment I stole for my own.

KING: Yes, unfortunately, that seems to be the case.

He folds the warrant.

KING: You did make me laugh.

He laughs.

That story you…well perhaps now isn't the best time. You've given me a few moments of laughter and that won't go unrecognized. The child will live, and let it not be said that I was without a heart. And yes, in time I might find my way to grant the Queen some privileges. All of that said, I'm afraid you're not quite fool enough for this place.

NABO: Sire!

KING: Yes.

Nabo laughs and shakes his bells furiously.

KING: Take him out.

The lights go to black on all except Louise. She slowly begins to unbutton her wet slip.

LOUISE: Taken to the woods and decapitated in one quick stroke to the back of the neck. Buried as a Christian beneath a great flowering tree. His name never spoken by anyone in court again. Nabo Sensugali. At the moment his neck cracked and split, Bontems carried me in his arms through the violent rainstorm.

Lights rise on the Mother Superior.

My mother sat…

Lights rise on the Queen in bed, cradling the air. These lights quickly fade.

LOUISE: I'm not yet finished. My mother sat…

Lights rise once again on the Queen in bed cradling the air.

LOUISE: In her bed singing and waiting for Nabo.

QUEEN: (*Singing.*) Go to sleep little one.

LOUISE: (*To the Queen.*) Are you my mother?

The Queen continues to sing the lullaby.

LOUISE: Is my father an African?

QUEEN: Go to sleep little one.

The lights fade on the Queen. The Mother Superior slowly makes her way toward Louise with a wedding gown in her hands. Nuns enter.

LOUISE: And my father's neck cracked and split his head tumbling to the ground with a grin still on his lips. And now I will stop waiting.

I have no family other than you, my sisters, and God. The king decreed them out of existence.

Louise ceases to speak as the nuns take off her wet slip and place her in the wedding gown.

LOUISE: And now I too will be lost to history.

She lies spread-eagle, face down on the floor as the lights fade.

END OF PLAY

COLOPHON

The cover title type is set in La Figura, a type designed with the feel of Italian Renaissance calligraphy. It was designed by Jim Marcus in 1998. Additional cover type is set in Futura, a geometric sans-serif typeface designed in 1927 by Paul Renner. It is based on geometric shapes that became representative of visual elements of the Bauhaus design style of 1919–1933.

The interior text is set with the font family of Berkeley Old Style. Berkeley—a classic and highly legible serif font—was originally designed in 1938 by Frederic W. Goudy as University Old Style for the University of California. That type font was redrawn and digitized as Berkeley Old Style in 1994 by designer Richard Beatty. The interior headline text is again set in Futura.

Interior stock is Rolland Enviro 100 Trade, 55# Cream made from 100% post-consumer recycled material by the Cascades Fine Paper Group of Canada. Cover stock is FSC Tango 12 point coated one side only with lay-flat matt film lamination.

Book design by Tracy Lamb, Laughing Lamb Design, Jackson Hole, Wyoming.

RECYCLED
Paper made from
recycled material
FSC
www.fsc.org FSC® C103567

Print production by Marquis Printing, of Cap-Saint-Ignace, Quebec, Canada. Marquis Printing is certified through the Forest Stewardship Council® (FSC®).

ABOUT WHIT PRESS

SUPPORT FOR THE INDEPENDENT VOICE

Whit Press is a nonprofit publishing organization dedicated
to the transformational power of the written word.

Whit Press exists as an oasis to nurture and promote
the rich diversity of literary work from women writers,
writers from ethnic and social minorities, young
writers, and first-time authors.

We also create books that use literature as a tool in
support of other nonprofit organizations working
toward environmental and social justice.

We are dedicated to producing beautiful books that combine
outstanding literary content with design excellence.

Whit Press brings you the best of fiction, creative nonfiction,
and poetry from diverse literary voices who do not have
easy access to quality publication.

We publish stories of creative discovery, cultural insight,
human experience, spiritual exploration, and more.

WHIT PRESS AND THE ENVIRONMENT
Whit Press is a member of the Green Press Initiative. We are committed to
eliminating the use of paper produced with endangered forest fiber.

PLEASE VISIT OUR WEB SITE WWW.WHITPRESS.ORG FOR OUR OTHER TITLES.

Seattle, Washington • Jackson Hole, Wyoming • www.WhitPress.org